THE BIBLE, CENTRES AND MARGINS

THE BIBLE, CENTRES AND MARGINS

Dialogues between Postcolonial African and British Biblical Scholars

Edited by
Johanna Stiebert and Musa W. Dube

LONDON · NEW YORK · OXFORD · NEW DELHI · SYDNEY

T&T CLARK
Bloomsbury Publishing Plc
50 Bedford Square, London, WC1B 3DP, UK

BLOOMSBURY, BLOOMSBURY ACADEMIC and the Diana logo are trademarks of
Bloomsbury Publishing Plc

First published in Great Britain 2018

A catalogue record for this book is available from the British Library.

A catalog record for this book is available from the Library of Congress.

ISBN: HB: 978-0-5676-6724-3
ePDF: 978-0-5676-6725-0
eBook: 978-0-5676-6726-7

Typeset by Newgen KnowledgeWorks Pvt. Ltd., Chennai, India
Printed and bound in Great Britain

To find out more about our authors and books visit www.bloomsbury.com
and sign up for our newsletters.

CONTENTS

Part II

Part III

CONTRIBUTORS

Mark S. Aidoo is Lecturer and Director for Special Programmes at Trinity Theological Seminary, Legon (Ghana). His research interests are Old Testament Interpretation, Wisdom Literature and Biblical Leadership. His most recent major publication is *Shame in the Individual Lament Psalms and African Spirituality* (2017).

Musa W. Dube is a biblical scholar based at the University of Botswana. Among other honours, she is Professor Extraordinaire in the Department of Religion and Classical Studies at the University of South Africa and a Humboldt award winner (2011). She studied New Testament at the universities of Botswana, Durham (UK) and Vanderbilt (USA). Her research interests include the New Testament in relation to gender, postcolonial criticism, translation, HIV and AIDS, and African studies. She is author of *Postcolonial Feminist Interpretation of the Bible* (2000) and co-editor, with Andrew M. Mbuvi and Dora Mbuwayesango, of *Postcolonial Perspectives in African Biblical Interpretations* (2012).

Katie Edwards is Director of the Sheffield Institute for Interdisciplinary Biblical Studies (SIIBS) and Senior Lecturer in the School of English at the University of Sheffield. Her research focuses on the function, impact and influence of the Bible in contemporary culture. She is especially concerned with intersections of gender, race and class in popular cultural reappropriations of biblical characters/ narratives. She is co-editor of the journal *Biblical Reception* (Bloomsbury) and of *Rape Culture, Gender Violence and Religion*, a three-volume series for Palgrave Macmillan, with Caroline Blyth and Emily Colgan (2018).

Mmapula D. Kebaneilwe is a womanist scholar and Senior Lecturer in Hebrew and Old Testament Studies at the University of Botswana. She completed her PhD with the University of Murdoch in Western Australia in 2012. Her research interests are wide, including Wisdom Literature, the Psalms, the Hebrew Bible and environmental issues, women, HIV and AIDS. She is a member of OTSSA, ACLARS, ATISCA and ASRSA, as well as BOLESWA).

Adriaan van Klinken is Associate Professor of Religion and African Studies at the University of Leeds. His research focuses on contemporary Christianity, gender and sexuality in Africa, with his current book project being on Christianity and queer politics in Kenya. He recently edited, with Ezra Chitando, two book volumes: *Public Religion and the Politics of Homosexuality in Africa* and *Christianity and Controversies over Homosexuality in Contemporary Africa* (2016).

Tsaurayi K. Mapfeka holds a BA (Hons) in Religious Studies from the University of Zimbabwe, an MTh from Africa University and an MA and PhD from King's College, London. His research interests are primarily in reading texts from the Hebrew Bible in their socio-historical contexts. His own positionality as a Zimbabwean migrant settled in the UK provides a heavy tint to these interests and, consequently, postcolonial and diaspora (transnational) dynamics feature prominently in his research.

Hugh S. Pyper is Professor of Biblical Interpretation at the University of Sheffield. His research interests centre around the often unnoticed effects that biblical texts continue to have on contemporary 'secular' culture in a postcolonial context. He has published on the interactions between biblical interpretation, translation and postmodernism, with Kierkegaard as a key figure. Recent publications include *The Unchained Bible: Cultural Appropriations of Biblical Texts* (2012) and articles on subjects ranging from the biblical influence on Tove Jansson's Moomin books to the role of the Old Testament in the ideology of Hindu nationalism.

Johanna Stiebert is Associate Professor of Hebrew Bible at the University of Leeds. Her research interests include Hebrew self-conscious emotion terminology, ideological and social-scientific criticism, family relations, gender and sexuality, as well as African-centred approaches. Her most recent books are *Fathers and Daughters in the Hebrew Bible* (2013) and *First-Degree Incest and the Hebrew Bible: Sex in the Family* (2016). She is co-lead (with Caroline Blyth and Katie Edwards) of the Shiloh Project, on intersections between religion and rape culture.

Nancy N. H. Tan is Associate Professor in Hebrew Bible at the Divinity School of Chung Chi College of the Chinese University of Hong Kong. She works on interpretations of women in the Hebrew Bible. Her current interests lie in the areas of the Second Temple Period, the Book of Judith and in promoting contextual interpretations for the marginalized in her own community. Her most recent publication is 'Hong Kong Sex Workers: Mothers Reading 1 Kings 3.16–28', in Gale A. Yee and John Y. H. Yieh (eds), *Honouring the Past, Looking to the Future: Essays from the 2014 International Congress of Ethnic Chinese Biblical Scholars* (2016).

Elizabeth Vengeyi is a PhD candidate at the University of Bamberg, Germany. Her research interests focus on the Bible and its relevance to contemporary Zimbabwean society. Her most recent publication is 'The Bible, Violence, Women and African Initiated Churches in Zimbabwe', which appeared in *The Bible and Violence in Africa*, edited by J. Hunter and J. Kügler (2016).

Gerald O. West teaches Old Testament/Hebrew Bible and African Biblical Hermeneutics in the School of Religion, Philosophy, and Classics at the University of KwaZulu-Natal, South Africa. He is Director of the Ujamaa Centre for Community Development and Research, a project in which socially engaged biblical scholars and ordinary African readers of the Bible from poor, working-class, and marginalized communities collaborate for social transformation. His most recent book is *The Stolen Bible: From Tool of Imperialism to African Icon* (2016).

Vincent L. Wimbush is the Founding Director of the Institute for Signifying Scriptures, an independent forum and organization of scholars, researchers, activists and others committed to constructing and promoting new modes of critical inquiry into social-discursive formation, as well as to cross-cultural, disciplinary-transgressive conversation about the politics of meaning (www.signifyingscriptures.org). His many influential publications include *White Men's Magic: Scripturalization as Slavery* (2012) and *Scripturalectics: The Management of Meaning* (2017).

FOREWORD

Vincent L. Wimbush
Institute for Signifying Scriptures, USA

As is the stated or presumed purpose of most scholarly collections of essays, *The Bible, Centres and Margins: Dialogues between Postcolonial African and British Biblical Scholars*, edited by Musa W. Dube and Johanna Stiebert, of Botswana and the United Kingdom, respectively, provides the reader fascinating conversations. According to the book title, the rubrics and themes of the colloquies that anticipated this publication, and as reflected within several of the included essays, the conversations are about 'the Bible' and, in relation to such, 'centres and margins'; or, about how self-ascribed but differently positioned and differently defined 'postcolonial' scholars engage the Bible and how through their engagements they name and analyse, but also reflect and, perhaps, further inscribe, textual and metatextual samenesses and differences.

A special feature of the conversations reflected in this particular book is that of the composition and categorization of the discussants: the latter are classified as postcolonial biblical scholars who are 'African[s]' (from various national, professional, and socio-cultural situations and of different ethnic identities, mostly from the southern part of the continent, and assumed all of them to be Black peoples); and postcolonial biblical scholars from the 'UK' (a seemingly more monochromatic and provincial cultural formation, assumed all of them to be only White peoples). The asymmetry in the group categorizations in the title is not the creation of the editors; this type of categorization has a history that has mostly been unquestioned. It appears that it was not the editors' aim to address and resolve the chronic historical problem inherent in the all too encompassing and overdetermined rubric 'African' in juxtaposition to the all too underdetermined and underanalysed 'United Kingdom' (as opposed to 'European') tag. The issues remain and beg, even provoke, more consideration, even more dialogue.

Indeed, notwithstanding the problematics of its title, this collection does move us along that path – of provoking more thinking about the 'dialogues'. In a way that is akin to the complex representation of self and meaning – 'hitting a lick with a crooked stick' – of the African American 'folk' (of early twentieth-century small town Florida, USA) whom novelist and folklorist Zora Neale Hurston 'discovered', some of the persons whom the editors of this book brought together in dialogues – through and beyond the formal responses – did indeed 'hit' on some of the key issues that their very composition and characterization as a circle of discussants raises. And even if this 'lick hitting' was done here and there, that is, in the different keys, tones, perspectives, degrees of coverage, orientation and focus, and unevenness of mastery that always mark individual contributions, insofar as it names and engages – crookedly, as it were – 'the Bible' as the 'crooked stick', the critical force of the collective cannot be denied.

The contributors are of course all Anglophones. Coming to terms with this difficult or haunting act means much – including the fact they have in common (among other things) 'King James' – the most important symbol of the English Bible: that is, the most powerful and enduring cultural-political achievement and problem of the English world. Even if not always identified and named, 'King James' functions much like the 'Constantine' of Dante's *Inferno* (Canto 19, 115), whose 'donation' wrought much evil, henceforth always needing to be addressed and resisted. So 'King James' raises the question how and precisely why 'it' figures as the common 'crooked stick' within the Anglophone world. On this side of colonial regimes, 'King James', the fraught sobriquet for 'the Bible' as fraught shorthand absolutely must be problematized; 'it' can no longer be taken for granted, at least not as the focus of scholarly cultural-critical (in distinction from un-self-reflexive religiously felt or dominant-culturalist) interest.

Over the last several decades, tracks have been laid for the advancement of critical thinking and conversation about the Bible in/and as part of the postcolonial world. Ever more dazzling and fancy methods and approaches to the Bible have been developed among self-styled postcolonial scholars – among and beyond the categories into which contributors to this book may be cast. But what we desperately need are approaches that return us to the most basic questions. This book is important because it provokes even if it does not answer some of these basic questions – Why bother with the Bible in the postcolonial situation? What is the point of conversation involving the Bible among postcolonial scholars so differently situated with different interests, politics, challenges, problems? For what is 'the Bible' (discursive-cultural-political) shorthand? What 'lick' does engagement with 'it' 'hit'? What does play with 'it' occlude? What does 'it' reveal or make more compelling? What is really being engaged, wrestled with? Why is so much time, energy invested in relationship to it?

The *donatio constantini* opens a window onto the long infra-European history having to do with discursive/textual claims, deceptions and manipulations on the part of the 'centre'. I have called such a phenomenon 'scripturalization'. For the sake of any type of salvation, the latter must constantly be unveiled, problematized and analysed. That is what the 'UK' (metonymic of the phenomenon of Constantine-turned-into-King James) represents as one side of the dialogue that this book provides us. The onus on those belonging to the 'UK', among other things, is to own their participation/collusion in the construction and maintenance of scripturalization as evil masquerading as 'donation' (as civilization, etc.). That such folk may also consider their having been betrayed or otherwise made vulnerable or sick by the phenomenon is worth noting.

Complexly located on the 'margins', if not altogether outside the empire, 'Africans' are required for their sakes if not for all to name even more pointedly and vocally and even more consistently and to sharply analyse, critique and resist, scripturalization. Their positionalities can and should afford them the perspective required for consistent critical orientation vis-à-vis the centre such that they can signify on what I have argued Olaudah Equiano discovered to be in terms of the deadly discursive play with the Bible – and the corresponding impact on non-white peoples – 'white men's magic'. But it is the now even more widely known saying (an alt-scripture?) that has for decades (in only slightly different versions) floated throughout the Anglophone Black Atlantic world – sometimes erroneously but understandably attributed to Desmond Tutu – that makes the most basic and disturbing point about the critical problem and the needed critical positionality:

> When the missionaries came to Africa they had the Bible and we had the land. They said, 'Let us pray'. We closed our eyes. When we opened them we had the Bible and they had the land.

Here it is: the Bible – not as text or object, but as a metonym for the relations of power with which (in this case, the British) empire was built and then 'donated' to the enslaved and colonized. This is what is at issue, what must always be the focus of critical discussion. The Bible/King James is a fraught abbreviation for that which the Anglophones – overdetermined 'African' and underdetermined 'British' scholars – now have in common, the significant site of interrogation for the English-speaking/reading self in the world. It is the English Bible – the 'donation', notwithstanding whatever other languages may come into the mix of textual play – that functions as a vector of sorts, as poignant and problematic indirection (crooked-ness) for the 'hitting of the lick'.

There is no doubt that some important licks are hit, some significant arguments are made, questions raised, by individual contributors to this book. These hits ensure this collection's strong place in the ongoing larger conversations among self-ascribed postcolonial scholars (of various fields of inquiry). The collection makes me hopeful, maybe even wistful, that we shall reach a time when we shall not so much do altogether without the 'stick' – as long as there is an Anglophone world it will surely be with us – but with less and less of its crooked-ness.

ACKNOWLEDGEMENTS

Many of the contributions in this book were first presented and discussed at research symposiums held in Leeds and Gaborone: events that would not have been possible without funding from the British Academy's International Partnership Fund. Three years of support ensured that students and scholars of the Bible from various parts of the UK, as well as from Nigeria, Ghana, South Africa, Botswana, Zambia, Zimbabwe and (in the final year) Hong Kong could meet and open a series of lively discussions, exchange ideas, ask questions, share stories, provoke and challenge and offer support.

At different times both editors were also given generous support by the Humboldt Foundation to spend time at the University of Bamberg, home of the Bible in Africa Studies (BiAS) series. Further financial contributions and hospitality were also provided by the Sheffield Institute for Interdisciplinary Biblical Studies (SIIBS), the Centre for Religion and Public Life (CRPL) of the University of Leeds, the University of Botswana and Kgolagano Bible College in Gaborone. What we have here is the fruit of a vibrant series of interactions and, we hope, the beginning of more.

ABBREVIATIONS

ABC	Australian Broadcasting Corporation
ACLARS	African Consortium for Law and Religion Studies
AICS	African Instituted (or 'Independent' or 'Indigenous') Churches
AIDS (or Aids)	Acquired Immune Deficiency Syndrome
ASEAN	Association of Southeast Asian Nations
ASRSA	Association for the Study of Religion in South Africa
ATISCA	Association of Theological Institutions in Southern and Central Africa
BDB	'Brown-Driver-Briggs', the abbreviation for *A Hebrew and English Lexicon of the Old Testament* (first published in 1906). The three authors of the original lexicon were Francis Brown, Samuel Rolles Driver and Charles Augustus Briggs.
BIAS	Bible in Africa Studies (Bamberg, Germany)
BNTS	The British New Testament Society
BOLESWA	An academic alliance between the Departments of Theology and Religious Studies at the Universities of Botswana, Lesotho and Swaziland
CNBC	Consumer News and Business Channel
CRPL	Centre for Religion and Public Life (University of Leeds)
HIV	Human Immunodeficiency Virus
HSRC	Human Sciences Research Council (South Africa)
ISS	Institute for Signifying Scriptures
JBL	*Journal of Biblical Literature*
JSNT	*Journal for the Study of the New Testament*
JSOT	*Journal for the Study of the Old Testament*
KTAV	Hebrew for 'to write'. The name of a publishing house based in New York.
LXX	The Septuagint, an early Greek translation of the Hebrew Bible and deuterocanonical books. Its name is represented by the Roman numeral for seventy on account of a story attributing translation of the Torah to approximately seventy Jewish translators.
NASB	New American Standard Bible
NBC	National Broadcasting Company
NHK	Nippon Hoso Kyokai ('Japan Broadcasting Corporation')
NIV	New International Version
NJB	New Jerusalem Bible
NKJV	New King James Version
NRSV	New Revised Standard Version
NTSSA	New Testament Society of South Africa
OTSSA	Old Testament Society of South Africa

OUP	Oxford University Press
RB	*Revue Biblique*
SADC	Southern African Development Community
SBL	Society of Biblical Literature
SBS	Special Broadcasting Service
SCM	UK-based press for theological publications. Originally affiliated with the Student Christian Movement.
SIIBS	Sheffield Institute for Interdisciplinary Biblical Studies
SOTS	The Society for Old Testament Study
TPP	Trans-Pacific Partnership
WLS	Wisconsin Lutheran Seminary
YHWH	The 'Tetragrammaton' ('four letters') transliterated from the Hebrew and representing the chief deity of the Hebrew Bible.

Chapter 1

INTRODUCTION

Musa W. Dube and Johanna Stiebert

This volume represents the culmination of a three-year project made possible through a British Academy International Partnership Fund. The project's working title was 'Biblical Studies in Southern Africa and the UK in Dialogue: Trends and Challenges', and one of many catalysts for its inception was the recognition that, for all the many historical connections between the UK and southern Africa, any dialogue between the two centres has been minimal, fragmentary and isolated. Whereas in English Literature there exists a sub-discipline called (not without controversy) Commonwealth Literature,[1] there is no such equivalent in Biblical Studies: no Commonwealth Biblical Studies convention, or journal, or discipline.

We, Musa Dube and Johanna Stiebert, are each of us resident in one of the dialogue centres: Musa is Professor of New Testament at the University of Botswana, and Johanna teaches Hebrew Bible at the University of Leeds. Events over the three-year duration, consequently, were held in England or Botswana.[2]

---

1. 'The Commonwealth' is an eclectic assemblage of some 53 independent nations, inclusive of the UK, that are associated by historical ties with the former British Empire. The majority of members are former colonies or protectorates of the one-time British Empire; English is spoken widely throughout; and the current British regent is the symbolic head of the Commonwealth. 'Commonwealth Literature' is a designation covering the literary works from these diverse territories, but it usually excludes UK literature – unless written by resident writers originally from a former colony/protectorate. The term has met with considerable resistance – vehemently so, from Salman Rushdie (1991). The term 'Commonwealth' (like 'British Academy', too) carries associations of patronage and colonialism – such as notions of exporting 'goodness' and 'civilization'. The designation 'Commonwealth Literature', alongside alternative terms (e.g. 'Postcolonial Literature in English' or 'World Writing in English'), is discussed fully by Ako (2004).

2. One consequence of 'Empire' and 'Commonwealth' is the English language as a common medium. Botswana has two official languages: English and Setswana. This makes dialogue between the centres possible. The dynamics have changed: Botswana is an independent democracy, prosperous and stable among its SADC (Southern African Development Community) neighbours; the UK is no longer the centre of an Empire, is

We have each had association with the 'Commonwealth' and have also each had direct prior encounter with the other dialogue partner. Musa is a Kalanga citizen of Botswana[3] who began her studies in her homeland before completing an MA at the University of Durham and, subsequently, a PhD in the USA. She has since had a distinguished career and is in the forefront of shaping postcolonial and feminist biblical scholarship, as well as theology of HIV and Aids in African contexts. Johanna was born in New Zealand,[4] and taught at the University of Botswana for three years before moving on to her current academic post in England (with a lengthy sojourn in the USA in between). While her interests in biblical interpretation are wide-ranging, the experience of teaching in Botswana has been transformative, as is reflected in several of her publications. The dialogue of the project has also embraced participants from other parts of southern Africa (South Africa, Zimbabwe, Zambia), as well as from beyond the two centres (Nigeria, Ghana, Hong Kong), developing over time a dynamic of its own. From the outset, the project was envisaged as inclusive and mutually supportive, bringing together junior and senior scholars. This is also reflected in this publication, which deliberately showcases the work of both established and emerging biblical scholars.

So why conduct such a dialogue in Biblical Studies? Above all, because there isn't one. Biblical Studies is encountering profound challenges (theological, secularist and economic) in both the UK and southern Africa. Christianity is gaining converts fastest in sub-Saharan Africa; the UK is seeing a decline in church attendance. But in spite of both historical and language associations, shared problems and stark juxtapositions, which should make for lively dialogue, the two centres seldom have opportunity for engagement. Our endeavour here has been to redress this, and to ask and begin to answer some of the following questions: How well do academics and students in the UK know and understand African-centred and generated approaches of biblical criticism? And how relevant do academics and students in southern Africa consider biblical interpretation from academic centres in the UK? How central and how marginal is each of us? What are the trends and challenges in our two centres of study and how can we effectively reflect on, teach and learn from each other?

about to leave the European Union and increasingly vulnerable and isolationist. Given these developments, as well as the inequalities and injustices of the colonial past and the globalized, Western-centric, capitalist present, dialogue remains vital. These meta-issues cannot be fully analysed or addressed here but they have left their mark in the chapters of this volume.

3. Following aggressive incursions from colonial wars in South Africa, Bechuanaland sought and obtained protectorate status from the British Empire in 1885. Following South Africa's withdrawal from the Commonwealth in 1961, the Republic of Botswana went on to attain independence and, simultaneously, membership of the Commonwealth in 1966.

4. New Zealand was a founder nation of the Commonwealth, attaining independence through the Statute of Westminster in 1931.

Both of us were conscious of, and Musa directly involved and instrumental in, the exciting work going on in Biblical Studies in Anglophone southern Africa.[5] In the UK, meanwhile, for all the assaults on the discipline,[6] Biblical Studies is continuing to sustain societies devoted to both the Hebrew and Greek testaments.[7] It is also true, however, that both dialogue partners are in many respects at the margin of the dominant centre that is the USA, the annual host of by far the world's largest gathering in Biblical Studies, the Society of Biblical Literature (SBL).[8]

This volume represents the fruits of the beginning of a new dialogue, of conversations, presentations and collaborations between scholars of the Bible meeting in Yorkshire (Leeds and Sheffield) and Gaborone over three consecutive years. In the first year (2012), Makhosazana ('Makhosi') Nzimande (formerly of the University of Zululand, since ordained in the Anglican Church of Southern Africa) visited England. Makhosi made a series of presentations in Leeds, Sheffield and Mirfield. These presentations gave a diachronic overview of Biblical Studies and critical reading methods in South Africa and contextualized Makhosi's own

---

5. One collection of essays demonstrating this vibrancy is West and Dube 2000. South Africa (to give one example from the region) has two large academic biblical associations, which meet annually, OTSSA (Old Testament Society of South Africa) and NTSSA (New Testament Society of South Africa). Each has a journal associated with it: *Old Testament Essays* and *Neotestamentica*, respectively.

6. Biblical Studies in the UK has received some hard knocks and, like other disciplines in the Humanities, is suffering the effect of harsh funding cuts. A number of institutions – among them the Universities of Leeds, Sheffield, Glasgow, Stirling, Bristol and Bangor – have seen a decimation of the discipline over the past decade (notably, in terms of number of teaching staff). While some of this might be accounted for in terms of what is characterized as 'the changing face of British society', with demographic shifts away from Christianity in the direction of other religious movements and with students attracted to other aspects of the study of religion, this does not tell the full story. Market forces and increased privatization in higher education have also taken their toll on the University of Botswana. Humanities subjects, including Biblical Studies, are particularly negatively affected.

7. Notable here are SOTS, the Society for Old Testament Study and BNTS, the British New Testament Society.

8. As proclaimed on its home page, SBL is 'the oldest and largest international scholarly membership organization in the field of biblical studies'. The Society was founded in 1880 and has over 8,500 international members. The catalogue for each meeting is the size of the phonebook for a small town. It is widely acknowledged that the annual SBL congress is *the* place to be for networking, encountering the 'celebrities' of the field, staying in touch with what is happening in the discipline and for recruiting students and exploring job opportunities. While membership is international and eclectic and while SBL certainly offers a smorgasbord of panels and papers, including on minority-interest matters of many kinds, given that the congress takes place in the USA, North Americans, naturally, predominate and there are very many scholars (especially from the Two-Thirds World) who are excluded.

Imbokodo criticism. The word *imbokodo*, which lends its name to Makhosi's distinctive method, is isiZulu and means 'grinding stone'.[9] This word evokes the rallying call of the women's protests of 1956, aimed at resisting racist Apartheid pass laws. The chant of which this word is a part is: *Wathint' abafazi, wathint' imbokodo, uzokufa!* This translates as, 'you strike a woman, you strike a grinding stone: you will be crushed!' The call asserts and exemplifies the persistence and resilience of the protesting women and Makhosi chooses the motif of the grinding stone to bring into the foreground of her readings the interests and concerns of black South African women. Therefore, hers is a postcolonial and therewith distinctly political form of reading, which seeks to bring about social justice. As Makhosi explains: '[*Imbokodo*] focuses on using the Bible as a weapon of struggle for redressing colonialism's negative historical effects and, most recently, globalization's impact' (Nzimande 2010: 137). Makhosi's influence on our project and our gratitude to her are considerable but due to her (hopefully not permanent) departure from academia she was, regrettably, unable to contribute to this volume.[10]

In the second year (2013), Johanna travelled to Gaborone and, together with biblical scholars from Botswana, as well as visiting scholars from Zambia and Zimbabwe, participated in presentations and dialogues hosted by the University of Botswana and Kgolagano Bible College. In the third year (2014), Musa travelled to England and presented at the Universities of Durham, Sheffield and Leeds, again with others making contributions and participating in discussions. Alongside the contributors to this volume, presenters at these events were: Bellina Mangena (Anglican Diocese of Natal, St. Alphege's Parish), James Crossley (St. Mary's University, Twickenham), Tarcisius Mukuka (St. Mary's University, Twickenham), Nelly Mwale (then MA candidate at the University of Zambia), Nyampa Kwabe (then PhD candidate at the University of Leeds, now at Theological College of Northern Nigeria), Rose Gabaitse (University of Botswana) and Malebogo Kgalemang (University of Botswana). Although, for various reasons, they did not contribute a chapter to this volume, their participation and contribution shaped the mood and directions of conversation in positive ways throughout the three years of the project.

Two publications were influential in the process of conducting the events that gave rise to this publication. The first is *Still at the Margins: Biblical Scholarship Fifteen Years after the Voices from the Margin*, edited by notable postcolonial scholar R. S. Sugirtharajah (2008). Our book is similar in that it discusses and evaluates the continuing impact of postcolonial criticism on Biblical Studies. It is distinct in that it opens up and then focuses on one dialogue – that between biblical scholars

---

9. IsiZulu is one of the eleven official languages of South Africa, dominant among the Zulu peoples centred in the KwaZulu-Natal region.

10. We sought permission to republish Makhosi's contribution to a dialogue project conducted in South Africa (Nzimande 2008). While Makhosi, the editors and the South African publisher all granted permission, the Europe-based publisher imposed a fee that was prohibitive for the budget of our project.

in the UK and in (mostly) southern Africa. The second publication is *African and European Readers of the Bible in Dialogue: In Quest of a Shared Meaning*, edited by Gerald O. West and Hans de Wit (2008). This volume (which has not received the circulation it deserves) is superficially similar to our volume and reports on exploratory discussions held over a few days at a gathering in South Africa. Our project, taking place over three years and offering a more sustained and in-depth encounter, draws the net more widely in terms of African contexts represented. Moreover, it features the UK as the other dialogue partner, whereas the 'European' readers of the title of West and de Wit's volume are all scholars from the Netherlands. Our project is thus more in-depth and somewhat differently focused but we have drawn from both volumes and discussed them in our meetings.

In what follows, this volume is divided into three sets of two chapters. Each set is followed by a response to reflect something of the dialogue initiated in our project and to stimulate more engagement and perspectives. The first set is by Mmapula Kebaneilwe and Katie Edwards. Katie reflects on whiteness, blackness and depictions of women in visual religious discourse, including biblical imagery, while Mmapula identifies distinctive techniques of African, particularly womanist, biblical scholars with particular focus on Proverbs 31. The two chapters are very different but each demonstrates that interpretation is marked by the context, including by the ideological forces, in which it occurs. Both also show that the injustices associated with colonialism, Apartheid and slavery have not been overcome but resonate – both in the independent post-colonies of southern Africa (as demonstrated by Mmapula) and in the heartlands of one-time colonial exploiters (as demonstrated by Katie's focus on popular culture from UK and US sources). The responder to these chapters is Nancy Tan, a postcolonial biblical scholar from Singapore based at the Chinese University of Hong Kong. Nancy's response draws inspiration from Mmapula and Katie's chapters and contributes a reflection on whiteness, purity and on the role of mothers in both Proverbs 31 and contemporary Chinese settings that is self-consciously shaped by the political context of Hong Kong and political manoeuvrings emanating from China.

The second set showcases two very different postcolonial-critical readings of biblical texts by Tsaurayi ('TK') Mapfeka and Mark Aidoo. TK, drawing on the experience of colonization in the context of his native Zimbabwe, explores the traces of imperialism in the book of Esther. Mark, meanwhile, uses the Akan office of the *okyeame* (an esteemed speaker) of Ghana to illuminate the power of words in Job. Both are emerging scholars and each in a distinctive way exhibits the dynamism and originality of African biblical scholarship and the interplay between biblical text and discrete African context. The responder is Gerald West who is well placed to situate both authors' contributions within African biblical scholarship. West characterizes African biblical scholarship as all of postcolonial, tri-polar and emphatic in terms of conceiving of the Bible as a place of struggle.

The final set of chapters explores postcolonialism from opposite directions. Elizabeth Vengeyi writes from Zimbabwe and probes how the imposition of missionary activity, ideology and translation have suppressed and distorted Shona worship and conceptualization of the Supreme Deity Mwari, with damaging effect on Shona identity and gender dynamics. Hugh Pyper, meanwhile, reflects on the practicalities and ironies of teaching postcolonial criticism in Sheffield and reinterprets the story of Babel as a story resisting homogeneity and celebrating diversity. The responder is Adriaan van Klinken who, inspired by these chapters, and bringing in his own empirical research on gender and sexuality in African Christianities, reflects on the notion of appropriation.

To enter into the spirit of the volume, we will next contribute accounts of our own encounters of 'the other place'. Hence, Musa weaves an account of her experiences in the UK and the USA through reflections on the possibilities and limitations of dialogue between biblical scholars from Two-Thirds and Western worlds. These reflections are shaped markedly by contemporary dialogue on the urgent topic of migration. Following this, Johanna describes and reflects on early and formative impressions of othered-ness, as well as on teaching in Botswana. Our hope is to have captured in this volume some of the energy and perspective-sharing that characterized this project. Our wish is to open a conversation and to invite and elicit more responses.

Works Cited

Ako, E. O. (2004), 'From Commonwealth to Postcolonial Literature', *Comparative Literature and Culture* 6 (2): 1–7.

Nzimande, M. K. (2008), 'Reconfiguring Jezebel: A Postcolonial *Imbokodo* Reading of the Story of Naboth's Vineyard (1 Kings 21:1–16)', in G. O. West and H. de Wit (eds), *African and European Readers of the Bible in Dialogue: In Quest of a Shared Meaning*, 223–58, Pietermaritzburg: Cluster and Leiden: Brill.

Nzimande, M. K. (2010), 'A Postcolonial *Imbokodo* Reading of the Book of Isaiah in South Africa', in H. R. Page, Jr. et al. (eds), *The Africana Bible: Reading Israel's Scriptures from Africa and the African Diaspora*, 136–46, Minneapolis: Fortress.

Rushdie, S. (1991), 'Commonwealth Literature Does Not Exist', in Rushdie, *Imaginary Homelands: Essays and Criticism 1981–1991*, 61–70, London: Granta.

Society of Biblical Literature (home page, 'About Us'). Available online: sbl-site.org (accessed 17 July 2017).

Sugirtharajah, R. S., ed. (2008), *Still at the Margins: Biblical Scholarship Fifteen Years after the Voices from the Margin*, London/New York: T&T Clark.

West, G. O. and M. W. Dube Shomanah, eds (2000), *The Bible in Africa: Transactions, Trajectories and Trends*, 72–102, Leiden/Boston: Brill.

West, G. O. and H. de Wit, eds (2008), *African and European Readers of the Bible in Dialogue: In Quest of a Shared Meaning*, Leiden: Brill and Pietermaritzburg: Cluster.

Chapter 2

BORDER CROSSING IN DIASPORIC ACADEMIC SPACE

Musa W. Dube

Black Princess in the Queen's Land

Having adopted Christianity as my religion in high school, I decided to study theology and religious studies at the University of Botswana for my first degree, to improve my faith. The University identified me as one of their outstanding students and prepared scholarships for me for graduate training, with a view to me becoming one of their future staff members. In 1988, I took my first journey into the belly of the Empire: I went to do my Masters in New Testament Studies at the University of Durham in the UK. I was hosted at St John's College, where I was the only black student. Oblivious of the conventional dress code in cold and wet Britain, I continued dressing according to the dictates of my desert country. I changed my clothes daily and unbeknown to me, I was rumoured to be a black princess: on account of both my dress and the novelty of my black presence in a relatively expensive and prestigious British University. Many could not understand how 'this African girl' made it to one of the British Ivy League Universities. I received attention befitting royalty from my fellow students, who brought coffee to my door every morning, did my laundry for the whole year, sent me flowers on Valentine's Day, and gave me many clothes (which, of course, were not to my taste). When sports teams were formed in St John's and the main sporting activity was rowing, I found myself highly in demand by various teams! I was black and so it was assumed 'she is good at sports'. Now, consider that in my desert country water is so rare that developing any skill in rowing is very unlikely (unless one happens to be from the Okavango Delta area) – it was comical.

When Christmas holidays arrived, I received numerous invitations to join families, and I decided to take up several, touring from Sussex, via London, to Manchester and back to Durham. In the various homes where I was kindly hosted the conversation of 'getting to know you' always included the question, 'Where are you from?' My answer was, 'Botswana in southern Africa'. Of course, no one knew about Botswana then, so they would say, 'Please bring the atlas so we can check where Botswana is located'. We would page through the atlas to southern Africa – but there was no Botswana. Instead, there was Bechuanaland, the colonial name for Botswana. Embarrassed, my hosts would close the atlas and say, 'We need to buy a new atlas!' Be that as it may, I was surprised at the old maps and my hosts' consistent obliviousness to the fact that colonial maps had been redrawn and the names changed by liberation movements.

Although my relationships with students in the hostel were largely positive, I encountered two challenges. First, my health was troubled throughout my stay in the UK. Second, classroom life was tough. It took the form of seminars, where we discussed authors and carried out exegesis of select biblical books. In general, I found myself struck into silence and quite angry at myself for this. Whenever I ventured to make my comments and observations, there were comments that usually went like this: 'Mmm ... that's very interesting. That is very interesting'. Such comments were followed by some seconds of silence, a lull of some sort, after which the class would take up other issues, raised by another student. Whatever I said and whatever I had perceived seemed to hold no particular importance. I was struck into silence again and again and began to question myself, wondering why my exegetical observations of the text were not worthy of any discussion. This became a vicious circle, for I became too tense, fearing that my silence now confirmed what the colonizer said about us – namely, that black people are just like infants, incapable of sophisticated thinking. I turned to thorough reading and preparation before class and still discovered that I was hitting on the rock of silence. When the last semester arrived, I began to prepare my dissertation and to seek a research area. My supervisor said, 'Why don't you do an African exegetical reading of the Bible?' Quite surprised by that suggestion, I repeated askance, 'an *African* reading of the Bible?' adding, 'what is that and how would I do it?' Everything at that moment came tumbling down. All bells were ringing – although, I confess, I did not hear the loud sirens. I was in shock.

So, if I was to do an *African* reading of the BIBLE, then what was the race of the exegesis that we had been doing for the rest of the year? Why was the race of our exegesis not named or revealed? And was there no training on African exegetical methods of the Bible, to start with? Why were they peripheral, or deemed unnecessary, or something that could only be pursued by an African student on their own? For the whole year our exegetical training had been named an 'objective', 'scientific' and 'neutral' way of reading the Bible. But now that I was being urged to do an African reading of the Bible, a subtext suddenly popped up like a log that has been hidden under water: namely, that the so-called neutral, scientific, objective readings, that aimed to seek out the intended meanings of the authors were not that at all. Rather, this was just another way of applying the European perspective, and making it appear as the universal, scientific neutral and objective approach (Segovia 1995). Now that I had been trained in the latter and been invited to do an African reading, which I had never seen or been taught in the classroom, I did not know how to read the Bible as an African. In fact, I did not even know that I had the right to read as an African – to assert my presence and my identity as a reader. Historical criticism had been training me to be a suppressed reader, who seeks only the intended and original meaning of the (European-like) author (Moore 1989). To read, and in reading assert my own identity had been openly disparaged as *eisegesis*, or reading into the text.

Whatever motivated my white male supervisor to make such a suggestion, and although I was shocked and disabled by my training, the suggestion was welcome. I was being challenged to speak in my own tongue. Resorting to a feminist exegesis that underlines direct experience and identity (see Dube 1997), I decided I wanted to construct a communal and inclusive African feminist Christology. I argued that Jesus as sole intermediary between God and people is exclusive, patriarchal and a colonial construct and that such a model can only be culturally oppressive for African people who embrace a community of intermediaries: namely, ancestors. Consequently, I proposed Mary the Mother of Jesus as our Ancestor side-by-side with Jesus her son (Dube 1990). My supervisor and I had our biggest argument about just how much status I could give to Mary the Mother of Jesus. I had argued that by giving birth to Jesus, the Son of God, *Mary was co-creator with God.* The phrase 'co-creator with God' brought about a heated argument – and that, unknown to me at the time, was a moment of finding my own voice and asserting it. Thinking about it now, I wish I had made an even more radical proposal, by suggesting that Mary was a 'co-creator with God together with the rest of the African Ancestors'! But would I have been awarded my MA? I wonder ...

My first journey into the belly of the Empire speaks about the prevailing stereotypes that are both external and those that the colonized have internalized, calling for a project of decolonizing minds as well as institutions. One of the challenges is to discover that in the colonial metropolitan centres, Two-Thirds World populations are still being seen through colonial maps and names: maps that were drawn by the colonizers, who still do not recognize that their formerly colonized subjects have struggled for and attained independence, redrawn the colonial maps and renamed themselves or corrected their colonially misspelt names. Coming upon colonial maps in the places where Two-Thirds World populations study and work means that their border crossing into the so-called First World is fraught with challenges, because they continue to be regarded as the infantilized and racialized subjects, supposedly lacking full humanity or intelligence. This explains the silence that follows our speech in the classroom and workspace: it is a replay of the historical situation of the colonized, who is being muted even while trying to voice their perspectives (Spivak 2010).

The Two-Thirds World voice continues to be smothered in First World academic spaces. This unspoken yet prevailing open text of the 'muted subject' can have a devastating impact on the self-esteem of the colonized, including in terms of how they study. They may find themselves tongue-tied because the atmosphere is unreceptive or hostile and because they feel themselves internally and externally colonized. This comes through in many subtle and sometimes ostensibly supportive ways, such as when what we say or write passes as 'interesting, very interesting' – but therewith concluding any discussion. This is captured, too, in the popular book series *The No. 1 Ladies Detective Agency*, written by Scottish author Alexander McCall Smith and since televised. The series is set in Botswana, featuring a woman who opens an investigative agency. This detective dates a man, Mr J. L. B. Matekoni, of whom it is said that he is 'a very good man ... He was just easy company. You could sit with Mr J. L. B. Matekoni for hours, during which he might say nothing very important' (McCall Smith 2000: 4). This depiction of the un-voiced Motswana (who is deemed 'very good') again confirms the stereotype of the easily dismissed (because by implication vacuous and 'primitive') colonized. Neither 'very good' nor 'very interesting' is indicative of high regard.

The challenge is, therefore, not just in the attitude of the Empire that members of Two-Thirds World populations study and work with. It is also in the content and structures of the institutions that they inhabit in the context of the West. My institutional context is the academy. My encounter with Biblical Studies in the Empire's centre was that the whole discipline was constructed in such a way that my academic questions became non-questions, or dismissed questions (Dube 1997:11–14). Historical criticism, the then-dominant method of reading in ways to bring out the 'objective,' 'neutral' and 'intended' authorial meaning, was a colonially informed approach that insisted on there being one meaning of the text and one universal way of reading – thereby suppressing heterogeneity (Segovia 1995). In other words, the questions and the terms were already established in the frame of Western ideologies that constructed the comments, questions and insights of the Other as 'very interesting' – but nothing more. With Two-Thirds World questions and observations/readings of the text dismissed and with Western cultural ways hailed as universal, they are urged to mimic the idiom of their colonial masters and, if they fail, they confirm the colonial stereotype of the infantilized subject.

This brings me to Gayatri Spivak's question: 'Can the Subaltern Speak?' Applying the question to the concerns of this chapter, can Two-Thirds World populations speak without their voices being co-opted by the language of Western institutions and by their methods of doing Biblical Studies? The question also highlights the psychological impact on the former colonized subjects, so vividly described by Frantz Fanon. Here I am recalling Fanon's account of his experience of travelling by train: he found himself occupying the whole seat, because nobody wanted to sit next to him because of his black skin (Fanon 1952: 92). In the silence and silencing of theological subjects of Two-Thirds Worlds, we discern refusal to engage, to the point where one wonders if they, too, are sitting and speaking alone or only to their own – such is the lack of serious dialogical engagement by Western scholars with perspectives from the Global South. Fanon's response is nausea, disgust. But is this response at racism, at himself, or both? Such ambivalence highlights the psychological impact of racism on Two-Thirds World populations – the subtle and not so subtle ways by which they are informed that they are welcome, but should refrain from bringing their cultural perspectives into the dialogue space. The 'welcome' is constraining, for it is actually the call to conform or be silent.

When Two-Thirds World populations serve and work in such colonially constituted programmes and institutions they can become so tamed and silenced that by the time they are freed to speak in their own tongue, to ask their own questions, they may have no idea how to do it anymore – because their professional training has been too Westernized and colonizing. Consequently, when one begins to give an African exegetical reading of the Bible, it happens tentatively and at the margins, for it may not have been taught in the white-dominant discourse of the Western academy. It still does not pass as central to the Western theological core subjects. To begin reading from one's own place as a citizen of the Global South, one has to decolonize one's own mind. The larger question therefore is: Are Western theological programmes colonizing structures, which assert the superiority of Western knowledge? How does, or indeed can, dialogue between Western and African biblical scholars occur in such contexts?

Arrival in the USA: What Is in Your Bag?

Two years after completing my British training, I had my bag packed and was travelling to the USA to embark on my PhD. Still traumatized by my muteness in the British classroom and by the shame of feeling somewhat ignored and sidelined, somewhat unworthy, I decided that I would do all that is possible to make sure that I actively participated in the classroom conversation – right from the start. I wanted to break the imposed silence. I even decided that if I have to go to a counsellor to discuss my classroom experience and the tension that I feel as a black student in a white classroom, I would do so. But before I could get to Vanderbilt University in Nashville, there was the national border patrol.

Those who have been to the USA are familiar with the border crossing, entry and customs cards they distribute and the questions these contain. It is all about what is in your travel bag: where have you been and what are you bringing into the USA that might be contaminating, dangerous and unacceptable. This includes agricultural products. And so when I was asked that question, I had to say, yes I have something in my bag. And what did I have? I had a teaspoon of Botswana soil in my bag. My mother had insisted that I should take a teaspoon of soil from my country and upon arrival I should sprinkle it in my glass filled with water, stir and drink. In this way I would be reunited with my country in the foreign land. The drinking of my native soil would heal me from suffering, from dislocation and displacement from my country, she said. This advice was given following the fact that I was very sick in Britain throughout my stay. But here at the border of the USA, the soil that my mother had advised would heal my body from dislocation, was taken and thrown away before I could drink it.

I was soon at Vanderbilt University, located in Tennessee, a southern state. If I was the only black student at St John's College of the University of Durham and one of very few black people in Durham more generally, here in the South there were a lot of black people. If in the UK the emphasis was on historical reading of the Bible, which insisted on neutrality, objectivity and scientific methodology, here I was another world away. The emphasis here was on a plethora of methods and theories, such as: narrative, reader-response, feminist, womanist, sociological and cultural criticism, as well as Two-Thirds World hermeneutics, among many more. I was even able to ask for a reading course on postcolonial theories and follow that route for my dissertation. Be that as it may, I found myself struggling with being a muted subject in the class, if in an unexpected way. My problem, of course, was the context of being black in a southern US state, moreover, a black student attending a prestigious university. As I walked across campus, black people were everywhere: sweeping floors, emptying trash cans, tending the gardens and cooking at the cafeteria. It was amazing how class could be so categorically racially determined – even well after the overthrow of slavery and victories of the civil rights movement.

The upshot was that I felt I did not deserve to be in the classroom. The subtext was that my place was out there with the black labourers – not doing the academic job of thinking. While the classes were not exclusively white, they were still predominantly white. My biggest struggle in the USA was coming to terms with my identity as a black person, with the history and repercussions of black enslavement and with the realization that black people largely remained at the margins of society. I recall how my usually bubbly son arrived from school looking sad. When I said, 'What's up? Why are you so down?' he said to me, 'Today we had a school trip to the prisons and all the prisoners were black'. What was amazing to me was that even an eight-year-old could not distance himself from the fate of fellow black people, neither did he miss that imprisonment in the USA is racially determined. Psychologically speaking, he too knew that the subtext was that his place as a black boy in the USA was in confinement.

Edward Said holds that 'crossing borders as well as the representative deprivations and exhilarations of migrations has become a major theme in the art of the postcolonial era' (1992: 308). There is no doubt that many of us have crossed manifold borders in the making of diasporic worlds. As Avatar Brah argues, in the age of globalization, travel from and to all directions has become so intense that those who are native and those who have travelled are both living in the diasporic space (2003). Border crossing is becoming a norm and the borders we confront are physical, cultural, institutional, racial, sexual and more (Guardiola-Saenz 2002). The borders that we have to confront are not just at points of entry – they exist also in our daily living, in public and private spaces, including in our places of study and work. And so, while I managed to cross the physical border into the USA, giving up my native soil in the process, at Vanderbilt University I had to deal with crossing historicized racial and class boundaries that forcefully impressed upon me that my place was not in the classroom but, on the basis of my race, outside with the workers.

At national borders we encounter border-patrol services. These serve as gatekeepers and as enforcers of law and determine who and what can and cannot enter (Guardiola-Saenz 1997). Similar patrols exist also at the other kinds of borders. How many times have you been asked about the contents of your 'travel bag', or to discard what you brought from your home country in order to pass? How many times have you felt that you are an outsider, even when you have seemingly been invited in? But Two-Thirds World populations need not despair, for it is also important to recognize that though they have been asked to discard some of the goods they brought, there are some that are successfully smuggled in. Borders are not watertight; borders are porous and permeable and they invite creative and subversive crossing.

As diaspora communities, we can begin the act of resistance first, by naming the borders that we face and identifying how these might limit what we say and how we say it. Second, we can name the goods that we are asked to remove from our suitcases. These are the goods brought from our countries, goods that are intimately connected with our identities and that exemplify the unique contribution we can make. Finally, although the border patrols are powerful and although sometimes it is not in our power to defy them without risking exclusion, we should never underestimate the power of our border crossing. As Leticia Guardiola-Saenz argues, we need to conceive of our border crossing as a defiant, even transgressive, act (2002: 135–51). The state of being dislocated and displaced can become a vantage point for prophecy over against the structures of oppression. As Said argues,

> it is not an exaggeration to say that liberation as an intellectual mission, born in resistance and opposition to the confinements and ravages of imperialism, has now shifted from the settled, established, and domesticated dynamic of culture, to its unhoused, decentred and exile energies, energies whose incarnation today is the migrant, and whose consciousness is that of the intellectual and artist in exile, the political figure between domains, between forms, between homes, and between languages. From this perspective, then all things are indeed counter, original, spare, strange. (1992: 332)

Leticia Guardiola-Saenz insists that 'crossing oppressive and tyrannical boundaries [reveals] new ways of redefining the borders of marginalised identities … contouring new territories that invite social transformation and political change' (2002: 143). Similarly, D. N. Premnath argues that '[b]eing in between borders gives one the ability to recognise where borders are and the identity they delineate. It provides a vantage point from which to examine and to critique. The act of border crossing opens up new locations for conversations and new alliances' (2007: 2). While this opens up possibilities alongside persisting challenges, I maintain that the dialogue between Two-Thirds World and Western World in Biblical Studies, too, continues within power relations that do not give equal voice to the dialogue partners (see Dube 2001).

Works Cited

Brah, A. (2003), 'Diaspora, Border and Transnational Identities', in R. Lewis and S. Mills (eds), *Feminist Postcolonial Theory: A Reader*, 537–612, New York: Routledge.

Dube, M. W. (1990), 'Mary as Our Ancestor: An African Feminist Search for Identity', unpublished MA thesis, University of Durham.

Dube, M. W. (1997), 'Towards a Postcolonial Feminist Interpretation of the Bible', *Semeia* 78: 11–26.

Dube, M. W. (2001), 'Divining Ruth for International Relations', in M. W. Dube (ed.), *Other Ways of Reading: African Women and the Bible*, 179–98, Atlanta: SBL.

Fanon, F. (1952), *Black Skin, White Masks* (trans. C. Lam Markmann), London: Pluto.

Guardiola-Saenz, L. A. (1997), 'Borderless Women and Borderless Texts: A Cultural Reading of Matthew 15: 21–28', *Semeia* 78: 69–81.

Guardiola-Saenz, L. A. (2002), 'Border-crossing and the Redemptive Power in John 7:53–8:11: A Cultural Reading of Jesus and the Accused', in M. W. Dube and J. Staley (eds), *John and Postcolonialism: Travel Space and Power*, 129–52, Sheffield: Sheffield Academic Press.

McCall Smith, A. (2000), *Tears of the Giraffe*, London: Polygon Books.

Moore, S. (1989), *The Literary Theoretical Criticism Challenge and the Gospels*, New Haven: Yale University Press.

Premnath, D. N. (2007), *Border Crossings: Cross Cultural Hermeneutics*, Maryknoll: Orbis Books.

Said, E. (1992), *Culture and Imperialism*, New York: Knopf.

Segovia, F. F. (1995), 'And They Began to Speak in Other Tongues: Competing Modes of Discourse in Contemporary Biblical Criticism', in F. F. Segovia and M. A. Tolbert (eds), *Reading from This Place, Vol. 1: Social Location and Biblical Interpretation in Global Perspective*, 1–32, Minneapolis: Fortress Press.

Spivak, G. (2010), 'Can the Subaltern Speak?' in R. C. Morris (ed.), *'Can the Subaltern Speak?': Reflections on the History of an Idea*, 293–308, New York: Columbia University Press.

Chapter 3

OF BORDERS, CROSSINGS, COLOURS AND BOTSWANA

Johanna Stiebert

Reading of Musa's experiences in Durham and Nashville has made me reflect on border crossings, too. This book has grown out of attempts to bring biblical scholars in the UK and in parts of Anglophone Africa (mostly in the southern reaches of the continent) into dialogue about our discipline. What has emerged is: first, each of us brings something personal to the dialogue and second, that such exchanges are sometimes unsettling, not least because of the self-questioning they generate. What follows is not a critical piece focused on a biblical text (a type of writing with which I am more familiar and more comfortable) but a reflection on Musa's border crossings and on how I respond and find my own counterparts to such.

The germination of a conscious awareness of identity, difference and the process of forming assumptions lies in my childhood, in Germany. Until the age of eleven (when I would move to New Zealand), I grew up in a secular family home in the suburb of a satellite town of the big trade city of Hamburg. I had parents who might be called progressive. They took part in anti-war and anti-nuclear power rallies; they were vocal feminists. We talked a lot in our home about racism, sexism and the horrors of Nazism. We discussed contemporary political events – the actions of the Baader Meinhof group, the conflicts in Israel.

In my child-world, the primary encounter with 'race' or 'otherness' involved *Ausländer*. This word literally translates as 'those from the lands outside', with the implication that we Germans were the insiders (although, tellingly, there is no word *Inländer*).[1] Where I grew up, *Ausländer* were predominantly Turkish[2] and had

---

1. In her essay in this volume, Edwards discusses how being white is tacitly assumed to represent 'neutrality', 'the norm', being 'unmarked' and 'unraced' – with acutely damaging effect, because of what it implies about being 'not white' (i.e. not-the-norm, marked, etc.). Being not-an-*Ausländer* functions rather like being white. It is the *Ausländer* who is 'other', 'not-the-norm', 'marked' and 'raced'. The word's denotation and its associations make this clear.

2. Persons of other groups or from other places were given the same label and Turks and Kurds and Greeks tended to form for me one amorphous group. My mother, from New

come to Germany since the post-war boom years coinciding with many Germans moving up into the middle classes and with the acceleration of industrialization and high demand for labour. As more and more Germans were not prepared to do work considered 'lowly', they looked to bringing in people from beyond Germany to do such work.

Ausländer were outsiders. They rarely became very integrated and they were not encouraged to become so. They lived separately in the kinds of houses most Germans did not want to and did not have to live in; and when I was little they had no rights to German citizenship. Even children born to German mothers and *Ausländer* fathers did not have German citizenship rights.[3] There were many *Ausländer* in my community and some children of *Ausländer* were in my class at primary school. After school a few of them would come to our house where my mother gave German lessons. But strong friendships did not form. The *Ausländer* children would not issue invitations to their homes or come to our birthday parties and we did not discern that there might be all kinds of reasons for this. We did not know that *Ausländer* parents might worry about non-halal food, or feel uncomfortable inviting German children to their modest homes, especially when their German language skills were often weak. *Ausländer*, even when they were *in* Germany remained *out*. And a bit of liberal good will did not go far in chipping away at this.

As for black Africans, there were none in my hometown when I was little. But, on trips to Hamburg, to visit family friends, or go to the museum, I would see black men (most often) on the trains. There were few black women, or black children, then. The majority of black Africans were students at Hamburg University. I embarrassed my mother on one occasion (I was about 3 or 4) by asking in a loud voice if we could take the black man in our train carriage home with us. I was clearly fascinated by this conspicuously different-looking person. Everything about 'Africa' was exotic and rather wonderful in my imagination. 'Africa' was the setting of *Born Free*, a place of yellow and red sanded deserts (with beautiful names

---

Zealand, who spoke German with an accent, was also an *Ausländer* but it was clear in my child-mind that she was a 'different sort' of *Ausländer*, one who was not instantly visibly recognizable, who was not assumed to do lowly work and whose children were accepted as 'proper Germans'.

3. This applied to children born in Germany prior to 1 January 1975 who did not have a German father. German citizenship would in such cases only be conferred if a child's German mother was unmarried – because her child might otherwise be stateless. I was born in New Zealand prior to 1975 but because my father is German, I was entitled to a German passport even if I never set foot in Germany. A child born to *Ausländer*, or with *Ausländer* paternity, meanwhile, even if they never left Germany, could not then obtain German citizenship. German citizenship law pertaining to children born in Germany, including in cases where neither parent holds German citizenship but where at least one holds a permit for legal residency, has become less restrictive only for those born on or after 1 January 2000.

like 'Sahara' and 'Kalahari'), thick jungles, mighty rivers and waterfalls and – most wonderful of all – magnificent creatures. Africa's people in my imagination were beautiful and wild – they could run fast, barefooted, through the savannahs, throw spears with stunning accuracy and climb palm trees with agility.

I cringe to think that I dressed up as a *Neger* (the German for 'negro' was in the seventies the standard word for anyone black and the designation 'Schwarzafrikaner' or 'Schwarzer' did not become widely used until the 1980s) one *Fasching*, the annual occasion when children go to school in costume. I had black face paint, a curly black wig and wore a short raggedy skirt made from an old white scarf. I also cringe now as I remember one of my favourite books as a child, *Zehn kleine Negerlein* ('ten little negroes'). In rhyme (often set to a catchy tune) the book tells of ten little black boys each of whom in turn succumbs to a horrid fate (one is made to disappear by a witch, another is eaten by a crocodile). These are my very earliest memories of blackness, Africa, otherness, foreignness.

A lot happened in between my early childhood and arriving on the African continent – to which I will fast-forward shortly. Briefly, my ten years in New Zealand marked encounters with 'othered-ness' that were altogether different from those with *Ausländer* in Germany. (While both Germany and New Zealand may qualify as 'Western', the term 'Western' can be so capacious as to risk being vacuous and – as with 'African' – qualification and nuancing of the term are necessary.) Now I, with my German accent, was marked out as different, though over time increasingly absorbed into the category called 'Pakeha', a Maori word, which refers to white New Zealanders who are (like my mother) predominantly of British descent. The Polynesian peoples who had migrated to the islands of New Zealand long before the arrival of the white settlers are called the Maori. By the time Pakeha turned up, in the wake of the 'discovery' of Aotearoa (the country's Maori name) by seafarers Abel Tasman and James Cook, the Maori had settlements all over the North and South Islands.

Today the Maori form a minority of New Zealand's population and constitute a demographic that is disproportionately beset by problems indicative of disadvantaged status. Maori are over-represented in the lower socio-economic echelons as well as in the prison population and under-represented in positions of social status and authority, including in higher education and business, pointing to entrenched systemic inequalities.

We arrived in New Zealand at the end of 1980 and moved to Wellington, the capital city. In 1981, in violation of the Gleneagles Agreement, New Zealand invited the Springboks, the South African rugby team, to come to New Zealand for a series of matches against the All Blacks. This became known as 'The Tour' and it split the population of New Zealand into two camps: those 'for' and those 'against'. The protests against the Tour were public statements against Apartheid but the Tour also mobilized internal investigations and protests concerning race relations and racially based inequalities within New Zealand. Maori rights movements, which were certainly active by this time, came to enhanced prominence in 1981 and the Tour in a significant way abetted the ratification of New Zealand's Treaty of Waitangi.[4] The Tour made clear that New Zealand is not the paradise of racial harmony as it was (and still is) sometimes depicted.

My family, like many families in the country, was split by the Tour. My grandfather found the protests an unnecessary 'fuss' disruptive of what, in his view, should have been a clash of two great rugby teams, free from politics. My mother, sister and I, however, were firmly on the 'against' side and these were to be for me the first protests I attended. In truth, however, I found the injustices afar, the institutionalized racist policy of South Africa, considerably more affecting and easy to see than the injustices that were staring me right in the face.

New Zealand in many demonstrable ways makes visible and promotes Maori language and culture. Many Pakeha know at least some Maori and have adopted tokens of Maori heritage – greenstone or bone carving pendants, for instance. All official documents and signs are in two languages, English and Maori, and there is a daily Maori news broadcast. But alongside these outfacing signs of inclusion are also deep countercurrents of tension and resentment. I have not lived in New Zealand for many years but every time I do return and find myself in conversation with Pakeha I hear lamentations about the 'Maori problem'. Sometimes there is sadness and white guilt about what is depicted as the decline of a proud warrior people but sometimes there are claims about social scourges, such as gang violence, or child abuse, or domestic violence more generally, being part of 'Maori culture', or there is hostility about Maori being given things (such as land, or social welfare benefits) 'for nothing'. Maori are often – sometimes in subtle ways, sometimes very blatantly – cast as undeserving spongers or natural born second-class citizens. New Zealand – for all its justly celebrated outstanding natural beauty – is no idyll.

Shortly after receiving my PhD, I applied for and was appointed to the role of Lecturer in the Department of Theology and Religious Studies at the University of Botswana. I had sent in my application and emailed the Head a few times. I had not been interviewed and I had not visited. I flew to Gaborone, via Johannesburg, in late December 1999. I would go on to spend three years teaching at the University of Botswana and those years – about which there is so much more to say – were for me transformative and wonderful. Not everything was wonderful, of course – but, for me at least, few things have made me feel more alive than coming to see pretty

---

4. The Treaty of Waitangi was signed on 6 February 1840 between a number of Maori leaders and representatives of the British Crown. The Treaty recognized Maori ownership of lands, forests and other properties but ceded to Queen Victoria's government the sole right to acquire land. The Treaty also conferred on Maori the rights of British subjects. There is, however, no consensus on quite *what* was agreed, given that English and Maori versions of the Treaty differ quite significantly. From the 1970s onwards, Maori grievances regarding particularly land claims gained considerable momentum and an inquiry was formed to examine breaches of the Treaty. This process received increased momentum following the Tour. There have been settlements for Treaty breaches, which have included reparation payments and apologies, but whether the Treaty is either honourable or whether it has been honoured is still a contested matter.

much every day that so much I had always taken for granted or understood in a particular way was actually more complicated, more rich – and also that there was more than one way of getting things done.

Sometimes, stereotypes were confirmed. Timekeeping was indeed 'a challenge' in Botswana. The German in me had me arriving at all meetings by the appointed time – and usually I would be waiting for quite some time on my own before any meeting would actually begin. I also learned, however, that adherence to punctuality is not a requirement for 'getting things done'. Things also got done in Botswana. One – rather typical – incident springs to mind. My computer was malfunctioning (remember the 'I LOVE YOU' virus?) and I needed help from one of the IT team. The time when the technician was due to come came and went. I sat in my office, waiting, getting gradually grumpier. Eventually, I strode over to the IT office, only to find the techie, the picture of relaxation, sitting in her swivel chair having a chat and a laugh with another colleague. By then I knew that behaviour that might have been acceptable in Germany (such as, gestures and words of indignation and reproof) would not be well advised. Instead, I joined in the conversation for a bit, then, when there was a gap, mentioned my computer problem. The techie thereupon came to my office and worked with patience and dedication until the computer was fixed, staying on long after the usual end of the working day. In my homeland the technician would probably have arrived on time or notified me of any lateness – but they would have clocked off punctually too. Things in Botswana got done – and often with more of the human touch.

The connections between peoples, families, communities also took their toll, though. I realized that I, from a more individual-centric culture, had had instilled in me a sense of self-sufficiency and independence. There are downsides to such inculturation but it also brings with it freedoms (providing one earns enough). Outside of work hours my time was often my own and I found Botswana a place where I could be very productive. I soon saw that my Motswana colleagues, while they had the same salary as me as well as – like me – a nice office with a good computer and access to a rather good library – did not tend to have it as easy when it came to conducting research. Quite simply, they had too many demands on them. Where I might get out insurance, the way to insure yourself in Botswana appeared to be to be loyal to your family and community. And this family or community could be quite extensive as well as quite demanding.

It struck me that my colleagues had a large number of drains on their resources. If their education and hard work had transpired in a good job, this came with responsibilities to those in their family who were less well off. My colleagues quite routinely supported children of family members, lent out their vehicle frequently, or hosted extended family for long periods of time. Saying 'no' was not an option and not contemplated. Whereas at first I thought that very many people in Botswana could not manage their time or incomes well, it became clear that for many their time or income was not only theirs to spend. Time was regularly consumed by commitments to family and friends. The generosity routinely extended to drive people around, or to wait with them in this or that place (and waits could be very long) was extraordinary to me.

Teaching in Botswana was very enjoyable – particularly, teaching Hebrew. All my students were at least bilingual (in Setswana and English). Many spoke three or more languages. There was never a complaint that Hebrew was 'weird' or 'too hard'. I gave up giving vocabulary tests because everyone learned all the words every time – effortlessly. Encouraging critical thinking was as difficult in Botswana as in other places I have taught. In Botswana, as I do now at the University of Leeds, I found it necessary to go right back to Bloom's Taxonomy and ask my students to summarize and describe the content of an article, then to analyse and then to evaluate it. Quite a few got hung up on what the 'right' analysis or evaluation was and found it puzzling when I would tell them that I was less interested in their opinion and more in the way they justified it.

More things stand out for me as I reflect on teaching in Botswana. I think often about my class on the Holocaust, or Shoah, as I prefer to call it (Stiebert 2009) in the Introduction to Judaism course. Growing up in Germany and going to school in the years commemorating four decades since World War II (there was a gruelling television programme called *Vor vierzig Jahren*, 'Forty Years Ago'), I had grown up with haunting images of rounded up Jews wearing the Star of David on their garments, of starved concentration camp survivors, and of mass graves filled with what looked like stick figures. I have struggled in a number of settings with teaching about the Shoah in ways that are respectful, avoid voyeurism and allow for absorbing, processing and discussing fully the events leading up to and of the Shoah. I don't think I've ever yet got it right.

What struck me about my class in Botswana was first that my students did not know much, sometimes even anything at all, about the Shoah. And then there was the shocked silence, whispered talk and next the statement, 'but the Jews the Nazis killed were *white*'. It dawned on me then that my students found whites committing atrocities against blacks understandable, to be expected – but white-on-white atrocity perplexing. They had most probably experienced plenty of racist treatment themselves – even though whites were a minority in Botswana and even though Botswana did not have institutionalized racism in the form of the Apartheid laws, for instance. Also, incongruously, they had in some way bought into an idea that whites were 'too civilized' to commit the crimes of the Shoah against other whites. White-on-white atrocity baffled them and they somehow seemed to find it worse than white-on-black atrocity. And on such occasions the extent of internalized suffering and negative self-evaluation became harshly clear to me, as did the fact that it had never struck me so consciously that I was white and that my whiteness conferred such nonchalant privilege.

Of course, being a white woman in Botswana in the early 2000s I stood out and I regularly had assumptions made about me. Such assumptions included that I was rich, for instance, and that I lived in a big house – which I did not. I was rarely believed when I said I was not married and had no children. When I walked to work (I did not have a car for the first year of my time in Gaborone), cars would stop and I would be offered lifts and asked if my car was broken. But none of the assumptions made about me was demeaning and I was not ever treated with suspicion, let alone cruelty. I have never felt that I 'deserved' bad treatment, or that it is 'understandable' if I were to be singled out for bad treatment, or that such treatment could be accounted for by the colour of my skin. After my class on the Shoah I learned that this is a luxury whiteness confers.

Another thing that stays with me is the scourge of HIV and Aids. The longer I was in Botswana the more students and fellow staff died. There was much fear and many death notices. Colleagues and students travelled regularly for funerals. Those were dying days. One day a notice was sent around by email, announcing the University's resolve to confront HIV and Aids at every opportunity and turn. This was in line with the advocacy of the then-leader, President Mogae, who made it his policy to raise the alarm about HIV and Aids and dispense information in every major public address. Free condom dispensers popped up on campus, as did a special unit offering testing and counselling. Posters proclaiming the ABC-campaign ('Abstain, Be Faithful, Condomise') became prominent and now all educators were being implored to educate about HIV and Aids in their classes.

I was not happy about this. After all, my training is in Biblical Studies – not in HIV and Aids awareness – and I was hired to teach courses on Hebrew, Greek, Old Testament Studies and Judaism, which surely have nothing to do with HIV and Aids. I felt righteous in my refusal. But then I was to have another reminder of how blinding privilege can be. This reminder took the form of Musa, who appeared in my office shortly after I sent an email to my colleagues expressing my displeasure at this voice-from-on-high telling me to teach something I was not qualified to teach or interested in teaching. Musa did not get cross with me and she did not say I was wrong. She looked tired rather than cross and she simply said something along the lines of, 'it's not really a choice, people are dying and we all *have* to do something'.

I also learned that Biblical Studies was a different thing in the setting where I was teaching. Engagement with and consultation of the Bible was all around. I had met before Jews and Christians who consulted the Bible and I would go on to meet (during my years in Tennessee) Christians who believe there is just one very clear interpretation of biblical texts. In Botswana many of my students were practising Christians. Moreover, spirituality traditional to Botswana as well as Christian spirituality, and both of these entwined, were ubiquitous. I learned that it was not easy to say 'I am agnostic' – much easier, instead, to say 'I am Jewish' (which is true, given my heritage, though I am not practising or devout). I also learned that the Bible was read with reverence and that reading the Bible was illuminated in terms of lived experience. And HIV and Aids were a painfully invasive and dominant part of lived experience and, therefore, infiltrated the reading and interpretation of biblical texts.

Living in Botswana and the research and publications of Musa and others in the area of HIV and Aids theology and biblical interpretation have made abundantly clear to me that 'text' is part of 'context' and that talking about HIV and Aids in my classroom was relevant and acutely important. I also found, the more I encountered it, that contextual types of criticism are exciting, opening up insights into the worlds within which texts are read and enlivening ancient texts and also the worlds in which they may have been written, used and interpreted.

I still stuck to my strengths in the classroom – focusing much on the biblical texts under discussion and probing with my students what they might mean and could mean – but I felt emboldened, too, to become much more interactive with my students. I began to read with them biblical texts alongside articles from *Mmegi* and other local newspapers, exploring how each text disclosed traces of its context. I learned more about Botswana and my students' perspectives and we talked also – in the class and one-on-one – about HIV.

I still feel heart-pain for my students and colleagues who succumbed to Aids – most often an awful death, often preceded by drawn-out suffering, as well as by stigma, social isolation and poverty. I am relieved that the dying days are past. HIV is still there but Botswana's health care provision is excellent and with advances in anti-retroviral medication HIV can now be managed, with people living *with* the virus, rather than dying *from* a disease contracted through the virus. Life expectancy for HIV-positive persons receiving the medication is comparable with the life expectancy for persons who are HIV-negative. And that is certainly worth celebrating.

I have not abandoned researching those areas of my subject that drew me into the vortex of Biblical Studies. What attracted me first was the Hebrew language, the tingle of reading something that had been recorded centuries earlier and then carefully handed down to be interpreted and reinterpreted through the ages. What attracted me was decoding a word, expression, paragraph, story, and contemplating how these were read, understood and applied long ago. Did a word like 'shame' or 'love' or 'sister', mean something similar to or different from what these words mean to me now? And if so, how and with what effect? I still find myself reinvigorated by my subject when I sit down with a page of Hebrew and a lexicon. I still ponder about decisions of translation when I move between Hebrew and English, or German. But my time in Botswana made me also into a biblical scholar with more animated interest in how biblical texts are shaped, thrown into relief or neglected in and by current contexts. How can I make sense of the intense interest in a handful of verses about same-sex sexual acts and do they illuminate anything at all about the complicated category we call 'gender identity'? How useful are concepts like 'sexuality' or 'patriarchy' or 'rape culture' and how do we qualify them both in biblical and contemporary worlds? It is these kinds of areas into which I find myself pulled now – and that was a journey about the pressure of the present begun in Botswana.

Also, while I already had strong views about social justice before I moved to Botswana, I tended to keep my academic work and my humanitarian and political activities separate. My academic work was, in many ways, a private delight, an opportunity to hide with arcane books and lexica and try to say something new about something ancient. The keen interest in the Bible as a living text and the pressure to read the Bible in the light of contemporary happenings made me aware of how *present* the Bible is – in its traces in idiom, in its reimaginings in fiction, art, film and advertising, in its resonance in law and social mores. And now – perhaps in part also because (in the wake of growing administrative burdens and family life) I now have less time for academic indulgence – there is more merging of my activist interests and my profession.

I do not believe that travelling or border crossing routinely makes us more open-minded or tolerant. Finding myself in a setting where I frequently had to explain or justify myself in response to assumptions (even though these were not hostile ones) probably made me more entrenched in myself in some ways. I certainly did find myself getting indignant and defensive at times, which shows up the limitations of my tolerance. Many of my fellow Germans as I was growing up complained about *Ausländer* not integrating, and I came to see the impossibility of integration while in Botswana, in part due to the comfort of withdrawing into familiarity. I grew despondent at my inability to learn much Setswana and resigned to speaking only English. It was less tiring to resort to ways I was used to doing things, rather than trying at all times to fit in, or follow suit. Crossing borders can be unsettling and isolating. I can only imagine (and not begin to understand) how crossing is experienced by economic migrants, or refugees, in desperate circumstances. Even when border crossing is done from a position of free choice, privilege and adventurousness it can cause dislocation and (not always self-chosen) separateness.

I did not grow up in a Christian home or with the Bible. My first encounter with the Bible was a trip to the local church with my school class while I was in primary school. The minister told us the story of Cain and Abel and two schoolchildren were chosen to act out the events. 'Abel' wore a sheepskin and the minister explained that he was the favoured one. Next, his brother Cain was jealous of him and killed him. God forgave Cain, marked him with a sign of protection, and Cain left home to start a new life elsewhere. I found the story bizarre and I remember thinking, 'that's not a very good story; is that what people listen to in church?'

In the story of Cain and Abel strife erupts in the family, within the territory of the familiar, driving Cain into the unknown where he will find no rest or familiarity again. In Jn 4.1-42, a story interpreted memorably by Musa (Dube 1992), the encounter is between Jesus and a Samaritan woman – two persons of dissimilar background and status – but the encounter yields a wealth of future hopes. Border crossing can take myriad forms – in these two stories it transpires in permanent instability and restlessness in one and in exciting possibilities in the other. What kind of traveller am I? I am still wondering about that but I recognize elements of both stories. And for all my agnosticism, I have found the Bible, as so often, a rich store of images for approaching an answer.

Works Cited

Dube, M. W. (1992), 'Jesus and the Samaritan Woman. A Motswana Feminist Theological Reflection on Women and Social Transformation', *BOLESWA Journal of Occasional Theological Papers* 1 (4): 5–9.

Stiebert, J. (2009), 'What's in a Name?: The African Holocaust', *Missionalia* 37 (2): 192–209.

Part I

Chapter 4

PADDLING THE BELLOWING WATERS AWAY FROM THE MARGINS: AFRICAN PERSPECTIVES OF PROVERBS 31

Mmapula D. Kebaneilwe

Introduction: Paddling Hard at the Margins

Speaking as a womanist, I will demonstrate that 'other' voices are continuing to exert efforts to penetrate the barriers erected not only by Eurocentric male modes of thought but also by privileged black American male liberation theologians and by white feminists. Such efforts have often felt like desperately paddling against bellowing waters away from precarious margins. Nonetheless, African scholars have read and are continuing to read biblical texts outside of Western academic strictures and conventions in ways that make them at home on African soil. As such, we, scholars from the so-called Third or Two-Thirds world continue to advance approaches to biblical interpretation that attempt to make sense of the Bible to the masses who read it as a meaningful document that contains answers to the plethora of difficult existential questions that characterize our lives.

Such approaches, however, are still struggling in the 'main stream' of theology and, hence, doing biblical theology as an African scholar is like paddling hard in the rapids and tributaries of the discipline. My conclusion is that paddling at the margins is set to last for a while since as Africans, more generally, we continue to face a multiplicity of challenges. Poverty, slow economic growth, unequal and unfair distribution of resources and wealth are highly prevalent in African countries (see Gyimah-Brempong 2002:183; Jenkins 2006: 67), as is exposure to deadly diseases, including malaria and HIV/AIDS (Gichaara 2008: 193). Africa is also plagued by insecurity of unstable governments, widespread government corruption and by militarism, as well as by gendered inequalities and intolerance towards members of minority sexual orientation (Oduyoye 2001: 22). While these challenges are not peculiar or confined to African nations, they at least seem to be more rampant on this continent than others (Jenkins 2006: 68). These challenges present themselves as forces to reckon with in my theologizing endeavours and as such can be likened to strong waves that make paddling hard. I will take up these ideas later in this chapter in an effort to show how African biblical scholarship has produced a unique kind of theology.

I concur with Tina Pippin when she asserts, 'Biblical Studies is at a crossroads between the past and ever-present hegemonic discourses and more recently resisting scholarship of the oppressed, the colonized and the disenfranchised' (2003: 170). Pippin's assessment concurs with my personal experience of the current landscape of biblical scholarship. As a womanist and scholar of the Bible I find myself having to resist voices from the past that to this day lead and dominate Biblical Studies and scholarship. At the end of the day, for all the gains made, I find myself still struggling at the margins. No wonder even R. S. Sugirtharajah, champion of minority interpreters, concludes in his reflection, fifteen years after the publication of his seminal *Voices from the Margin* (first published in 1991), that the supremacy of the Western academy, of North American and European voices, persists. He concludes that the enterprise of the 'other' (be this Asian, African, Latin American, etc.) continues to be at the periphery and efforts to shake off the exotic or novelty labels attached to us are mostly in vain (2008: 8–21).

On a more positive note, Paul Gifford accurately states, however, that while Africa's traumatic encounter with the West has led to a damaged self-understanding, independent Africa is active in resisting Western domination (2008: 203–19). That is, Africans, in multiple ways, are affirming their traditional heritage and asserting their identity by resisting Western intellectual hegemony – including in the domain of Biblical Studies (Gifford 2008: 203). In Andrew Mbuvi's assessment (2017: 149), therefore, African Biblical Studies is both innovative and reactionary. He maintains that it is innovative because it refuses to be confined by methodologies and principles that govern Biblical Studies in 'the West' and reactionary because it charts a course that seeks to pursue interpretations, which make the Bible relevant to present realities. This is the point I wish to explore in this chapter by sampling select works by African biblical scholars which demonstrate this dynamism. Thus the intention is to show that African scholars are engaged in biblical interpretation that can be termed 'African'. My argument is that such a stance is indicative of not only a resisting scholarship that says 'no!' to long-time domination by Eurocentric and North American hegemonic discourses and voices but also of an affirmation of the self that is at home with itself.

Africa is a vastly varied continent and discrete contexts will present distinctive experiences and complexities. Hence, there are internal variegations and every individual has a specific and personal context (or multiple contexts) within the wider African context. Importantly, as African scholars, theologians and interpreters of the Bible, we can pride ourselves in knowing that our efforts are motivated and propelled by who we are, including our experiences of enduring and overcoming oppression and colonization by European colonizers and by contemporary pressing realities of globalization. Whatever the specific case might be, such complexities usually leave their imprint on interpretation and this will hopefully be demonstrated in the samples presented in this chapter.

Gerald O. West (2000) insists that African biblical scholarship is marked and characterized by both missionary/colonial encounter and close association with ordinary African readers of the Bible. Consequently, he continues, African biblical interpretation tends to subscribe to the imperative of contextualization.

This in essence means that African theologies respond to and are particularly self-consciously shaped by pressing sociopolitical and cultural realities, including those of deprivation and persistent health challenges alluded to earlier. This is variously accounted for, including in terms of what might be described as an affinity between biblical narratives and themes, on the one hand, and realities of African societies, on the other. Or, in other words, many biblical stories and motifs might be said to have acute relevance for settings of hardship. Hence, Philip Jenkins explains the role and resonance of the Bible and biblical interpretation in the global South as follows:

> the Bible has found a congenial home among communities who identify with the social and economic realities it portrays, no less than the political environments in which Christians find themselves. For the growing churches of the global South, the Bible speaks to everyday real-world issues of poverty and debt, famine and urban crisis, racial and gender oppression, and state brutality and persecution. The omnipotence of poverty in these societies promotes awareness of the transience of life, of the dependence of individuals and nations on God, and of the untrustworthiness of the secular. (2006: 67–8)

It is our struggle that characterizes and makes distinctive our biblical interpretations. But that which defines us also puts us and keeps us at the margin, paddling hard.

In what follows, I will discuss first, the phenomenon called 'inculturation' and next, the interpretations of three African biblical scholars who all examine the Hebrew Bible wisdom text of Proverbs 31.10-31. I will focus on publications by Madipoane Masenya and Ezra Chitando and compare and contrast these with one of my own. My aim is to analyse how we read this text and to identify the features characteristic of each of us and of African biblical scholarship more generally. From this (albeit narrow) sample I hope to distil some broader patterns but also to illustrate diversity within them.

What Is Inculturation?

In his overview of contemporary theologies in Africa, James Nkansah-Obrempong (2007) explains that in the post-independence and post-missionary eras from the late 1950s to the late 1980s, two major theologies rose to prominence: the theology of inculturation or contextualization and the theology of liberation. It is the former of these that I wish to pursue at this juncture. Its many practitioners describe inculturation variously and I will not attempt to provide an exhaustive definition here but rather an outline of what inculturation criticism with reference to the Bible entails. Inculturation involves an encounter between biblical text and a particular cultural context. It seeks to inform, transform and remake the culture through this encounter in order to bring about a new creation (Odozor 2008: 585; cf. Magesa 2014: 7). Paulinus Odozor (2008) explains that the Hebrew Bible is from a Jewish world, but that it went on to infuse the Church and other non-Jewish environments over many centuries – hence, the Bible has a long history of establishing a relationship with the many cultures in which it has taken root.

At the heart of inculturation is the matter of *making the Bible relevant* to the context in which it acts. As noted by West, biblical interpretation in Africa involves an interaction between the Bible, the African context and the act of appropriation, which is performed by the interpreter, whom West designates the 'real reader' (2015: 21–31). Accordingly, the reader/interpreter enables the conversation between the biblical text and the situational context. West insists that engagement between the biblical text and the African context is a fundamental aspect of African biblical scholarship (2015: 21). He further asserts that Western forms of interpretation have been considerably more reluctant to acknowledge that text and context are always, whether overtly or covertly, in a dialogical conversation (2015: 21–2). Moreover, African biblical scholarship has tended much more focally to take into consideration the significance of the reader in making possible a conversation between text and context. This, in turn, highlights both the identity of the reader and the reader's situational context.[1]

Is Inculturation African?: The Bible, Africa and the African Interpreter

It is important to explain that usage of the term 'African' in this chapter is a loose one. One has to acknowledge that Africa is a vast continent with diversified contexts and peoples. We can hardly speak of how all Africans read and interpret a given biblical text for there will be as many interpretations as there are interpreters (Jenkins 2006: 68). The peoples of Africa are variegated at all levels including in terms of socio-economic, political and religious identities, sexual orientation, gender, and so forth. Depending on who and where one is, and even one's associations, one is likely to read a text differently from one's neighbour (Dube 2003).

But, as has already been pointed out earlier, several factors contribute to Africa's contextual and inculturated interpretation of the Bible, which gives it a distinctive flavour especially when viewed alongside most Western interpretations. I know that the term 'Western' is also problematic and also descriptive of considerable stratifications and diversities. Like Jenkins (2006), I am not seeking to advocate a simplistic kind of geographic determinism that destines religious belief. What must be underscored, instead, is that each interpreter is influenced by manifold socio-economic factors in their interpretation of the Bible and it is unlikely that even two different individuals in one country, or town, or street, will have the

---

1. For a full discussion of these matters see Ukpong (1995; 2000) and West (1997; 2000; 2015).

same interpretation of a text. Nonetheless, I will argue that there are certain general characteristics that mark African biblical interpretation as distinctive from Western interpretation.

There is a saying in southern Africa that links the Bible with loss of land. It states aphoristically that when Western missionaries came to Africa they had the Bible and we, Africans, had the land. They asked us to pray, and when we finished praying they had the land and we had the Bible.[2] The saying serves as an important starting point for African hermeneutics including inculturation interpretation. As Masenya asserts, the Bible has been used since the time of the earliest missionaries and continues to be used by the powerful against the powerless. Against the specific backdrop of sub-Saharan Africa's HIV and AIDS contexts, Masenya explains that the Bible was used thus by Western imperialists, whites, men, the rich and is used now, too, by the powerful – and here we are thinking of African leaders, men, pastors and so forth – to perpetuate the oppression, marginalization and discrimination of the powerless: such as minority groups, women, and children – to mention just a few.[3] These power dynamics, which incorporate an overarching patriarchal culture that is still very much alive in most if not all of Africa (Gichaara 2008; Kebaneilwe 2012; Maundeni 2016: 140–1), contribute to the complexity and multiplicity of factors that give shape to African biblical scholarship.

To paraphrase the words of and add to Jenkins's elaboration on African interpretation (2006: 68), I insist that the persistence of poverty, disease, corruption, patriarchy and homophobia in Christian African societies has promoted awareness of the transience of life and of the dependence of African societies and nations on the Bible and its God. Such pressingly felt relevance of the Bible is less prominent in Western societies and this may be due to more stable and prosperous socio-economic, political and cultural conditions. Studies show that biblical interpretations from richer Western countries tend to be most liberal (Jenkins 2006: 68) and West points out that scholars of Western academic traditions ask questions of the Bible using a range of critical methods – such as historical-critical, socio-historical, literary, or semiotic ones (1997; 2000). West further asserts that the degree of emphasis on such questions for inquiry separates Western scholars from African scholars (cf. LeMarquand 2006: 68). Contextual dimensions of reading biblical texts, meanwhile, which are more in the foreground in African biblical interpretation, are not absent in Western interpretation but may be unacknowledged, even unrecognized (LeMarquand 2006: 68). I align myself with Grant LeMarquand, however, that the context of any interpreter, even when it is not described or acknowledged as significant, nevertheless forms the substructure on which interpretation is founded.

2. Editors' note: Please see the Foreword by Vincent Wimbush on this saying.

3. See Masenya's unpublished paper (no date), which is available online, for a fuller discussion.

It is my assertion that African biblical interpretation is predominantly inculturation hermeneutics. In such hermeneutics the text is explicitly interfaced with specific contextual issues and situations.[4]

Madipoane Masenya on Proverbs 31

Masenya (1997; 2011) advances a distinct interpretive perspective from which to view Proverbs 31.10-31. She describes it as 'a reading for the liberation of African and in particular, Northern Sotho women' (1997: 55). The hermeneutic, therefore, is womanist, promoting the rights of African women, and hence, by definition, political or ideological. For Masenya the woman of Proverbs is an ideal and role model whose example can and should be emulated by Sotho women (1997: 62).

Masenya maintains that, as is the case with much of Scripture, both the positive and the negative roles of women are viewed from a male perspective with this pericope being no exception (1997: 62). She asserts that women in ancient Israelite society were most often the household managers and this is why Proverbs 31 refers to *bayetah* 'her house/hold' (vv. 15, 21, 27) (1997: 63). Moreover, for Masenya the use of *balah* 'her lord/master' for the husband is ironic, but also makes sense in the context of patriarchal culture (1997: 63). She notes that while it is good for a wife to care for her husband (v. 23), it is the portrayal of the one-sidedness of this nurturing that is problematic, since it casts the woman as primary caregiver for husband, children and servants, with no explicit expression of any reciprocal care for her. Something similar, Masenya continues, is often borne out in African families of South Africa, where women have many demands on them without their own needs or demands being met in return (1997: 63). Masenya demonstrates that, read from her *bosadi*/womanhood perspective, the poem of Proverbs 31.10-31 can be read as empowering for women in that, being household managers, they are in control of certain activities from which they make a contribution to the family, but that such a role should not be used to confine women and their talents only to the household (1997: 64). As she explains, with men of her own community often going away to work as migrant workers in cities (1997: 64), women often had to lead in non-domestic spheres as well – and would do so with competence: just as the woman of Proverbs does in her business transactions, such as when she purchases a field.

Masenya, therefore, uses the woman of Proverbs to reflect on women of her own Sotho community. She identifies parallels with women in antiquity (e.g. autonomy and leadership in managing the household) but also reads critically to draw attention to women's (often unmet) needs: alongside caregiving, women also require and deserve care; moreover, their abilities can confer benefit outside of the domestic sphere too – both in antiquity and in contemporary settings particular to Masenya's own community. Masenya is clearly drawing on her own

---

4. While I am focusing particularly on Masenya, Chitando and my own interpretation, I am aware also of the extensive work on this pericope by Nzimande (2005).

socio-historical context when she comments on the woman of Proverbs 31.10-31 caring for the poor and needy (v. 20), which reminds her of wealthy white women reaching out to the indigenous poor (1997: 64). But it is also reminiscent for her of the African spirit of socialism/humanism called *ubuntu* (1997: 64). Masenya thus contends that caring and compassion are (quint)essential in African culture (1997: 65). Finally, Masenya comments on the hard work and tireless industry of the woman of Proverbs. She is insistent that hard work should not be the preserve of women, as may be implied in the poem, but that work should be shared and with fair remuneration (1997: 65). Often and unjustly, she points out, this is not the case, with women earning less than men for the same work. Masenya concludes on a strong note that 'marriage should not serve as an institution in which the status of one is defined in terms of the other, and that marriage should not be idolized' (1997: 65). Masenya's reading of Proverbs 31, then, is notable for interpreting the biblical text by incorporating her own context, as well as advocacy for women in the light of gender-based injustice.[5]

Ezra Chitando on Proverbs 31

Chitando, in his reading of Proverbs 31.10-31 for and within the context of the HIV/AIDS crisis in his native Zimbabwe, maintains that the *eshet hayil* (Hebrew for 'woman of strength') exemplifies a 'good wife' (2004: 154). He explains that the poem has gained popularity in his community because it promotes social values and ideals concerning women that the original Hebrew context shares in common with the contemporary Zimbabwean context. Hence, a wife who is industrious and financially astute, for instance, is celebrated in both cultures (2004: 154).

Chitando, like Masenya, also ascertains, however, that the poem entrenches patriarchal principles and hence, for different reasons, not only feminists but traditionalists too have reason to affirm it (2004: 154). Thus the poem projects the image of a self-sacrificing woman who seems preoccupied with bringing honour to her husband and whose reward consists in winning his praise (2004: 154). Moreover, Chitando, also like Masenya, reading critically from the position of his context, points out that while the ideal of a married woman sacrificing herself for her family (vv. 12, 29) may hold appeal and deserve admiration, it is an ideal which, given the realities of HIV/AIDS in Zimbabwe, demands interrogation (2004: 154). Chitando describes the powerlessness of women who try to negotiate safer sex

---

5. Nzimande's unpublished work on Proverbs 31 is not discussed here. Her method, however, has some similarity with that of Masenya's. Nzimande names her reading strategy *Imbokodo* (isiZulu for 'grinding stone'), which recalls the rallying call of Zulu women during the 1956 protests against Apartheid pass laws. Nzimande explains that this strategy uses 'the Bible as a weapon of struggle for redressing colonialism's negative historical effects and, most recently, globalization's impact' (2010: 137). Like Masenya's method, Nzimande's focuses on negative effects on women and women's rights and freedoms in particular.

in marriage in the patriarchal cultural context of Zimbabwe and how unfaithful husbands expose their wives to the risks of HIV infection. In such circumstances, being a dutiful and self-sacrificing wife poses risks – even deadly ones (2004: 155). Like Masenya, Chitando points to a lack of reciprocity: hence, wives are called to 'do no harm to their husbands' (v. 12) but husbands are not called on to do likewise. Following the text uncritically, therefore, could place women at risk. Consequently, Chitando urges that, given the risks of HIV prevalence, wives need to protect themselves from infection and prioritize self-protection over submissive obedience to husbands (2004: 155).

Chitando insists that in both contexts (the ancient Israelite and the Zimbabwean) a wife is extolled for prudence (2004: 155). However, in the prevailing economic crisis in contemporary Zimbabwe, women's ability to provide for their families has been seriously compromised. The economic crisis has instead led Zimbabwean women into temporary economic exile, which has led to an increase in their vulnerability (2004: 154). Chitando advocates that 'the good wife' in the Zimbabwean HIV and AIDS context is not (just) doting and self-sacrificing but, above all, actively seeking knowledge about the pandemic and proactively guarding against vulnerability to infection (2004: 156). The 'good wife' is the one who challenges corrupt and oppressive measures in high places and demands accountability, championing the rights of the downtrodden and outcasts. While traditional readings of Proverbs 31.10-31 continue to promote docility and domesticity, liberating interpretations should shake off inherited traditions that contribute to suffering and death. This, Chitando contends, can empower women in the face of HIV and AIDS (2004: 157). Again, then, we have here an interpretation that reads the ancient text alongside particular contextual circumstances and uses it for advocacy in the service of contemporary human rights.

Mmapula Diana Kebaneilwe on Proverbs 31

In a recent publication (2016), I use the text of Proverbs 31.10-31 to encourage Batswana women to engage in businesses, from small-scale to international ones, as this may improve their own lives as well as those of their family members and of the nation at large (Kebaneilwe 2016: 250). My research was propelled by the discovery that, in Botswana,[6] women have lower levels of income, education and professional skills when compared to men. The same has been documented in previous research about the status of women in Africa more generally (Owusu and Samatar 1997; Ntseane 2004). Studies further indicate that in developing countries – and this includes Botswana – women tend to be relegated to informal and less prosperous and prestigious economy such as street vending and the sale of second-hand clothing (Kebaneilwe 2016: 257; Ntseane 2004: 37 and Batsalelwang

6. The name of the country is 'Botswana'. Its citizens are 'Batswana' (plural; singular: Motswana). The national language of Botswana is Setswana.

and Dambe 2015: 25). This, in turn, confines women in business to marginal socio-economic sectors.

Gender inequity in Africa has given men advantages over women, including in the area of business, capital and loan accessibility (Owusu and Samatar 1997: 268–9). In Botswana the issue persists despite the government's efforts to curb gender inequality in the country (Maundeni 2016: 140). For instance, in an effort to empower women in the area of business, the government of Botswana set up a Women's Affairs Department under the Ministry of Labour and Home Affairs. This department is awarded funds annually to help support individual women, women's collectives and women's organizations to start businesses. For all these efforts, a recent report shows that women in Botswana still gravitate mostly to the informal business sector and continue to be greatly underrepresented in larger businesses and especially as CEOs (Chief Executive Officers) (Batsalelwang and Dambe 2015: 25 and Kapunda and Moffat 2014: 1).

In my interpretation of the biblical text against the backdrop of the context outlined above, I argue that the woman at the centre of Proverbs 31.10-31, like Batswana women, lives in a culture with accentuated gender roles (Kebaneilwe 2016: 256). In ancient Israel as in Botswana, a woman's dignity is associated first and foremost with her role as wife and mother (Lang 1986 *passim*). For all this, however, the woman described in Proverbs 31 navigates her way through the patriarchal culture to explore and realize her potential as a businesswoman alongside her domestic roles (Kebaneilwe 2016: 256).

Peggy Ntseane (2004: 37) makes the point that women who engage in business in Botswana are *both* entrepreneurs *and* domestic servants for their families. The woman in the text, therefore, could offer Batswana women in business good counsel and courage to persist in their businesses and like her transcend stereotypical and solely family-focused roles and expectations. The woman in our text cares for her husband in the home and, similarly, a Motswana woman is expected to serve her husband, doing the housework and tending to him. Ntseane has argued that such cultural expectations affect Batswana women negatively and limit their horizons, so that their businesses almost invariably remain small (2004: 38). My argument is that in the absence of any quick fix for the problem, Batswana women could learn from the woman of Proverbs 31. Like her they need to be proactive and work within and against a culture that otherwise tries to curtail their options and opportunities. She is not a super woman, but a courageous woman who explores her own potential despite obstacles (Kebaneilwe 2016: 256).

Identifying Characteristics in Inculturation Interpretation

Observable from the review above is that the African scholars under scrutiny have tended towards readings and interpretations of Proverbs 31 that pay attention to the context of the interpreter and of the specific audience. Masenya, Chitando and I have each dealt with the text from the perspective of a specific contextual slant with profound personal relevance to which we explicitly draw attention. All of us approach the text from a distinct positionality and while our interpretations differ, for each of us the text and its interpretation in the light of contemporary circumstances convey ideological messages. Each of us uses the text for political advocacy – to promote gender equity among Sotho women and men, to empower Zimbabwean women at risk of HIV infection, to embolden Batswana women to venture into business. Emphasis is consistently placed on defining the meaning of *eshet hayil*. Masenya reads from a womanist/womanhood perspective that is aimed at the liberation of South African women, more particularly, Northern Sotho women. She insists that even though idealized, the qualities of the woman in Proverbs 31.10-31 relate to real-life human women and can be emulated. Masenya demonstrates that read with Northern Sotho women in mind, and cognizant of their lived experiences, the interpretation of the biblical text can be informative and empowering to the women of her community.

Similarly, Chitando reads from and for the Zimbabwean HIV/AIDS context. His conclusion is that in the face of HIV/AIDS, the 'good wife' is the one who protects herself. She cannot be there for her husband, her children, or the poor, if she is made vulnerable to infection and disease. Informed by the painful realities of HIV/AIDS and poverty, one can see that Chitando cannot brush off such realities but instead strives to find an empowering message from the text. He sees a similarity between the portrait of the *eshet hayil* and married women in his Zimbabwean context. Both function in and transcend the patriarchal context that stacks the odds against them. But he sees an *eshet hayil* in his context as well as in Proverbs as a woman who is proactive and, in the context of Zimbabwe, who protects herself from HIV infection and courageously challenges patriarchal powers that are oppressive and unjust.

Continuing along similar lines, I too insist that the portrait of *eshet hayil* is that of a courageous woman. For me the woman at the centre of Proverbs 31.10-31 is brave, industrious, daring and resilient, and because of that she resists and transcends patriarchy. Informed by my own Botswana context, I argue that she rises above the stereotypical definition of womanhood in a patriarchal culture and hence is a model for all enterprising women, especially Batswana women who are in, or who aspire to be in, business. It is because of her courage and resilience that the woman makes it to the top and from that portrayal Batswana women can learn that one can work within a patriarchal system and eventually rise above it to reach one's full potential.

Conclusion

From the brief discussion above, it is fitting to say that African biblical interpretation is heavily, and often overtly, influenced and shaped by the African context. Consequently, it undoubtedly qualifies as inculturation hermeneutics as per the definition given earlier. It is observable in these examples that in Africa the Bible has found a congenial home in which it is treated as informative and packed with life, relevance and wisdom. I have observed that the three readings of Proverbs 31.10-31 by three different scholars, all from Africa – more specifically, Southern Africa: with Masenya from South Africa, Chitando from Zimbabwe and myself from Botswana – present distinct interpretations of the same text. The common denominator for all three interpretations, however, is that all are borne of the interpreter's context. Each of us scholars seeks to address intimate and lived experiences. Perhaps one can conclude that the African context demands a contextual reading and an appropriation. For instance, the challenges of HIV and AIDS, which Chitando's reading confronts, or the manifold gender-based inequities addressed by Masenya and myself cry out for justice. And the Bible is one source for seeking this justice. All of us acknowledge that the Bible can collude with patriarchy and even contribute to injustice: Chitando points out that an obedient wife is a wife who may be vulnerable to HIV infection; Masenya makes clear that the care extended by the good wife needs to be reciprocated and I admit that the Motswana woman who is inspired by the *eshet chayil* is nonetheless double-burdened by the expectation of having to be a nurturer and housekeeper as well. But all of us also find great hope and a source of strength in the biblical text and the talented woman it presents.

Finally, much of African biblical interpretation is inculturation hermeneutics. Texts are read to address and confront real-life issues faced by real-life people. Something is learned both from the ancient text and from the contemporary context of the interpreter and reader, with the two deliberately brought together in a dynamic dialogical process. The result is that the message of the biblical text becomes alive and imbued with relevance in the new context. Such inculturation approaches are not prominent in biblical interpretation from Western contexts though they may indeed be relevant and meaningful there too. For now our interpretations, those of Masenya, Chitando, myself and of most other African inculturation scholars of the biblical text, remain in the maelstrom of the peripheral waters of Biblical Studies' mainstream. In time, may the current take us and our findings farther and farther still.

Works Cited

Batsalelwang, J. and M. Dambe (2015), 'Women's Dominance in the Informal Sector in Gaborone, Botswana', *International Journal of Gender Studies in Developing Societies* 1(1): 25–39.

Chitando, E. (2004), '"The Good Wife": A Phenomenological Re-Reading of Proverbs 31:10–31 in the Context of HIV/Aids in Zimbabwe', *Scriptura: International Journal of Bible, Religion and Theology in Southern Africa* 86: 151–9.

Dube, M. W. (2003), 'Social Location as a Story-Telling Method of Teaching in HIV/AIDS Contexts', in M. W. Dube (ed.), *HIV/AIDS and the Curriculum: Methods of Interpreting HIV/AIDS in Theological Programmes*, 101–12, Geneva: World Council of Churches. Available online: http://www.wwc-coe.org/wcc/what/mission/hiv-curriculum-index.html (accessed 3 March 2017).

Gichaara, J. (2008), 'Women, Religio-Cultural Factors and HIV/AIDS in Africa', *Black Theology* 6 (2): 188–99.

Gifford, P. (2008), 'The Bible in Africa: A Novel Usage in Africa's New Churches', *Bulletin of the School of Oriental and African Studies* 71 (2): 203–19.

Gyimah-Brempong, K. (2002), 'Corruption, Economic Growth, and Income Inequality in Africa', *Economics of Governance* 3 (3): 183–209.

Jenkins, P. (2006), 'Reading the Bible in the Global South', *International Bulletin of Missionary Research*, 30 (2): 67–73.

Kapunda, S. M. and B. D. Moffat (2014), 'Employment Trends and Poverty Reduction: The Case of the Informal Sector in Botswana', *Journal of Social and Economic Policy* 11 (1): 1–12.

Kebaneilwe, M. D. (2012), 'This Courageous Woman: A Socio-Rhetorical Womanist Reading of Proverbs 31.10-31', unpublished PhD diss., Murdoch University.

Kebaneilwe, M. D. (2016), ' "A Woman of Courage": An Interpretation of the Biblical Hebrew Perspective in Relation to Women and Business in Botswana', *Botswana Notes and Records* 48 (1): 250–9.

Lang, B. (1986), *Wisdom and the Book of Proverbs: An Israelite Goddess Redefined*, New York: Pilgrim Press.

LeMarquand, G., (2006), 'Siblings or Antagonists? The Ethos of Biblical Scholarship from the North Atlantic and African Worlds', in D. T. Adamo (ed.), *Biblical Interpretation in African Perspective*, 61–85, Lanham, Oxford: University Press of America.

Magesa, L. (2014), *Anatomy of Inculturation: Transforming the Church in Africa*, Maryknoll, NY: Orbis Books.

Masenya, M. (n.d.), ' "For Better, For Worse" ': Revisiting the Use of the Christian Bible in HIV and AIDS African Contexts'. Available online: http://www.google.com/url?url=http://208.72.3.146/uploadedFiles/hiv_aids/MM%2520presentation%25202%2520October%25201.doc&rct=j&frm=1&q=&esrc=s&sa=U&ved=0ahUKEwjmqvaO6P3RAhVrCcAKHQeLCC4QFggVMAA&sig2=PKZVBqNCj6e4pH1VfQitVw&usg=AFQjCNFtnfo6Hph5XUC-cSY8G9RrcxGQUg (accessed 26 February 2017).

Masenya, M. (1997), 'Proverbs 31: 10–31 in a South African Context: A Reading for the Liberation of African (Northern Sotho) Women', *Semeia* 78: 55–68.

Masenya, M. (2011), 'The Woman of Worth in Proverbs 31:10–31 Reread through a Bosadi (Womanhood) Lens', in F. Faix, H.-G. Wünch and E. Meier (eds), *Theologie im Kontext von Biographie und Weltbild*, 79–96. Available online: http://gbfe.org/wp-content/uploads/2013/02/GBFE-Jahrbuch-2011-Masenya.pdf (accessed 2 March 2017).

Maundeni, T. (2016), 'Gender Equality and Women's Empowerment in Botswana: Progresses and Challenges', in N. Awortwi and H. Musahara (eds), *Implementation of the Millennium Development Goals: Progresses and Challenges in Some African Countries*, 139–62, Addis Ababa: OSSREA.

Mbuvi, A. M. (2017), 'African Biblical Studies: An Introduction to an Emerging Discipline', *Currents in Biblical Research* 15 (2): 149–78.

Nkansah-Obrempong, J. (2007), 'The Contemporary Theological Situation in Africa: An Overview', *Evangelical Review of Theology* 31 (2): 140–50.

Ntseane, P. (2004), 'Being a Female Entrepreneur in Botswana: Cultures, Values, Strategies for Success', *Gender and Development* 12 (2): 37–43.

Nzimande, M. K. (2005), 'Postcolonial Biblical Interpretation in Post-Apartheid South Africa: The *Gebirah* in the Hebrew Bible in the Light of Queen Jezebel and the Queen Mother of Lemuel', unpublished PhD diss., Brite Divinity School, Texas Christian University.

Nzimande, M. K. (2010), 'A Postcolonial *Imbokodo* Reading of the Book of Isaiah in South Africa', in H. R. Page, Jr. (gen. ed.), *The Africana Bible: Reading Israel's Scriptures From Africa and the African Diaspora*, 136–46, Minneapolis: Fortress.

Odozor, P. I. (2008), 'An African Moral Theology of Inculturation: Methodological Considerations', *Theological Studies* 69 (3): 583–609.

Oduyoye, M. (2001), *Introducing African Women's Theology*, Sheffield: Sheffield Academic Press.

Owusu, F. and I. A. Samatar (1997), 'Industrial Strategy and the African State: The Botswana Experience', *Canadian Journal of African Studies* 3 (2): 268–99.

Pippin, T. (2003). 'On the Blurring of Boundaries', in R. C. Bailey (ed.), *Yet With a Steady Beat: Contemporary U.S. Afrocentric Biblical Interpretation*, 169–76, Leiden: Brill.

Sugirtharajah, R. S., ed. (2008), *Still at the Margins: Biblical Scholarship Fifteen Years after the Voices from the Margin*, New York: T&T Clark.

Ukpong, J. S. (1995), 'Rereading the Bible with African Eyes: Inculturation and Hermeneutics', *Journal of Theology for Southern Africa* 41: 3–14.

Ukpong, J. S. (2000), 'Developments in Biblical Interpretation in Africa: Historical and Hermeneutical Directions', in G. O. West and M. W. Dube Shomanah (eds), *The Bible in Africa: Transactions, Trajectories and Trends*, 11–28, Leiden/Boston: Brill.

West, G. O. (1997), 'On the Eve of an African Biblical Studies: Trajectories and Trends', *Journal of Theology for Southern Africa* 99: 99–115.

West, G. O. (2000), 'Mapping African Biblical Interpretation: A Tentative Sketch', in G. O. West and M. W. Dube Shomanah (eds), *The Bible in Africa: Transactions, Trajectories and Trends*, 29–53, Leiden/Boston: Brill.

West, G. O. (2015), 'Biblical Hermeneutics in Africa', in D. B. Stinton (ed.), *African Theology on the Way: Current Conversations* (International Study Guides), 21–33, Philadelphia: Fortress.

Chapter 5

WHITE IS PURITY: CHRISTIAN IMAGERY, POPULAR CULTURE AND THE CONSTRUCTION OF WHITENESS

Katie Edwards

In this chapter, I will demonstrate that while contemporary US and UK popular culture[1] explores and critiques the raced and gendered embodiment of Christian imagery, it continues to betray a deeply problematic religious history of race relations. Using feminist scholarship, critical whiteness theory and an analysis of evangelicalism's troubled history of race, I will show that the structures of whiteness are fundamental for popular culture. Indeed, the representation of a black woman as Christ or Virgin Mary is simultaneously subversive and problematic due to Anglo-American Christianity's history of cultural and political investments in whiteness.

Pivotal for the evangelical tradition are the Baptist revivals of the eighteenth and nineteenth centuries (Bartkowski 2001: 17). Revivals, or large meetings that comprised the 'Great Awakenings', marked periods of increased interest in Christianity – though not necessarily in the church. Fervent preachers travelled to campsites, where spiritual conversions were marked by displays of intense emotion (Bartkowski 2001: 45). These preachers believed that churches had become too formal, and they took it upon themselves to take the message of Christ directly to the people (Douglas 2005: 137). Evangelical theology emphasized individual salvation through a relationship with Jesus Christ (Douglas 2005: 140). John Bartkowski remarks, 'historical evidence suggests that early Baptist evangelicalism – with its focus on the individual believer's direct relationship with God and its employment of an ecstatic worship style – posed a direct challenge to secular and non-evangelical mechanisms of social stratification' (2001: 18). In other words, women and African Americans were assigned a direct relationship to God, unmediated by a spiritual authority. This direct spiritual connection challenged formalized Protestant structures that privileged only white men's connection to God. Formal Protestants, therefore, viewed revival meetings unfavourably, as

---

1. The majority of popular culture examples examined here originate in the USA. Their influence and impact, however, extends to the UK and far beyond.

potential sites of social contamination, where men, women, whites and blacks mixed freely (Bartkowski 2001: 47–8).

Despite the seemingly egalitarian structure of revival meetings, their potential for social justice advocacy was, however, severely limited by the evangelical focus on individual salvation. Enlightenment thought uplifted the individual and inspired 'religious disestablishment', empowering individuals to be responsible for their own spiritual lives (Douglas 2005: 141). But this focus on individual salvation made it possible to 'virtually ignor[e] the [systemic] inhuman social conditions to which black people were subjected' (Douglas 2005: 142). The Great Awakenings were responses to what was perceived as widespread evil in America: drinking alcohol and engaging in sexual sin or other lewd behaviour (Douglas 2005: 137). Far from being considered a sign of 'evil times', the institution of slavery, however, was even supported by revivalists because it enabled the conversion of enslaved black people to Christianity (Douglas 2005: 142). Instead of condemning slavery, revivalists condemned and preached against sins of the body, and historically, African Americans are defined by their bodies.

Nancy Wadsworth asserts that race and religion do not operate independently of one another; rather, religion is a powerful discourse that has given meaning to race. In other words, it is not by coincidence that evangelicalism enabled existing racial hierarchies to go unchallenged. She writes, 'American categories of race and religion were constructed in relationship to one another' (2008: 312). Christianity and whiteness became co-constitutive in colonial North America. As Ladelle McWhorter explains, the present notion of race was first created for economic reasons: 'The white race was established as a legal and economic category in colonial and then in U.S. law and policy as a way of co-opting the European-American portion of the labour force ... so that enslavement of a subset of the total labour force – the African American portion – could proceed unhampered' (2009: 73). In order to control a rowdy labour force that originally consisted of Europeans, Native Americans and enslaved Africans, power and servitude became coded through race. Enslaved black people had no ties to governments that could protect their rights and no knowledge of the landscape and were therefore the easiest to control (McWhorter 2009: 69). In the early 1700s, the religious category 'Christian' was deployed as a justification for superiority rather than whiteness: those labourers who were not Christians were legally forced into lifelong service (McWhorter 2009: 70, 74). But, as Charles Mills demonstrates, 'race' eventually replaced 'religion' as a differentiating marker because religious difference is mutable and can be overcome by conversion (1997: 23). Despite the shift away from using religion as a discriminatory marker, Christianity was later used by some opportunistic Southern white Americans to justify the practice of slavery.

Situating the White Popular Cultural Viewer as Neutral Subject

In contemporary popular culture the viewer is asked to identify as white and with white Christian imagery. Popular cultural images are framed by such assumptions

Figure 5.1 This advertisement for Nivea skin cream provides a blatant visual representation of associations between whiteness, purity and superiority/desirability. It was removed, following complaints of racism (see 'Nivea removes "white is purity" deodorant advert branded "racist"', BBC News).

of a characteristically 'neutral' white perspective. Whiteness allows for the images' subject position to seem neutral, universal, or even irrelevant. Critical whiteness theorists demonstrate that the slippery notion of whiteness bears both political and cultural implications. As George Lipsitz writes, 'As an unmarked category against which difference is constructed, whiteness never has to speak its name, never has to acknowledge its role as an organizing principle in social and cultural relations' (1998: 47). Because North American and English culture has historically privileged whiteness politically, economically and socially, whiteness is viewed as the norm. White people seem unraced; they are simply people. Anyone who is not white is particular, different, and commonly punished for diversion from the norm. Because white people seem to be 'just people', they can claim to speak for all people: 'because we are seen as white, we characteristically see ourselves and believe ourselves seen as unmarked, unspecific, universal' (Dyer 1997: 45). Whiteness seems neutral and unbiased.

The political philosophy that complements the seeming neutrality of whiteness is liberalism. Classical liberalism, rooted in the social contract theories of Western philosophy, is the political notion that the individual is entitled to rights. The liberal subject is widely understood to exist independently of race, sex, or class. However, rights-based discourse has been historically constructed around the white, middle-class, Christian, property-owning male (Winnubst 2006: 25). Raced, gendered and classed individuals have fought for rights with group-based identity claims. Because white people seem unraced, they appear to be individuals without a group affiliation. The language of liberal individualism is, therefore, used to justify group-based policies that benefit whites (Lipsitz 1998: 21). The claim to neutrality, or the claim that whites exist as individuals without a racial affiliation, is politically salient for whiteness, enabling structures of white supremacy to stay intact. Whites appear to gain achievements through merit, despite the reality that political and economic structures are organized to privilege whiteness.

However, whiteness does not operate uniformly without regard to a person's class, gender, or sexual orientation. Lipsitz writes, 'whiteness never works in isolation; it functions as part of a broader dynamic grid created through intersections of race, gender, class, and sexuality'. Whiteness, moreover, is aligned with particular expressions of masculinity, patriarchy, and heterosexuality (1998: 72). The co-configuration of whiteness and patriarchy is illustrated by the evangelical construction of the family. Though evangelicalism originated as a comparatively socially egalitarian expression of Christian faith, evangelical values eventually converged with patriarchal Victorian ideals as evangelical Christianity entered the mainstream (Bartkowski 2001: 20). The evangelical philosophy about gender, sex, and power can be located in the volumes of literature about marriage and the family: 'the family is considered by religious conservatives to be the most important of social institutions' (Lienesch 1993: 52). The most popular evangelical literature about the family espouses traditional gender roles (Bartkowski 2001: 5). Men and women are understood to be essentially different, as can be summarized with, 'while men are rational, women are emotional, intuitive, and nurturing' (Bartkowski 2001: 65). Deriving from this, because men are understood to be more rational, it is deemed natural that they be the leaders of their families. The value placed on rationality in Enlightenment thought, a concept that is both raced white and gendered male, is reflected in evangelical family values.

This concept of hyper-rational faith aligns with Enlightenment discourse around Christianity as the rational religion. The Enlightenment's epistemological shift from God to Man caused Christianity to relocate the presence of the divine within (white) men (Dyer 1997: 16). The period of the Enlightenment did not impair the authority of Christianity as long as Christianity was framed as a rational religion (Douglas 2005: 121). John Locke, the father of liberalism, also 'essentially epitomized the "rational" Christianity that emerged during the Enlightenment' (Douglas 2005: 121). The posing of Christianity as rational provided the justification for unconverted Africans being classified as irrational and therefore bestial (Mills 1997: 22). Because both the social contract and modern Christianity were influenced by similar Enlightenment discourses, they operate simultaneously to maintain structures of whiteness and patriarchy.

Kelly Brown Douglas explains how the influence of the Enlightenment on American Christianity reifies the association between whiteness and Christianity (2005: 110–11). She writes, 'Christianity's alliance with Platonic/Stoic thought was the primary troubling alliance that laid the foundation for a terrorizing Christian legacy in relation to black bodies' (2005: xv). Platonic and Stoic thought enforced a dualism that honoured the mind and demonized the body (Douglas 2005: xv). Whites tended to assume that Africans lacked the ability to reason and were vulnerable to the unbounded passions and desires of their bodies (Douglas 2005: 117). As Douglas writes, 'according to Enlightenment spirit it follows that white people should rule over black people – mind over body/reason over passion' (2005: 118). Platonic discourses multiplied in order to explain the inferiority of African Americans and thereby justify the institution of slavery.

Embodying Christian Icons as Black Women

Richard Dyer writes about the symbolic connotations of the colours white and black. The colour white is used to connote purity, holiness, and goodness (Fig. 5.1), while black is widely used to mark evil, darkness, or filth (1997: 63). The symbolic attachments to these colours frequently transfer to groups of people raced as 'white' or 'black' (1997: 68). Therefore, whiteness is associated with the realm of the divine; white represents light, joy, peace and truth (1997: 73). Dyer writes, 'white people's whiteness enables them to inhabit without visual contradiction the highest point in the Enlightenment's understanding of human development, that of the subject without properties; the beauty of their skin, just because it is nothing "particular and positive", is the beauty of this intellectual ideal' (1997: 110). Whiteness in this reasoning connotes both intellectual and spiritual enlightenment.

Furthermore, whiteness represents the pinnacle of human achievement; all men strive to reach this level of pureness and knowledge that is attributed to white men already due to the colour/colourlessness of their skin (Dyer 1997: 152). The slippage between symbolic connotations of the colours white and black and attribution of characteristics to entire populations based on skin tone uplifts 'white' people and condemns 'black' people, who are associated with sin and evil. Stoic and Platonic thought, moreover, both espouse 'antisexual/antibody attitudes' (Douglas 2005: 27). Striving for holiness required transcending the desires of one's own body: 'The body was essentially condemned for being the source of the very sexual desires that ostensibly tainted humanity and thus separated humans from God' (Douglas 2005: 30). White culture's sexualization of black bodies allowed all black bodies to be associated with evil. This enabled the widespread lynchings of blacks, many of which were attributed to allegations of sexual threat black men posed. By lynching these bodies, white, Southern Christians felt as though they were casting out evil from their Christian communities (Douglas 2005: 66). The blackness of black bodies was the unspoken proof needed for Christians in a culture that uplifts whiteness as transcendent and holy to support the slave trade, lynch black folks, and later to support Jim Crow laws and oppose the Civil Rights Movement.

The association of the black body with sex and sin takes multiple forms; hence, Ange-Marie Hancock writes about the role of disgust in public policies that benefit minorities. She argues that 'women who exist at the intersection of marginalized race, class, and gender identities' elicit a reaction of acute disgust from the North American public most often reserved for sexual deviance (2004: 6). Given the history of American Christianity's collusion with whiteness, some viewers experience a visceral response also to any portrayal of Christ or the Virgin Mary that undermines white patriarchy. Additionally, I will argue that gendered structures of whiteness are so integral to the culture of American Christianity that they have folded into evangelical theology. Consequently, blackness and femaleness pose particular problems for the notion of spiritual transcendence in a culture that privileges whiteness and maleness.

Transcendence of the body is imperative for Christian theology, which reinstates the white male as the subject of Christianity (Dyer 1997: 24–5). The incarnation of God as a man in the figure of Jesus Christ, who transcends his body by also being fully spirit, poses a particular challenge for those who are defined by their bodies rather than by mind or spirit. Thirteenth-century theologian Thomas Aquinas already was of the opinion that 'Christ had to be incarnated as a male because only males possess full humanity' (Ruether 2009: 94). St Augustine, too, defended the notion that just men are fully human because they possess *both* body and mind. The relationship between men and women is that of mind over body (Ruether 2009: 93). Jesus's moral authority derives from his ability to overcome his human flesh, yet women and people of colour are essentially embodied (Nelson 1978: 12). Women are defined by their bodies, particularly by their reproductive capacity and motherhood (Dyer 1997: 27). Furthermore, women's bodies are innately sinful, because original sin is attributed to Eve, the proto-woman (Ruether 2009: 94).

Blackness is also defined by the body: 'the black body in particular is seen as paradigmatically a body' (Mills 1997: 51). In addition, blackness is likened to moral depravity and hypersexuality, the antithesis of rationality (Mills 1997: 46; Douglas 2005: 123). Black women's bodies are threatening to white masculinity because of their sexual provocation. This concept is documented as early as the fourth and fifth centuries CE when monks in the Egyptian desert indicated that the Ethiopian, or black, woman was a sexual threat to the monastic life (Byron 2002: 102). The notion of sexual threat continues today in the myth of the black male rapist (McWhorter 2009: 142). Douglas writes, 'platonized Christianity demonizes the body and sexuality, thereby implying the demonization of sexualized people' (2005: 123). In other words, bodies of women, people of colour, as well as of queers are deemed innately sinful as a result of the mind/body dichotomy. The body and sexuality are suspected of obstructing the purity of a white, masculine spiritual life (Nelson 1978: 19).

Just as the social contract is dependent on an abstracted subject that is independent of the body, Christianity relies on the overcoming of the body by the spirit or the mind. The figure of Jesus Christ reinforces the supposed neutrality of the liberal subject. Christianity claims that the figure of Jesus is an example for all humans despite the particularity of his body, which is the same body that is the 'neutral' subject of the social contract (Mills 1997: 53). The emphasis on God's incarnation as a human minimizes the race and sex of Jesus's body. Just as Jesus is celebrated as human rather than male, white people are commonly understood to be humans without a race: 'There is no more powerful position than that of being "just" human. The claim to power is the claim to speak for the commonality of humanity' (Dyer 1997: 2). Whiteness proclaims to transcend race and thereby transcend bodies, demonstrating its pure spiritual nature (Dyer 1997: 24–5). Meanwhile, Jesus is said to have lived a pure spiritual life that transcended bodily desires, thereby exemplifying whiteness. Though historically Jesus was not 'white' per se, he has been whitened in the Western practice of Christianity (Dyer 1997: 17). Renaissance images already portrayed him predominantly as fair and blue-eyed (Dyer 1997: 68).

Popular Culture: Trapped in Tropes

The question, then, is: Are there any examples of popular culture that successfully undermine these systems of whiteness and patriarchy in their rendering of a black woman as Christian icon?

On the first day of US Black History Month, Beyoncé revealed her second pregnancy in a series of striking and beautiful images re-appropriating classical and religious iconography. The central image, posted on her Instagram account, depicts the artist and activist in the style of the Virgin Mary: wearing a veil, surrounded by a halo of flowers. The announcement and accompanying image quickly became the most liked post on Instagram and numerous press articles appeared, attempting to decode the symbolism in Beyoncé's visual essay.

While *The Guardian* and *Vox* picked up on the Virgin Mary imagery and its associations with authority and virtue, *The New York Post* went furthest, dedicating its front page to the 'Beymaculate Conception'.

The Virgin Mary is traditionally represented in art as a white woman. Often her complexion takes the palest possible hue, apparently connoting holiness and innocence. As Dyer writes, 'in Western representation, whites are overwhelmingly and disproportionately predominant, have the central and elaborated roles, and above all are placed as the norm, the ordinary, the standard. Whites are everywhere in representation' (1997: 102). Whiteness, then, occupies a position of cultural hegemony as 'normal' and neutral (Smith 2004). And religious iconography that – quite literally – represents whiteness as divine is a means of reproducing white power and superiority.

Beyoncé's re-appropriation of Virgin Mary iconography offers a biting critique of this supreme exemplar of feminine whiteness and the ideology that constructs and perpetuates it. In a historical moment when white supremacy was echoed in the 'America First' slogan of US President Donald Trump, Beyoncé simultaneously dislodged 'white' from its central place in religious iconography and Trump from his monopoly of press headlines.

Beyoncé is no stranger to the appropriation of religious iconography to challenge cultural norms. Cultural critic and theorist bell hooks coined the term 'oppositional gaze' in 1992 to 'see, name, question and ultimately transform' oppressive racialized images. In 2013, Beyoncé released the video for *Mine*, in which she is also portrayed as the Virgin Mary, this time recreating Michelangelo's *La Pietà* (Fig. 5.2), literally surrounded by whiteness, to enact the oppositional gaze and subvert the racist and sexist ideas around ownership and black women.

Christian imagery offers prescriptive images of socially approved women. As Douglas argues, 'positive images define what female "goodness" looks like and urges women to imitate the qualities of these images' (2005: 20). Images of the Virgin Mary are central to Western culture as a symbol of ideal femininity that equates whiteness with beauty, purity and virtue, and artistic representations of the Mother of Christ have helped to define how women are publicly represented.

Beyoncé does not only convey a powerful and iconic image of black femininity in her pregnancy announcement images. Images of the Virgin Mary usually depict her fully clothed, including a head covering. The Virgin Mary's attire routinely suggests chastity, purity and (sexual and spiritual) virtue. But Beyoncé recreates and subverts this ideal by posing in mismatched lingerie, cradling her pregnant belly, and in doing so fuses elements of the 'Jezebel', one of the most prominent stereotypes of black women, with Virgin Mary imagery. This boldly challenges concepts of both 'acceptable' female sexuality and racialized stereotypes.

Black women came to be associated with Jezebel, another stereotype based on a biblical character, during slavery when 'the Black woman as Jezebel was a perfect foil to the White, middle-class woman who was pure, chaste and innocent' (Douglas 2005: 19). The Jezebel stereotype was used to rationalize sexual atrocities against black women and its insidious influence persists in contemporary culture. Hence, sociologist Anthony Cortese found that in popular culture black women are often othered, animalized and exoticized, associating women of colour with primitivity and wild sexuality. For example, where all women are objectified and hypersexualized in advertising, black women are far more often marked as hypersexual *and* subhuman, or to take novelist Alice Walker's famous words: 'Where white women are depicted as human bodies if not beings, black women are depicted as shit' (Walker 1981: 52).

The cultural residue of the Jezebel stereotype means, therefore, that black women continue to be more vulnerable to sexual assault and, as psychologist Carolyn M. West explains: 'Black women may receive a double-dose of cultural rape myths, those that target all survivors and those that claim black women especially for deserving the assault' (2008: 189). In the images accompanying her pregnancy announcement, Beyoncé simultaneously confronts and undermines the historical racial and sexist stereotypes of the Virgin Mary and Jezebel, and responds to the association between whiteness and purity that remains very much alive in Anglo-American culture.

Figure 5.2 Michelangelo, *La Pietà* (Creative Commons image).

In July 2017, Beyoncé publicly released the first official photo of her twins – one-month-old Rumi and Sir Carter (Harmon 2017). The image – which, again, quickly became one of the most liked on Instagram – echoes her pregnancy announcement from February, once again referencing religious and classical icons: this time both Botticelli's Venus and, in what has become something of a signature move for her, the Virgin Mary.

Beyoncé's birth announcement, then, is an extension of the divine feminine theme she invokes in her earlier pregnancy announcement, as well as in her performance at the 2017 Grammy Award Ceremony (Blair 2017). By referencing religious iconography, and particularly Virgin Mary symbolism, Beyoncé simultaneously reinforces and subverts dominant cultural narratives of motherhood. Her representation of motherhood, moreover, draws also from the Black Madonna tradition in which Mary – and sometimes Jesus – is represented in paintings and statues with dark skin. This tradition is associated with power, miracles and ancient mother goddesses – but it too has been subjected to whitewashing and used as a tool to perpetuate racism. Hence, Catholic authorities have attempted to downplay or even erase any racial element of the Black Madonna by insisting that the darkness of these statues is not original but caused by external influences, such as oxidization.

Figure 5.3 Black Madonna and Child, Chartres Cathedral (Creative Commons image).

The famous Black Madonna at Chartres Cathedral (Fig. 5.3), for example, was the subject of controversy in 2014 after it was repainted as part of a refurbishment – turning the Black Madonna white in the process. In a scalding article for the *New York Review of Books*, American architecture critic Martin Filler (2014) laments:

> Whenever and however Chartres's Black Madonna acquired its mysterious patina – through oxidation or smoke from candles and incense – it was familiar as such to centuries of the faithful until its recent multicoloured makeover, which has transformed the Mother of God into a simpering kewpie doll.

In her account of her post-college travels, black feminist writer bell hooks also critiques European worship of the Black Madonna. For all the Black Madonna veneration, she found Europe to be rampant with racism: the worship of a black woman did nothing to 'alter the politics of domination outside, in that space of the real' (1994: 86).

A (Black) Woman's Place

Beyoncé, then, draws on a complex tradition of political resistance to disrupt white supremacist narratives of black motherhood. But her representations have not gone without criticism.

Beyoncé's pregnancy and birth images have been critiqued, for instance, for glorifying, glamourizing and romanticizing motherhood. Sharon Kellaway, an Irish woman who also just gave birth to twins, parodies Beyoncé's Instagram birth announcement to show ordinary women's experience of motherhood, saying that the singer looked 'so unrealistic' (Stewart 2017). Certainly, Beyoncé's perfectly honed post-pregnancy body is not common to most new mothers. Celebrity pregnancies are hyper-commodified and the shot of the celebrity post-partum figure is even more desirable in the public domain than a photo of the baby. Beyoncé has controlled the representation of her body by managing and releasing her own image. But the capability of a celebrity with extreme wealth, a management team, personal trainers and stylists, chefs and round-the-clock childcare, to make a speedy return to socially accepted standards of beauty is used to control 'ordinary' women.

Film and media academic Rebecca Feasey observes that 'irrespective of the reality of celebrity pregnancy, delivery or the ensuing maternal role, what is represented is an orchestrated and deliberately considered image of motherhood' (2012: 93). The tabloids and gossip magazines have been quick to congratulate Beyoncé on her almost immediate return to shape – thereby presenting her to women readers as an example of appropriate post-pregnancy body discipline and linking women's maternal bodies to 'good' or 'bad' motherhood. As sociologist Meredith Nash argues 'a fit, risk-free, flexible, and responsible body is the mark of a good mother' (2012: 63).

Beyoncé's images have also been criticized for reinforcing a pro-natalist narrative, which insists that women's value lies in motherhood. Beyoncé's 'endless Virgin Mary/Sun goddess routine' at the Grammys exercised *New York Post* journalist Naomi Schaeffer Riley, who responded:

> Why is it that in an era when women are constantly insisting that they should not be defined by their traditional, biological roles, we have fetishised motherhood to such an extent? ... Our cultural imperative to elevate motherhood to both the most important thing in the world and the hardest thing in the world is getting out of control. (2017)

Disrupting Stereotypes

Riley was promptly rebutted by Australia-based Tongan writer Meleika Gesa-Fatafehi: 'The article is written by a white woman who shames motherhood, especially black motherhood' (2017). Gesa-Fatafehi makes a powerful point. The criticisms of Beyoncé's Virgin Mary imagery fail to address the racial politics of motherhood and the overtly political statement Beyoncé makes in her use of religious iconography. She draws from the most culturally influential imagery to disrupt dominant stereotypes of black motherhood.

US feminist writer Amber E. Kinser writes:

> Women of color ... have historically been more concerned with having the children they choose, rather than being forced to produce children through slavery or rape or forced to stop producing children through sterilisation; keeping their children, rather than seeing them sent off to assimilation boarding schools, sold off as slaves, or taken from them because nonwhite mothering practices are distrusted; and raising their children in ways they've determined are best for their families, rather than having their cultural values, histories, and ways of speaking denigrated in schools, public policy, and other institutions such as healthcare and media. (2010: 112)

In her pregnancy and birth images, Beyoncé thus effectively negotiates a terrain most closely associated with whiteness – 'good' motherhood.

Ruether demonstrates that white supremacist culture manifests in multiple and sometimes contradictory portrayals of 'others'. Black bodies have been characterized as sexually dangerous if not properly controlled: 'But, on the other hand, when properly humble and submissive, the elderly black male becomes the Uncle Tom, who, with his wife, Mammy, loves and nurtures the white child in preference to their own children' (2009: 102). Coded in the notion of religious stereotypes is race and gender. Embodying Christ and the Virgin Mary as something other than white does not just challenge religious stereotypes, it challenges racism and sexism.

Structural Racism vs Individual Racists

Simplifying the structural issue of racism to a problem of stereotypes and individual judgments is reflective of the broader evangelical approach to race. Evangelicals tend to attribute the problem of racism to interpersonal conflicts and prejudiced individuals (Tranby and Hartmann 2008: 343). In such a scheme, racism can be overcome by developing better cross-racial relationships between individuals. Racism is not viewed as a structural problem that requires government interference (Wadsworth 1997: 368). This interpersonal approach inevitably leads to racist stereotypes: 'it is not accidental that evangelical ideals lead into negative racial stereotypes; these ideals actually need such stereotypes and prejudices to explain, justify, and legitimate the social inequalities they almost inevitably produce' (Tranby and Hartmann 2008: 346). Because evangelicalism is rooted in individualist notions of salvation and a personal relationship with Christ, evangelical values align with the individualist tenets of liberal capitalism. Ascribing to the US belief of equal opportunity, 'they tend to see racial inequality as separate from systemic structures and policies, to hold blacks accountable for their problems, and to believe that, if blacks are subordinated, it is because they suffer from relational dysfunction and a lack of responsibility' (Tranby and Hartmann 2008: 348). Because a structural analysis of racism is outside the evangelical framework, evangelicals then have no other choice but to blame black Americans for their own subordination.

Defenders of liberalism reject the suggestion that the system is centred on the white male subject and subscribe to the idea that the USA is in fact a meritocracy. The result is what scholars might call 'laissez-faire racism' or 'neoracism' (Bobo, cited in Tranby and Hartmann 2008: 342; Lipsitz 1998: 5). By denying the privileges of whiteness, blacks are then blamed for their own suffering, resulting in racist stereotypes that further perpetuate systems of inequality. Neoracism and the investment in white privilege unify the Christian Right with fiscal conservatives (Lipsitz 1998: 15–16). The purportedly 'neutral' subject of the liberal social contract has the same qualities as the 'neutral' subject in North American Christianity. White patriarchy is reinstated in the Christian faith due to its individualist values. The white male liberal subject is enabled through a system that invisibly supports his interests and blames others for their subordination.

Neoracism is more subtle and difficult to pinpoint than more explicit forms of racism that motivate one person to cause harm to another. One way neoracism operates is through 'the equation of whiteness with American civic identity' (Tranby and Hartmann 2008: 347). Eric Tranby and Douglas Hartmann write, 'many of the key values of the liberal American civic identity – freedom, individualism, independence, equality of opportunity, etc. – derive from the blending of evangelical Christianity and Enlightenment philosophy' (2008: 343). The combination of Christianity and Enlightenment values resulted in evangelicalism being regarded as the 'quintessential American faith' (Douglas 2005: 134). Therefore, evangelicals' defence of North American culture is the result of an investment in white identity and privilege: 'Because the norms and values that form the evangelical idea of "American-ness" are implicitly white, the demands for increased recognition for minority groups is perceived as a threat to these values and norms' (Tranby and Hartmann 2008: 348). Beyoncé's portrayal of the Virgin Mary as black and female undermines evangelicals' cultural and national investments in whiteness.

The equation of whiteness with American-ness, rooted in religious conceptualizations of Manifest Destiny, has had very poor results for people of colour, who have been historically subjected to slavery, colonialism, political exclusion, and even genocide (Wadsworth 2008: 321). Christ's spiritual transcendence is replicated in nationalist narratives about manifest destiny: 'US exceptionalism hangs on a narrative of transcendence' (Puar 2007: 8). The USA is somehow spiritually enlightened through its embrace of Christianity as a sort of national religion, which speaks to US exceptionalism and the nation's sacred mission (Puar 2007: 8). This notion of exceptionalism can also be derived from the biblical concept of an elect people: 'North Americans continued to promote racist themes of a unique election of an "Anglo-Saxon" American people as God's elect, associated both with superior political institutions (democracy) and with superior moral-religious traditions' (Ruether 2009: 100). The discourse shifted from identifying those who accept Christ as the chosen people to identifying the chosen people as white. The notion of spiritual transcendence, which is tied to white masculinity, is used to demonstrate the greatness of Christ and the Christian faith, and therefore the US nation.

Conclusion

Popular culture ultimately reifies structures of whiteness and patriarchy. Simply embodying Christ or the Virgin Mary as a black woman is enough to expose the anxieties of the evangelical community regarding race, gender and power.

I have argued that popular cultural images are fundamentally rooted in the role of whiteness in bodily transcendence. As long as the mind and the spirit are attributed to white masculinity and non-whites and non-masculinity are relegated to the realm of the body and sexual desire, evangelicalism will continue to reify structures of whiteness, patriarchy, colonialism, heterosexuality and national exceptionalism. As Douglas writes, 'inasmuch as evangelical Protestant traditions substantially embrace Platonized theology they will continue to be predisposed to troubling connections with unjust power' (2005: 146). As racism becomes less acceptable in society at large, evangelicals take up issues of racial reconciliation in their own communities (Wadsworth 2008: 329). Alliances have been forged between black and white Christians regarding the conservative family values agenda; however, white evangelicals seem to expect that blacks will assimilate into the culture of white evangelicalism without changing in any way their political trajectory (Wadsworth 1997: 367). Mills writes, 'Whereas before it was denied that non-whites were equal persons, it is now pretended that non-whites are equal abstract persons who can be fully included in the polity merely by extending the scope of the moral operator, without any fundamental change in the arrangements that have resulted from the previous system of explicit de jure racial privilege' (1997: 94). By asking black Christians to support the structures of white patriarchy, whiteness is reified and structural racism goes unchallenged. Popular culture colludes with systems of racial privilege by ultimately failing to undermine them.

Works Cited

Bartkowski, J. P. (2001), *Remaking the Godly Marriage: Gender Negotiation in Evangelical Families*, New Jersey: Rutgers University Press.

Beyoncé (2013), *Mine* (ft. Drake) [Music video], Parkwood Columbia. Available on YouTube.

Blair, O. (13 February 2017), 'Grammys 2017: Watch Beyoncé's Performance in Full: The Night Belonged to One Woman', *The Independent*. Available online: www.independent.co.uk (accessed 27 August 2017).

Byron, G. L. (2002), *Symbolic Blackness and Ethnic Difference in Early Christian Literature*, New York: Routledge.

Cortese, A. J. (2007), *Provocateur: Images of Women and Minorities in Advertising*, New York: Rowan and Littlefield Publishers

Douglas, K. B. (2005), *What's Faith Got to Do with It? Black Bodies/Christian Souls*, New York: Orbis Books.

Dyer, R. (1997), *White: Essays on Race and Culture*, New York: Routledge.

Feasey, R. (2012), *From Happy Homemaker to Desperate Housewives: Motherhood and Popular Television*, London: Anthem Press.

Filler, M. (14 December 2014), 'A Scandalous Makeover at Chartres', *New York Review Daily*. Available online: www.nybooks.com (accessed 27 August 2017).

Gesa-Fatafehi, M. (February 2017), 'Beyoncé's Babies Are Miracles and Mothers Are Goddesses', *Affinity Magazine*. Available online: www.affinitymagazine.us (accessed 27 August 2017).

Hancock, A.-M. (2004), *The Politics of Disgust: The Public Identity of the Welfare Queen*, New York: New York University Press.

Harmon, S. (14 July 2017), 'Beyoncé publishes photo of her twins on Instagram', *The Guardian*. Available online: www.theguardian.com (accessed 27 August 2017).

hooks, b. (1992), *Black Locks: Race and Representation*, Boston: South End Press.

hooks, b. (1994), *Outlaw Culture: Resisting Representations*, New York: Routledge.

Kinser, A. E. (2010), *Motherhood and Feminism: Seal Studies*, Boston: Da Capo Press.

Lienesch, M. (1993), *Piety and Politics in the New Christian Right: Redeeming America*, Chapel Hill: The University of North Carolina Press.

Lipsitz, G. (1998), *The Possessive Investment in Whiteness: How White People Profit from Identity Politics*, Philadelphia: Temple University Press.

Ma, Remy (date of release: 28 August 2007), *Shesus Khryst* (hosted by Superstar Jay) [Album]. Available online: https://mobile.datpiff.com (accessed 27 August 2017).

McWhorter, L. (2009), *Racism and Sexual Oppression in Anglo-America: A Genealogy*, Indianapolis: Indiana University Press.

Mills, C. W. (1997), *The Racial Contract*, Ithaca: Cornell University Press.

Nash, M. (2012), *Making 'Postmodern' Mothers: Pregnant Embodiment, Baby Bumps and Body Image*, London: Palgrave Macmillan.

Nelson, J. B. (1978), *Embodiment: An Approach to Sexuality and Christian Theology*, Minneapolis: Augsburg Publishing House.

'Nivea removes "white is purity" deodorant advert branded "racist"' (no author) (4 April 2017). Available online: www.bbc.co.uk (world-europe-39489967) (accessed 18 August 2017).

Puar, J. K. (2007), *Terrorist Assemblages: Homonationalism in Queer Times*, Durham, NC: Duke University Press.

Riley, N. S. (18 February 2017), 'Having a Baby Isn't a Miracle and Doesn't Make You a Goddess', *New York Post*. Available online: www.nypost.com (accessed 27 August 2017).

Ruether, R. R. (2009), *Christianity and Social Systems: Historical Constructions and Ethical Challenges*, New York: Rowman & Littlefield Publishers.

Smith, P. (2004), 'Whiteness, Normal Theory, and Disability Studies', *Disability Studies Quarterly* (Spring) 24 (2) (no pagination).

Stewart, A. (17 July 2017), 'Beyoncé: Cork mother's parody goes viral', BBC News NI. Available online: www.bbc.co.uk (accessed 27 August 2017).

Tranby, E. and D. Hartmann (2008), 'Critical Whiteness Theories and the Evangelical "Race Problem": Extending Emerson and Smith's *Divided by Faith*', *Journal for the Scientific Study of Religion* 47 (3): 341–59.

Wadsworth, N. (1997), 'Reconciliation Politics: Conservative Evangelicals and the New Race Discourse', *Politics and Society* 25 (3): 341–76.

Wadsworth, N. (2008), 'Reconciling Fractures: The Intersection of Race and Religion in United States Political Development', in J. Lowndes, J. Novkov and D. T. Warren (eds), *Race and American Political Development*, 312–36, New York: Routledge.

Walker, A. (1981), *You Can't Keep a Good Woman Down*, New York: Harcourt Brace Jovanovich.

West, C. M. (2008), 'Mammy, Jezebel, Sapphire, and Their Homegirls: Developing an "Oppositional Gaze" Toward the Images of Black Women', in J. C. Chrisler, C. Golden and P. D. Rozee (eds), *Lectures on the Psychology of Women* (4th edn), 186–99, Boston, MA: McGraw-Hill.

Winnubst, S. (2006), *Queering Freedom*, Bloomington: Indiana University Press.

Chapter 6

RESPONSE: BETWEEN RESISTING WHITE AND REFLECTING BLACK: A HONG KONG RESIDENT'S RESPONSE AND PERSPECTIVE

Nancy N. H. Tan

Introduction

I have been asked to respond to the chapters by Katie Edwards and Mmapula Kebaneilwe.[1] In essence, Katie's chapter exposes the subtle and unsubtle cultural symbolizations of whiteness as 'purity'. She outlines the historical development of Occidentalism of black bodies in contrast to white and, in particular, the symbols of Christianity embodied in white against the evil and sinfulness embodied in black. Katie goes on to show how black bodies have resisted this cultural suppression by embodying Christian symbols. Mmapula's chapter delineates the development of African biblical scholarship and the struggle of African biblical scholars to gain recognition in Euro-US-dominated academia. She presents the interpretations of Proverbs 31.10-31 by African biblical scholars, illustrating how they employ inculturation as an approach that contrasts with Western methodologies. Both chapters share one theme: they wrestle with the Western/white 'normative' cultural stereotyping that is imposed on non-white cultures.

I would like to respond to these thought-provoking chapters from my own stance as a non-white, female Singaporean Peranakan-Chinese[2] ethnic, and as a biblical scholar who has resided in Hong Kong for over a decade. The general public in Hong Kong is currently demoralized, lamenting the inevitable loss of democracy to the 'yellow power'. Living in Hong Kong has been the most enriching stage of my life journey. It has taught me to appreciate the people of Hong Kong's struggle for democracy and suffrage, human rights and free speech.

---

1. I have sought permission to address both authors by their given names, instead of their surnames, or the names of their forefathers. From here on, I will use first names.

2. 'Peranakan Chinese', or 'Straits-born Chinese', pertains to the descendants of Chinese immigrants who moved to Peninsular Malaysia and Singapore between the fifteenth and seventeenth centuries. In Malaysia, the Peranakan-Chinese self-identify also as Baba Nyonya.

I deeply admire how the courageous younger generation has attempted to make their suffering of injustice heard – fully cognizant of their predictable failure, yet persevering, because they must not submit silently to bullying.

This chapter will begin by responding to Katie's chapter on 'White Is Purity' and show how East Asians in general, and Chinese in particular, idolize whiteness. In the second section, I will illustrate this by indicating how Hong Kong scholars have interpreted Proverbs 31.10-31 and contrast this with the African interpretations found in Mmapula's chapter. In the third section, I seek to take seriously the economic situation of women in the developed countries of East Asia, including China, in reinterpreting the *'ēšet-ḥayil*, 'the woman of strength or worth'. I argue that the *'ēšet-ḥayil* is not an appropriate model of the perfect wife and mother. In the fourth section, I extend my argument that the *'ēšet-ḥayil* is only portrayed in economic terms and is an imaginary figure in a man's dream. In the fifth section, I seek to address and identify the issue of oppression reflected in the two chapters from the stance of postcolonial resistance. This is to confront the colonizing tendencies of China in the global market economy and China's impact in ASEAN[3] regions. Finally, I return to Proverbs 31.10-31, and propose how we might treat this pericope in more meaningful and just ways.

Idolizing 'White Is Purity'

In the book *Becoming Yellow*, Michael Keevak outlines how Western colonizers of the sixteenth century described many East Asians, especially the Chinese and Japanese, as 'white', until finally they were deemed 'yellow' in the eighteenth century (Keevak 2011). Among some of the possible reasons for this shift, one cultural-political one, as noted by Katie, is that by the eighteenth or nineteenth centuries, 'white' had become synonymous with Christianity (cf. Keevak 2011: 124–42). While the East Asian peoples were deemed highly civilized, they were considered inferior on account of their religion(s) when compared with Christians: East Asians were, consequently, 'heathens' and 'sinners'. Earlier, the missionaries had considered them potential targets for conversion, but when East Asians proved resistant to the gospel, the designation 'white' came to be rejected, and dropped out of Western literature on East Asia. In Keevak's analysis, it was only in the nineteenth century, when Chinese and Japanese began to migrate to the West in large numbers and when Japan became a colonial power, that East Asians were labelled a 'yellow peril'. From here on out the term 'yellow' for the races of the area became commonplace.

The symbolization of colours for race in relation to skin colour tones might seem a non-issue. Nevertheless, during their colonial rule, 'whites'[4] took this

---

3. ASEAN refers to the Association of Southeast Asian Nations.

4. The colour designations when applied to human beings do not 'work' literally. They pertain to peoples in ways that are first and foremost ideological and also hierarchical.

symbolization forward ideologically by defining 'whiteness' in terms of supremacy and purity, and tying it to Christian symbols of sinless-ness. In contrast, non-whiteness is associated with the opposite of purity and superiority. Katie shows how white people defined the colour black and, consequently, black people as 'sin'-ful, and 'evil'. Katie highlights the recent resistance to this from Beyoncé, for example, who announced her second pregnancy with pictures of herself adorned in symbols of the Virgin Mary.

While whites were colonizers of much of East Asia, Christianity is to this day not a dominant religion for most of the people here,[5] and, in comparison to Africa (once labelled 'the black continent'), the impact and resistance in terms of contrasting colour symbolization of bodies is less evident. One example of the way 'white as purity' *has* influenced Chinese and Indians is an insistence that brides wear white instead of red, the traditional celebratory colour. But for Chinese and Indians white symbolizes above all death, and that is why Chinese call whites 'ghosts' (鬼 *gui*), with a pejorative overtone. White clothes are used for mourning and funeral purposes. It was probably the memorable appearance of Queen Elizabeth II in her wedding dress, alongside glamorous images from Hollywood that broke the staunch tradition among Chinese and Indians, and led them to accept that modern fashionable wedding gowns are white. Hence, towards the mid-twentieth century, white wedding gowns came into vogue. Still, Chinese and Indian weddings today (regardless of whether they are Christian or not) usually have brides wearing at least two gowns: with one, usually, white and the other often red.

For East Asians, white can symbolize purity, but its association with Christian symbolism has somehow become watered down. Undoubtedly, a remnant of colonial influence has descended into subconsciousness and become an archetype. For instance, the Singapore flag is red and white, where white is said to signify 'pervading and everlasting purity' and red, 'universal brotherhood and equality of men [sic]' (National Heritage Board).[6] (How sadly sexist!)

In the last two decades or so, 'white as purity' has affected the East Asia region in a different way, and one that has escalated in recent months. Propelled largely by the hype of South Korean culture, the desire to bleach skin white has overtaken the region. According to Sharon Lee's (2016) report, this trend began in the early 1990s and continues to flourish today, perhaps even more so because of the increasing idolization of Korean celebrities, fashion, cuisine, language and culture, facilitated through popular drama serials that are distributed throughout the world (Lee 2016: 2–5). In Korea, this obsession with whiteness has become a serious social issue and efforts from feminist sectors at all levels strive to counter this craze (Lee 2016: 12–14) but have apparently not been successful.

It has now been twenty-five years and not only have these efforts failed but the phenomenon has also spread to the rest of the East Asian region, including

---

5. South Korea is an interesting exception to this tendency.

6. By comparison, white in the flag of Malaysia is simply negative space, to highlight the red stripes (see 'Malaysia Flag Facts').

China. Lee reports that the motivation for skin bleaching stems from the desire to emulate idealized white women who are perceived as educated and modern, 'having control over their bodies and sexualities and [exercising] the freedom to make their own decisions' (Lee 2016: 8; see also Mohanty 2003: 227). In the last decade this desire to look like white women has escalated to include plastic surgery to attain more 'Western-like features': meaning, bigger eyes and breasts, and sharper noses (Lee 2016: 3). The recent observation about Korean beauty pageant contestants looking exactly alike is a good indication of how youth of today want to become a particular version of white (Lee 2016: 5; Francis 2013). Moreover, this goal is aspired to not only by females, but, increasingly, by East Asian males as well (Lee 2016: 29).[7]

In the last few months, China has caught 'Ivanka Fever' 伊万卡热, (Fan 2017; Hernández 2017; Karl et al. 2017). Legions of Mainland Chinese women are hailing Ivanka Trump as their role model. She has become their inspiration and they aspire to look like her, be like her and become her. Ivanka is white, has conventionally beautiful features, is voluptuous and a successful entrepreneur as well as mother. Some postulate that due to a combination of the one-child policy and China's economic boom, very many Chinese females in their twenties and thirties come from prosperous, advantaged and indulged backgrounds. Ivanka, from an affluent and powerful family, may be more glamorous and commanding than they could hope for but she is nonetheless a magnet for aspirational Chinese women. Importantly, too, Ivanka married a rich man (Karl et al. 2017). Idolization of her has escalated to the point where Chinese women go under the knife to look like her. Apparently, cosmetic clinics are jumping on to the bandwagon and promising the possibility of Ivanka features through skin bleaching, eye and nose surgery, chin surgery, liposuction and breast enlargement (Papenfuss 2017).

I find 'Ivanka Fever' particularly ironic in the light of Chinese censorship policies. China's history of enforcing its brand of communist ideals through censorship is common knowledge. While in the last decade or so an increasingly open economy seemed to signal a more permissive stance, when President Xi Jinping took charge, vigorous censorship in all forms of the media began in earnest and acquired the form of extensive legal restriction. For example, China TV must no longer produce programmes that promote or include anything from a list of subjects that is eight pages long (Beech 2017). This 'catalogue' was issued on 31 December 2015, when it was announced that the list was in compliance with Xi's speech made in 2014: 'Art and culture will produce the most positive energy when the Marxist perspective on art and culture is firmly established' (Beech 2017). Xi denounced all 'negative' aspects of life as indicative of 'foreign' and 'hostile' culture and prohibited any notion of emulating 'Western-ness' (whatever precisely this might mean). Television programmes now ban portrayals of fraud (family or

---

7. Recent reports indicate that males in the Philippines, for example, have caught the desire to look more white and are practising cosmetic skin bleaching (Lasco 2017; Pe 2016; Woo 2012).

business), as well as of drugs, homosexuality and even displays of cleavage. What is pertinent to our discussion here is that among the things listed as banned is 'depictions of "luxurious lifestyles" ' (Beech 2017) – which would surely include depictions of the lifestyle of privileged multimillionaire Ivanka Trump, which has generated such frenzied emulation.

Strangely, a humble, fictional, *yellow-orange* (italics mine) bear, clad only in his red top, hobbling around looking for honey or his friends, is officially banned for promoting 'Western' values (Ross 2017); but the real-life Ivanka Trump is lauded, despite her undeniably luxurious lifestyle, her ever-presence in the White House as the 'unpaid' advisor to the President, her dabbling (together with her also unelected husband) in US politics, and her questionable ethics towards workers in her factories in developing countries, including China (Kinetz 2017; Bassett 2017; Varagur 2017). Chinese censorship and Chinese political leaders overlook all of these! There is reprimand for Winnie the Pooh[8] but not for wanting to look like glamorous and ostentatiously wealthy Ivanka Trump. Perhaps white is not just purity; perhaps, the wealthy white who is full of *bling*, is blinding also.

White Is Canonical

White as representing Christianity is attended by the notion that white is *the* canon. While conservative and evangelical Christians may claim they have the only inerrant Bible and the only rightful interpretation of this Bible, the historical reality is that the dogma they live by was formulated in and by the West. East Asian biblical scholarship also looks to the West in order to train and educate potential scholars and teachers for our seminaries. Thus, my teachers graduated from institutions in the UK or the USA and I, too, furthered my education in the UK.[9]

Mmapula rightly mentions that in geographical territories that are experiencing unstable politics, and poorer socio-economic conditions, and where cultural traditions are under threat, such as in many African countries, biblical interpretations tend to be more contextual than in Western countries. Indeed, in comparison to much of the continent of Africa, Hong Kong, economically speaking, thrived and became affluent under British colonial rule. Hong Kong, since 1 July 1997 designated a Special Administrative Region, continues to flourish as a financial hub under the watchful eyes of China. Thus, it seems Hong Kong is not, perhaps, pressed to read the Bible against the 'Western' grain.

Biblical scholars in Hong Kong who undertake contextual interpretations are insignificant in number, and are mostly connected to the Divinity School

---

8. According to one report (' "Oh Bother": Chinese censors block Winnie the Pooh' 2017), the children's book character was banned due to a meme comparing the bear with Xi Jinping, which apparently caused the head of state much embarrassment.

9. Like Musa Dube, I am an alumna of the University of Durham. Editors' note: Musa's experience of studying at Durham and Vanderbilt Universities is recounted in this volume.

of Chung Chi College, the Chinese University of Hong Kong. Hence, I learned about contextual interpretation from Chichang Li (also known as Archie C. C. Lee), who teaches 'cross-textual hermeneutics' there (Li 1996; Tan and Ying 2010) and also from Philip P. Y. Chia, another scholar resident in Hong Kong (2010a; 2010b; 2012; 2013). But most of the scholars from whom I learned about the method were far from Hong Kong. Hence, I learned from books by scholars such as Elisabeth Schüssler Fiorenza about doing feminist interpretations of the Bible from the perspective of one's own social context and experiences, as well as from publications by bell hooks, Kwok Pui Lan, R. S. Sugirtharajah and Musa Dube – to name a few.

The majority of biblical interpreters in Hong Kong, meanwhile, right up to the present, practise primarily grammatico-historical approaches (Ho 2004). Needless to say, the commentaries and books available in translation in local bookstores for seminarians and laypeople also use such methods. Seminaries and Bible Colleges offer 'Old/New Testament Survey' courses and textbooks are often by evangelical authors, such as L. S. Lau's translation of Tremper Longman III and Raymond B. Dillard's *An Introduction to the Old Testament* (1999), originally published by Zondervan, which contains an evangelical interpretation of the historical data relevant to the biblical period. Contextual interpretations are still avoided and deemed too 'liberal' or 'political' and as not compatible with church tradition.

The two most popular commentary series in Hong Kong are the Bible Study Commentary Series and the Tien Dao Bible Commentary Series, both published by Tien Dao Publishing House. When it comes to the book of Proverbs, the first is a translated commentary by E. G. Woodcock (1998) and the second is by Barbara M. Leung Lai (2005), a local Chinese scholar, who graduated from the University of Sheffield. Both exemplify standard grammatico-historical approaches, giving selective attention to the Hebrew original, points of translation and literary structure, and focusing most closely on explaining the face-value meaning of texts. Both give interpretations that reflect Christian assumptions with only occasional reference to Jewish interpretation.[10]

Leung interprets Proverbs 31.10-31 as referring to an ideal wife, whose delight it is to please her husband alone. While Leung acknowledges that the *'ēšet-ḥayil* is Wisdom personified (2005: 185), the section on women's perspectives states (approvingly) that marriage, and being a diligent wife by the grace of God, are central to the text (2005: 244–7). This articulation echoes evangelical commentaries from the United States.

Another essay by Elaine Goh, a Malaysian Chinese, offers an intertextual reading of the *'ēšet-ḥayil*, interfacing Ruth and Proverbs 31.10-31, from a Chinese

---

10. Neither interpretation pushes any boundaries, nor does either stray from convention. There is only superficial treatment of dating and authorship, and while there is mention that portions of Proverbs might not have been written by Solomon, there is no reference made to the possibility of post-exilic influence, for example. Neither reflects consideration of ideological factors.

woman's perspective (Goh 2015). Like Leung, Goh affirms that the woman of Proverbs 31.10-31 is Wisdom personified, but alongside this, she gives credence to the woman's (idealized) characteristics as affirmative for Chinese women of today.[11] But how apt and how relevant is the *'ēšet-ḥayil* really for contemporary women of Hong Kong and East Asia more widely?

An East Asian Interpretation of the *'ēšet-ḥayil*

I completed my doctoral research on the motif of the Foreign Woman of Proverbs 1–9 in 2004 and concluded then that interpreting the *'ēšet-ḥayil* as the extension of Woman Wisdom (see Proverbs 1, 8 and 9) as well as the counterpart of the Foreign Woman, was the most emancipatory approach (cf. McCreesh 1985). I personally think that to treat this woman as a real person is oppressive for women, regardless of status (be it socio-economic or cultural). For me, to understand her as an exemplar only builds up expectations of what a female should be or become. It cuts both ways: that women themselves try to measure up to this model (and internalize a sense of deficiency), *and* that others use her as the benchmark (exerting external pressure). I can appreciate in Mmapula's chapter how biblical interpreters attempt in different ways to read the text in the light of the lives of African women, highlighting empowering elements, and rejecting those elements that are not empowering, because this acknowledges the futility of being or becoming like *'ēšet-ḥayil*.[12]

Next, I want to reinterpret the *'ēšet-ḥayil* by taking seriously the livelihoods of women as wives and mothers in the developed countries of East Asia, starting with the pursuit of looking like the ideal white women mentioned in the first section. I will show that the *'ēšet-ḥayil* is outdated in the aspirational sector of my part of the world.

First, what is extremely troubling about the *'ēšet-ḥayil* is that she is faceless. (Perhaps this makes it more possible to map on to her a wide range of interpretations? She is, in some ways, a blank canvas.) What is described about her is that her body is a well-clothed machine that produces wealth. Wealth remains an aspiration but the face is also extremely central as a marker of success – sometimes in ways that are acutely troubling. As mentioned earlier, facial skin bleaching and cosmetic surgery, undertaken in order to look like the ideal white woman, is connected to becoming successful and competitive in today's economy

---

11. Goh, following Sakenfeld (cf. 2003: 129), mentions that when *'ēšet-ḥayil* is ascribed to Ruth the designation is 'freed' of its confines in Proverbs 31.10-31, where it refers particularly to married mothers. According to Goh, all working women, irrespective of marital status or motherhood, can be worthy of the designation *'ēšet-ḥayil*.

12. Being as industrious and competent as the *'ēšet-ḥayil* is as impossible as becoming like Ivanka Trump, the beautiful, rich right-hand woman to the world's most powerful man: both are constructed and unattainable fantasies.

(Lee 2016: 15–16; Lasco 2017). If people do not have the 'right' look, they are denied opportunities (Lee 2016: 28; Wen 2013: 79–98).[13] This perspective applies to both genders, only more so to women (Nisen 2013; Reed 2016).[14] Lee has problematized this as 'lookism' (2016: 1, 27; cf. Safire 2000) and unfortunately, as troubling as this behaviour is, it is prevalent in the workplace (Lee 2016: 28; Wen 2013: 79–98; Lasco 2017). The maxim found in v. 31 'Looks are fleeting … but the woman who fears YHWH is to be praised' – may be admirable, even true, but it is not the pitch geared at the aspirational East Asian woman of today. Looks may be fleeting and deceiving, but they land women with opportunities and get women to the top in the here and now. Assuredly, it is a beautiful woman who will be praised by all. This is 'the motto' (Lee 2016: 21). While we may resent it, it is a fact of life and someone without the right kind of look has to work harder even if the pay is lower.

Commentators note that in Proverbs 31.22 the *ēšet-ḥayil* makes an effort to dress well (e.g. Fox 2009: 896; Leung 2005: 187). I have heard preachers who exaggerate this mention, saying that the *ēšet-ḥayil* beautifies herself; but the text only mentions that she seeks purple cloth for herself and her family, in reference to her tailoring skills (vv. 23–24). To be covered in well-designed and costly materials is not sufficient in today's world: the face, hair and body must match. This means a lot of effort and expense, including scrubbing, exfoliating, massaging, moisturizing, masking, eye-brow pruning, shaving, botox injections and all the nips and tucks. Moreover, sourcing the best services and products to accomplish these efforts is part and parcel of the task. Anyone who does not do all or at least many of the above is not considered a sufficiently diligent woman. The woman who does not pay attention to her face and body does not find herself dating, in a relationship or married, and there is no need to even consider motherhood. At the same time, the wife who does not take care of her general appearance is expected to take some responsibility for her omission if her spouse strays.

Second, the *ēšet-ḥayil* defines womanhood only as wife and mother. This stereotype of womanhood is, again, out of date. Aspirational women are now educated and financially independent, and marriage is no longer as urgent a requirement as it used to be half a century ago. This is not to suggest that the pressure for marriage does not exist in this part of the world, but that the society is more open towards a woman's choice to remain single, as well as towards single parents, or childless marriages.

Third, where motherhood is concerned, the role of *ēšet-ḥayil* actually pales by comparison with the duties expected of a mother today. When her child is born,

---

13. There are other social experiments that have been conducted, alongside Lee's, that bear out similar results (e.g. Paglicawan 2014). In China, having the right looks is crucial for improved opportunities and success (e.g. 'Young Graduates Turning to Plastic Surgery' 2013; 'Don't Hate Me Because I'm Beautiful' 2013).

14. Lasco (2017) reports that both Korean and Philippino men express the belief that if they look more white, this will have 'social and economic gain' for them.

the contemporary mother ensures there is funding set aside for the child's future education. She starts early education at home as soon as the baby starts to babble. She charts its every milestone, makes notes, takes a lot of pictures, makes scrap books, ensures every health check is strictly adhered to, plans playgroups, registers for early childhood programmes, and seeks the best affordable nursery and kindergarten. When the child starts nursery – as early as three years old – the mother dutifully attends every 'Meet the Parents' event at school, and discusses with the teachers how best to help her child learn and socialize. By kindergarten, the mother has sought out the best school, tuition centres and tutors for all subjects, including music and extra-curricular subjects, and the best self-improvement programmes available to build her child's resilience and self-esteem in order to secure future success and competence. She attends to her child's academic needs and monitors the progress of her child's test and examination scores. The mother is an active participant in the chat group with the child's form teacher. Her child has the most up-to-date and organized stationery, computer, software programmes and applications. The mother discusses with other parents how to ensure their children have the best school holiday outings, camping and/or tour experiences – whether locally or abroad.

Today every mother is judged on her parenting in all the tasks mentioned above, regardless of whether or not she holds a full-time job. The *'ēšet-ḥayil* falls rather short in terms of this portrayal of motherhood. The only association between her and her children, which we find in the passage, concerns the preparation of food for them before dawn breaks (v. 15); she ensures there is ample provision for the winter (v. 21) and her children rise up to praise her (v. 28).

The Chinese have a popular folk song about motherhood which every child learns to sing. The lyrics go like this:

世 上 只 有 妈 妈 好
有 妈 的 孩 子 像 个 宝
投 进 了 妈 妈 的 怀 抱
幸 福 享 不 了

世 上 只 有 妈 妈 好
没 妈 的 孩 子 像 根 草
离 开 妈 妈 的 怀 抱
幸 福 哪 里 找?

Mothers are the best in the world
Those who have mothers are like a treasure
To be embraced in her bosom, it is where one finds happiness
Mothers are the best in the world
Those without mothers are like a blade of grass
To leave the embrace of your mother, where can one find happiness?

These simple lyrics encapsulate the powerful bond that is expected to exist between mother and child. There is no need for a father (in the song). It is about the singular relationship between mother and child. Contrastingly, we find no portrayal of the *'ēšet-ḥayil's* feelings for her child/ren. She is not described as having one-on-one time with them; her children are not her sole, or even top, priority; this does not appear to be part of her idealization. The *'ēšet-ḥayil* is thus reflective of an ideal very different from that of the contemporary East Asian mother or wife.

The *'ēšet-ḥayil* Lives in a Man's Dream

In this section, I will argue that the *'ēšet-ḥayil* of Proverbs is portrayed primarily in economic terms and is not about a 'real' woman. Instead, she is merely a figment of the imagination in the male mind, a 'dream-wife'.[15] This fantasy wife lives and does everything for her husband to ensure that his needs are met. In v. 11 we find the word *šālāl*, used only to refer to 'plunder' or 'loot' when taking the possession or property of someone else (BDB *ad loc.*). Why would the man need *šālāl*?[16] This may refer to his dream that there is no need to go to war, and that he might receive ample supplies for his household without fighting for them: his dream-woman will provide riches for him. In v. 12, the man reiterates that this dream-woman only has his interests at heart. There is no reciprocity here. He is the sole beneficiary and recipient of all the goodness – he gives nothing back.

From vv. 13–27, we find a full account of how the *'ēšet-ḥayil* covers all the basic expenses for running the household. She weaves and sews, she plans, buys and plants, she sells and earns. She does not need to report or discuss matters with her husband. This portrayal clearly betrays that she lives only in his dream and will only act according to his wishes. There will be no ideas conflicting with his and there is no compromise needed. In his dream, he does not need to rise early to toil or to attend to his children. He can sleep and laze in his bed until he wishes to wake up, and food will be waiting for him (v. 14). He dreams of some exotic spices – perhaps a savoury from Babylon he loved before returning to Yehud? Only she knows it and ensures that it will be part of his meal (v. 15). And in his dream, why shouldn't there be red wine? Thus he will own a vineyard and she shall plant it, harvest and manufacture wine for him (v. 16). She can do all this, because she is his lean, mean and strong machine, ever ready for all the back-breaking tasks

15. Interestingly, Christine Roy Yoder also interprets the *'ēšet-ḥayil* in economic terms. Yoder retrieves the everyday ancient Near Eastern trade and legal documents from the period of sixth to fourth centuries BCE, which mention women and concludes that this poem reflects the profiles of diverse types of women of ancient Persia known through these documents. Conceivably, the poet of Proverbs 31.10-31 constructs an ideal wife and personified Wisdom out of a combination of real and admirable foreign women (Yoder 2003), while at the same time countering the seductiveness of foreignness (Tan 2008).

16. Yoder discovers legal marriage contracts which detail women's dowries and describes cases where husbands helped themselves to the dowry. She therefore interprets the word 'loot' as referring to a husband 'plundering' his wife's dowry (2003: 434–6).

of a vineyard (v. 17). She is a sensible woman and will consider all that she has accomplished. She ensures that there is always light in the house (v. 18): indeed he can be carefree about life's mundane needs and his own fortune; his rest is soothed by the thought of her constant work (v. 19).

Oh yes, a proper religious man and a wealthy one must also be charitable. So here is his dream-woman at work again – she bears his name and in his name she reaches out to the poor (v. 20). He does not need to contact the poor directly, physically and has fulfilled his obligations. He has sent his ambassador.

When she has to trade her crafts, she must showcase her wares and skill through her own adornment, as all merchants do (vv. 22, 24). Through all her good works, he dreams he shall become popular and influential. He will sit at the city gate with the elders and hold his head up high, respected by his community (v. 23).

He laughs as he finishes painting this female figure in his dream – she is strong and dignified and as long as he is happy and well taken care of now and forever, she will surely be happy too (v. 25)! As a true YHWH-worshipper, and mother of his children, she must only speak the words of the patriarchal tradition: they are, after all, from the Torah (v. 26; cf. Proverbs 1.8; 6.20). Indeed, a YHWH-fearer she must be (v. 30). Above all, however, it is important that this dream-woman manages and provides for every aspect of the household diligently, and is never an idler (v. 27). By now the man has painted a picture-perfect dream for himself: How beautiful this dream would be and how praiseworthy (vv. 28–31)! He must end by emphasizing an imperative to all the world: Honour all her diligent works, otherwise his money-making dream shall come to naught (v. 31)!

This poem does not reflect care about the *'ešet-ḥayil* as a person (cf. Goh 2015: 86). She is given no rest; she is not said to be loved and cared for by her husband. In his view, she lives on praises alone. Praises are the only lubricant to maintain this machine. Her laughter is his (v. 25); she is attributed no emotions of her own – good or bad. One such dream-woman is sufficient for his household. It really does not matter if she is beautiful or not (v. 30) because he can have concubines to live off their wealth. This is his perfect dream come true! The *'ešet-ḥayil* is his winning lottery ticket to life.

The beginning of the poem in v. 10 already tells us that this woman *cannot* be found. The opening verse is a rhetorical question. At the end of the poem, this is also said of her: that she alone exceeds all good women (v. 29). The reality is that in a patriarchal world, women rarely have the mobility and independence to make financial and legal decisions apart from the male figure in the household. There is, and can be, only one *'ešet-ḥayil* – and she does not exist.

Resisting Oppressive Economic Forces

Both Katie's and Mmapula's chapters identify oppressive forces against humanity and against womankind in particular. Katie's chapter exposes how colonial powers bully black bodies and successfully encode into the language colour symbols that prioritize white over black. Mmapula also charts how postcolonial

Africa copes, not only with the after-effects of the devastation of the land, and the impoverishment of the people and their culture, but also with the consequences of a Westernized and patriarchal biblical interpretation that continues to oppress black bodies, especially women's bodies. These two chapters present the ongoing postcolonial resistance of black bodies, and in this section I want to raise concerns about today's rising superpower and the oppressive forces that accompany it.

Reading these two chapters as a resident of Hong Kong, it is difficult not to relate the theme of resistance against oppressive powers to my own context. This leads me to ponder the constant and invasive threat of Chinese control over Hong Kong, despite the promise of autonomy until 2037 (Lam 2017), as well as the imperializing economic power of China in the contemporary global market. If we, in the twenty-first century, are still coping with postcolonial resistance to white supremacy, have we learned from our history how to confront the oppressive forces of a new superpower on the stage?

China of two decades ago and China of today are not the same (Gill 2016). Today, China is a formidable economic power, second only to the United States and it has been predicted China will overtake the United States in the next few years (Bajpai 2017). China's escalating economic strength makes President Xi more powerful than any Chinese leader before him. Since his appointment, he has sworn to preserve the ideals of Marxism in and for China (Beech 2017). He has stepped up China's domination over the region: for example, by marginalizing Taiwan through third-party negotiations or measures (Watt and Zamorano 2017) and by exerting territorialism over the Spratly Islands amidst the yet to be finalized debates over ownership (Buckley 2016).

China has also been accused of recolonizing Africa – and yet, many African states are opening their doors to Chinese enterprise (Esposito et al. 2014; French 2014; Tiffen 2014; Smith 2015). China is pouring money into Africa by building infrastructure in exchange for the natural (including mineral) resources to support China's increasing consumer needs and demands. However, the possibility of a debt-crisis amounting to US$ 86 billion hitting African nations seems imminent; and China's increasing military presence in Africa has also raised concerns (Albert 2017).

The economists in ASEAN countries are probing China's rising power and questionable ethics of trade. A recent NHK World programme,[17] called 'Global Agenda', aired on 9 June 2017 in Tokyo. The feature was entitled 'Asia's Economy: Changing Roles, Shifting Realities'[18] and debated the recent uncertainties in the economic world brought about by changing roles after President Donald

17. NHK stands for 'Nippon Hoso Kyokai', 'Japan Broadcasting Corporation'. NHK is Japan's only public broadcaster.

18. The programme is available as video on demand: https://www3.nhk.or.jp/nhkworld/en/vod/globalagenda/20170610/. The panel consists of Simon Tay (host), Michael Stumo (USA), Daisuke Iwase (Japan), Victor Gao (China) and Khong Yuen Foong (Singapore).

Trump pulled the United States out of the Trans-Pacific Partnership, leaving China 'eager to fill in the political vacuum' (Sink et al. 2017). It asks how these uncertainties are affecting ASEAN today, and raises issues about the supremacy of the United States' role in policy-making prior to pulling out, and the 'behaviour' and political motivation of China's trade role in Asia.

The example given is China's investment in making Hambatonta (Sri Lanka) the prominent port in the region. It was built with Sri Lanka's permission and China's monies. This situation resulted from a period of poor business in the port, leading to Sri Lanka's debt to China reaching US $8 billion, a sum it was estimated would take four hundred years to repay. China then drew up a debt relief program for Sri Lanka, requiring the country to surrender the port for ninety-nine years, and thus ceding sovereignty of the port to China. Sri Lanka now laments that Hambatonta will soon become a Chinese colony (Meyers 2017; Mourdoukoutas 2017).

On a macro level, China's strategic move is designed to take control of the Middle Eastern oil transport routes. And China's plan seems to solidify as China signs an agreement with Malaysia to build a harbour along the Malacca Straits costing US $9.73 billion (Reeves 2017). China's bilateral ties with Malaysia seem to open an avenue for an increased presence in the region. Socioculturally, we are seeing how the influx of Chinese is shaping Malaysia and her people (Sukumaran and Liu 2017; Tho 2017). The Malaysian Chinese are protesting against 'perks' such as land ownership given to Mainland Chinese, when earlier they were given only restricted rights of ownership (Kamarudin 2017). Culturally, the local Chinese language is also affected by the influx of Mainland Chinese. Politically, there are concerns about the increase in Chinese ships in the area and suspicions about a military agenda (Holmes 2017; Jennings 2017).

Becoming a prosperous economy is the currency for stability in many developing countries, but at what sacrifice to the people, their rights and sovereignty in their own lands? Will nations help each other resist and overcome superpowers in their domination, along with the abusive erosion of human rights and free speech? For the passage in Proverbs 31.10-31, the male's dream of becoming wealthier, is at the cost of personhood for 'ešet-ḥayil. And the various interpretations of Proverbs 31.10-31 outlined in Mmapula's chapter should serve as a prophetic warning for readers today about the consequences of colonization, oppression and abusive treatment of humankind, especially women.

Re-appropriating Proverbs 31.10-31 for Today's Readers

In the above sections, I have argued why interpreting the 'ešet-ḥayil as a real person is not only irrelevant to today's women of my setting, as well as discriminatory to all womankind, but also that such an interpretation departs from the intent of the biblical passage. In this section, I would like to propose an alternative take on this passage.

In lived Jewish tradition Proverbs 31.19-31 is not, generally, treated in literal or prescriptive terms. This passage is conventionally sung every Friday evening before Kiddush to the woman of the house, usually the mother, during the Sabbath rites. It is a customary song, sung to her regardless of whether she meets any (let alone all) of the descriptions of *ešet-ḥayil*, but in appreciation for all that she is and has done.

The Christian hermeneutical position is often more restrictive than this Jewish practice. Unfortunately, I have heard of Chinese churches advising reading this passage to women on Mother's Day (Goh 2015: 80), often with negative outcomes, since many women feel it is a reminder of shortcoming, or even a judgement of them – for not living up to the expectations of husbands or children, or of not being significant economic providers to the household.

In view of my interpretation of Proverbs 31.10-31, I propose that this poem be treated like a 民谣 *minyao* in the Chinese genre. A *minyao* is similar to a folk song or poem. It originates among locals and is passed on orally from one generation to the next. In terms of content, *minyao* are varied. There is no restriction in terms of length and rhyme or when they are used. I would suggest that Proverbs 31.10-31 be sung to the youth, regardless of gender. It is not to be sung in praise of anyone, but as a fun song, similar to a wake-up call to all youth to abandon their unrealistic dream of becoming wealthy through marriage or at the expense of someone else's hard work and suffering. It is a call to the reality that we are responsible for working hard for our own future, and our partners and spouses are to be loved, cherished and appreciated for who they are, regardless of what they can or cannot do.

Conclusion

Katie's chapter on 'White Is Purity' shows how Western colonization continues to haunt us in both conspicuous and subtle ways through its colour coding and symbols. Africans as well as African Americans, on the one hand, and East Asians, on the other, seem to respond to 'White Is Purity' by running in opposite directions. East Asians, as I have demonstrated, especially among the aspirational elite, seek to emulate whiteness – in one extreme form this is exemplified by idolization of Ivanka Trump. Among black Africans and African Americans there is instead more overt resistance, as is demonstrated by the readings discussed by Mmapula and with superstar Beyoncé embodying Christian symbols in a prominent and proud display of her black body.

The second section takes up Mmapula's inculturation interpretations of Proverbs 31, explaining why the portrayal of *ešet-ḥayil* is largely irrelevant to the lives of women in developed East Asian countries in three ways:

(1) She has no face, while in the contemporary world a beautiful face is of paramount importance in creating opportunities for success and also marriage.
(2) She is defined only as a wife and married mother, while singleness and motherhood outside of marriage are becoming more prevalent and acceptable.

(3) She is portrayed as distant from her children, while mothers in East Asia are intimately (over?)involved in every aspect of their children's development and education.

In the third section, we see again how African biblical interpretation operates in resistant ways. Meanwhile people of Hong Kong and China often embrace the notion that 'white is canonical' and Chinese biblical interpreters model themselves on conventional, grammatico-historical Western scholars. I also explain why I think that to interpret the *ēšet-ḥayil* as a concrete woman is demoralizing and unhelpful for womankind, and I argue that she is only an image in a man's dream of becoming rich and living a carefree life. I attempt to show that the *ēšet-ḥayil* is only portrayed in economic terms and is merely the man's money-making machine. In my fourth section, I point out the pressures faced by developing countries to get rich, and how they are becoming vulnerable to the rising superpower of China. How China runs the country and exerts dominance in Hong Kong and the ASEAN region should serve as a significant reference point for developing countries when they welcome the 'yellow currency' into their lands. Just as the man only dreams of getting rich in Proverbs 31.10-31 and ignores a personal engagement and appreciation of *ēšet-ḥayil*, will our dreams of becoming rich also exploit and abuse the human dignity of others? I conclude this response by proposing treating Proverbs 31.10-31 as a *minyao* to sing to all youth in order to wake them up from their get-rich-easy-through-marriage dreams. Hopefully, this interpretation promotes an awareness of more just and fair treatment of all humankind.

Works Cited

Albert, E. (17 April 2017), 'China in Africa', Council on Foreign Relations (New York). Available online: https://www.cfr.org/backgrounder/china-africa (accessed 28 June 2017).

Baculinao, E. (20 April 2017), 'Ivanka Trump Has Huge Chinese Fan Club Worshiping "Goddess Ivanka" ', *NBC* (New York). Available online: http://www.nbcdfw.com/news/politics/Ivanka-Trump-Has-Chinese-Fan-Club-Worsh iping-Goddess-Ivanka-419972023.html (accessed 25 June 2017).

Bajpai, P. (8 February 2017), 'The World's Top Ten Economies', *Investopedia*. Available online: http://www.investopedia.com/articles/investing/022415/worlds-top-10-economies.asp (accessed 25 June 2017).

Bassett, L. (13 June 2017), 'The Women Who Make Ivanka Trump Clothes Can't Afford to Live with Their Children', *The Huffington Post*. Available online: http://www.huffingtonpost.com/entry/ivanka-trump-women-clothing-factory_us_59402d7de4b003d5948b6d05 (accessed 25 June 2017).

Beech, H. (6 March 2017), 'China's Censors Are Leaving the World's Most Populous Nation with Very Little to Watch on TV', *Times*. Available online: http://time.com/4247432/china-tv-television-media-censorship/ (accessed 25 June 2017).

Buckley, C. (15 December 2016), 'China Suggests It Has Placed Weapons on Disputed Spratly Islands in South China Sea', *New York Times*. Available online: https://www.nytimes.com/2016/12/15/world/asia/china-spratly-islands.html (accessed 25 June 2017).

Chia, P. P. Y. (2010a), 'After Crossing: The Relevance of Public Culture to Biblical
    Interpretation', in N. N. H. Tan and Y. Zhang (eds), *Essays in Honour of Professor Archie
    Lee*, 212–24, Hong Kong: Divinity School of Chung Chi College.

Chia, P. P. Y. (2010b), 'Biblical Studies and Public Relevance: Hermeneutical and
    Pedagogical Consideration in Light of the Ethos of the Greater China Region (GCR)',
    in E. Schüssler Fiorenza and K. H. Richards (eds), *Transforming Graduate Biblical
    Education: Ethos and Discipline*, 93–107, Atlanta: SBL.

Chia, P. P. Y. (2012), 'Biblical Studies in a Rising Asia: An Asian Perspective on the Future
    of the Biblical Past', in R. Boer and F. Segovia (eds), *The Future of the Biblical Past*,
    81–95, Atlanta: SBL.

Chia, P. P. Y. (2013), 'Occupy Central: Scribal Resistance in Daniel, the Long Road to
    Universal Suffrage', in J. Aitken, J. Clines and C. Maier (eds), *Interested Readers: Essays
    on the Hebrew Bible in Honor of David J. A. Clines*, 247–63, Atlanta: SBL.

'Don't Hate Me Because I'm Beautiful' (31 March 2013), *The Economist* (London).
    Available online: http://www.economist.com/node/21551535 (accessed 28 June 2017).

Esposito, M., T. Tse and M. Al-Sayed, (30 December 2014), 'Recolonizing Africa: A
    Modern Chinese Story?' *CNBC*. Available online: http://www.cnbc.com/2014/12/30/
    recolonizing-africa-a-modern-chinese-story.html (accessed 25 June 2017).

Fan, J. (11 April 2017), 'China and the Legend of Ivanka', *The New Yorker*. Available online:
    http://www.newyorker.com/news/daily-comment/china-and-the-legend-of-ivanka
    (accessed 26 June 2017).

Fox, M. V. (2009), *Proverbs 10–31: A New Translation with Introduction and Commentary*
    (Anchor Yale Bible, Vol. 18B), New Haven: Yale University Press.

Francis, J. (19 March 2013), 'The K-Pop Effect', *SBS* (Australia). Available online: http://
    www.sbs.com.au/news/dateline/story/k-pop-effect (accessed 28 June 2017).

French, H. W. (10 June 2014), 'A Place in the Sun: Why 1 Million Chinese Migrants Are
    Building a New Empire in Africa', *Quartz*. Available online: https://qz.com/217597/
    how-a-million-chinese-migrants-are-building-a-new-empire-in-africa/ (accessed 26
    June 2017).

Gill, J. (21 April 2016), 'China in Africa: Empire-builders or Alliance-makers?' *Times
    Higher Education* (London). Available online: https://www.timeshighereducation.com/
    comment/china-africa-empire-builders-or-alliance-makers (accessed 26 June 2017).

Goh, E. W. G. (2015), 'An Intertextual Reading of Ruth and Proverbs 31.10-31, with a
    Chinese Woman's Perspective', in J. Havea and P. H. W. Lau (eds), *Reading Ruth in Asia*,
    73–87, Atlanta: SBL.

Hernández, J. C. (5 April 2017), 'The "Goddess" Yi Wan Ka: Ivanka Is a Hit in China',
    NY Times. Available online: https://www.nytimes.com/2017/04/05/world/asia/
    ivanka-trump-china.html?_r=0 (accessed 26 June 2017).

Ho, C. Y. S. (2004), 'Biblical Scholarship in Hong Kong', *SBL Forum*. Available
    online: https://www.sbl-site.org/publications/article.aspx?ArticleId=290 (accessed 26
    June 2017).

Holmes, O. (5 April 2017), 'Chinese Patrol Ships Keep Presence around Malaysian Reefs',
    The Guardian (London). Available online: https://www.theguardian.com/world/2017/
    apr/05/ chinese-patrol-ships-keep-presence-around-malaysian-reefs (accessed 26
    June 2017).

Jennings, R. (17 April 2017), 'Discovery of More Chinese Ships Adds Pressure on
    Normally Passive Malaysia', *Voice of America*. Available online: https://www.voanews.
    com/a/discovery-of-more-chinese-ships-adds-pressure-on-normally-passive-
    malaysia/3812961.html (accessed 26 June 2017).

Kamarudin, R. P. (13 January 2017), 'Chinese Do Not Want Chinese in Malaysia', *Malaysia* Today. Available online: http://www.malaysia-today.net/chinese-do-not-want-chinese-in-malaysia/ (accessed 26 June 2017).

Karl, R. E., Y. Mao and L. Jaivin (17 April 2017), 'Unpacking China's Curious Ivanka Fever', *The Business Insider*. Available online: http://www.businessinsider.com/unpacking-chinas-curious-ivanka-fever-2017-4 (accessed 26 June 2017).

Keevak, M. (2011), *Becoming Yellow: A Short History of Racial Thinking*, New Jersey: Princeton University Press.

Kinetz, E. (30 May 2017), 'Activists Investigating Ivanka Trump Supplier in China Arrested, Missing', *Chicago Tribune*. Available online: http://www.chicagotribune.com/news/nationworld/politics/ct-ivanka-trump-supplier-investigation-arrested-20170530-story.html (accessed 27 June 2017).

Lam, J. (29 April 2017), ' "One Country, Two Systems" for Hong Kong Could Be Scrapped if It Is Used to Confront Beijing, Official Says', *South China Morning Post* (Hong Kong). Available online: http://www.scmp.com/news/hong-kong/politics/article/2091747/one-country-two-systems-hong-kong-could-be-scrapped-if-it (accessed 27 June 2017).

Lasco, G. (25 February 2017), 'Why More Asian Men Are Using Skin-Whitening Products', *SBS* (Australia). Available online: http://www.sbs.com.au/news/dateline/article/2017/02/27/why-more-asian-men-are-using-skin-whitening-products (accessed 28 June 2017).

Lee, S. H. (2016), 'Beauty Between Empires: Global Feminism, Plastic Surgery, and the Trouble with Self- Esteem', *Frontiers* 37 (1): 1–31.

Leung Lai, B. M. (2005), *Proverbs* (Tien Dao Bible Commentary), Hong Kong: Tien Dao.

Li, C. (1996), 'Cross Textual Hermeneutics on Gospel and Culture', *The Asian Journal of Theology* 10 (1): 38–48.

Longman III, T. and R. B. Dillard, (1999). *An Introduction to the Old Testament*, trans. L. S. Lau, Taipei: Campus Evangelical Fellowship.

'Malaysia Flag Facts'. Available online: http://malaysiaflag.facts.co/malaysiaflagof/malaysia-flag.php (accessed 27 June 2017).

McCreesh, T. P. (1985), 'Wisdom as Wife: Proverbs 31.10-31', *RB* 92: 25–46.

Meyers, J. (25 February 2017), 'Sri Lankans Who Once Embraced Chinese Investment Are Now Wary of Chinese Domination', *Los Angeles Times*. Available online: http://www.latimes.com/ world/asia/la-fg-sri-lanka-port-2017-story.html (accessed 27 June 2017).

Mohanty, C. (2003), *Feminism without Borders: Decolonizing Theory, Practicing Solidarity*, Durham, South Carolina: Duke University Press.

Mourdoukoutas, P. (5 April 2017), 'Ten Years from Now, China Will Still Own Sri Lanka's Hambantota Port', *Forbes*. Available online: https://www.forbes.com/sites/panosmourdoukoutas/2017/04/05/ten-years-from-now-china-will-still-own-sri-lankas-hambantota-port/#99fc27911680 (accessed 27 June 2017).

National Heritage Board ('National Flag'), the Singapore Government. Available online: http://www.nhb.gov.sg/resources/national-symbols/national-flag (accessed 27 June 2017).

Nisen, M. (9 September 2013), 'Beautiful People Get More Job Interviews', *Business Insider* (New York). Available online: http://www.businessinsider.com/beautiful-people-get-more-job-interviews-2013-9 (accessed 28 June 2017).

' "Oh Bother": Chinese Censors Block Winnie the Pooh over Meme Comparing Him to Xi Jinping' (no author) (17 July 2017), The Telegraph. Available online: http://www.telegraph.co.uk/news/2017/07/17/oh-bother-chinese-censors-block-winnie-pooh-meme-comparing-xi/ (accessed 20 July 2017).

Paglicawan, M. (2014). 'Job Interview Experiment: Do Good Looks Count during the Job Hunt?' *Dailypedia* (Philippines). Available online: https://www.dailypedia.net/2014/06/job-interview-experiment-do-good-looks-count-during-the-job-hunt/ (accessed 28 June 2017).

Papenfuss, M. (17 March 2017), 'Chinese Plastic Surgeons Offer to Transform Patients into Ivanka Trump', *The Huffington Post*. Available online: http://www.huffingtonpost.com/entry/ivanka-china-plastic-surgery_us_ 58cb4edce4b0ec9d29da9a17 (accessed 27 June 2017).

Pe, R. (1 October 2016), 'Yes, Asia Is Obsessed with White Skin', *Inquirer Business* (Philippines). Available online: http://business.inquirer.net/215898/yes-asia-is-obsessed-with-white-skin (accessed 28 June 2017).

Reed, W. (5 January 2016), 'China's Male Skin Care Market Continues to Bring Big Opps', *Cosmetics Design Asia* (France). Available online: http://www.cosmeticsdesign-asia.com/Market-Trends/China-s-male-skin-care-market-continues-to-bring-big-opps-in-2016 (accessed 28 June 2017).

Reeves, H. (12 April 2017), 'China's New Malaysian Invasion: Both Friends and Foes in Beijing', *ASEAN Today*. Available online: https://www.aseantoday.com/2017/04/chinas-new-malaysian-invasion-both-friends-and-foes-in-beijing/ (accessed 27 June 2017).

Ross, E. (14 March 2017), 'Why Is China Banning Winnie the Pooh and other Foreign Picture Books?' *Newsweek*. Available online: http://www.newsweek.com/china-ban-books-children-567565 (accessed 27 June 2017).

Safire, W. (27 August 2000), 'The Way We Live Now: 8-27-00: On Language; Lookism', *New York Times Magazine*. Available online: http://www.nytimes.com/2000/08/27/magazine/the-way-we-live-now-8-27-00-on-language-lookism.html (accessed 28 June 2017).

Sakenfeld, K. D. (2003), *Just Wives? Stories of Power and Survival in the Old Testament and Today*, Louisville, KY: Westminster John Knox Press.

Sink, J., T. Olorunnipa and E. Curran (24 January 2017), 'China Eager to Fill the Political Vacuum Created by Trump's TPP Withdrawal', *Bloomberg*. Available online: https://www.bloomberg.com/politics/articles/2017-01-23/trump-s-withdrawal-from-asia-trade-deal-viewed-as-boon-for-china (accessed 27 June 2017).

Smith, D. (12 January 2015), 'China Denies Building Empire in Africa', *The Guardian* (London). Available online: https://www.theguardian.com/global-development/2015/jan/12/china-denies-building-empire-africa-colonialism (accessed 27 June 2017).

Sukumaran, T. and C. Liu (26 March 2017), 'Why are Chinese Moving to Malaysia by the Thousands?' *The South China Morning Post* (Hong Kong). Available online: http://www.scmp.com/week-asia/geopolitics/article/2080869/why-are-chinese-moving-malaysia-thousands (accessed 27 June 2017).

Tan, N. N. H. (2008), *The 'Foreignness' of the Foreign Woman in Proverbs 1–9*. (Beiheft zur Zeitschrift für die alttestamentliche Wissenschaft 381), Berlin and New York: Walter deGruyter.

Tan, N. N. H. and Z. Ying (eds) (2010), *Cross Textual Boundaries: A Festschrift in Honor of Archie Chi Chung Lee for his Sixtieth Birthday*, Hong Kong: Divinity School of Chung Chi College of the Chinese University of Hong Kong.

Tho X. Y. (1 January 2017), 'At Home with Another Language', *The Star* (Malaysia). Available online: http://www.thestar.com.my/news/education/2017/01/01/at-home-with-another-language/ (accessed 27 June 2017).

Tiffen, A. (17 August 2014), 'The New Neo-colonialism in Africa', *Global Policy Journal* (Durham, UK). Available online: http://www.globalpolicyjournal.com/blog/19/08/ 2014/new-neo-colonialism-africa (accessed 27 June 2017).

Varagur, K. (13 June 2017), 'Revealed: Reality of Life Working in an Ivanka Trump Clothing Factory', *The Guardian* (London). Available online: https://www. theguardian.com/us-news/2017/jun/13/revealed-reality-of-a-life-working-in- an-ivanka-trump-clothing-factory (accessed 27 June 2017).

Watt, L. and J. Zamorano (13 June 2017), 'Panama Switches Diplomatic Recognition from Taiwan to China', *ABC News*. Available online: http://abcnews.go.com/ International/ wireStory/panama-switches-diplomatic-recognition-taiwan-china-47997104 (accessed 27 June 2017).

Wen, H. (2013), *Buying Beauty: Cosmetic Surgery in China*, Hong Kong: Hong Kong University.

Woo, J. (9 October 2012), 'More Men Opt for Plastic Surgery', *The Wall Street Journal* (New York). Available online: https://blogs.wsj.com/korearealtime/2012/10/09/ more-men-opt-for-plastic-surgery/tab/interactive/itp/public/page/archive.html/ (accessed 28 June 2017).

Woodcock, E. G. (1998), *Proverbs – A Topical Study* (Bible Study Commentary, trans. K. F. Nip), Hong Kong: Tien Dao.

Yoder, C. R. (2003), 'The Woman of Substance (*ēšet-ḥayil*): A Socio-Economic Reading of Proverbs 31.10–31', *JBL* 122 (3): 427–47.

'Young Graduates Turning to Plastic Surgery for Job Market "Advantage" in China's Tough Market' (29 June 2013), *National Post* (Toronto). Available online: http:// nationalpost.com/news/young-graduates-turning-to-plastic-surgery-for-an- advantage-in-chinas-tough-job-market/wcm/c3057ea3-ba05-4818-9280-c1211349c3c0 (accessed 28 June 2017).

Part II

Chapter 7

EMPIRE AND IDENTITY SECRECY: A POSTCOLONIAL REFLECTION ON ESTHER 2.10

Tsaurayi K. Mapfeka

Introduction

This chapter aims to show that power dynamics have a decisive effect on the way the Bible in general and the book of Esther in particular are read. I will focus primarily on Esther 2.10, which reads as follows:

לא–הגדה אסתר את–עמה ואת–מלדתה כי מרדכי צוה עלה אשר לא–תגד

'Esther did not reveal her people or kindred, for Mordecai had charged her not to tell.'[1]

That biblical texts are products of a long and complex process of composition and redaction is a matter of quite considerable scholarly support and consensus, as is aptly summed up by Douglas Knight when he says, 'the literature of the Bible or at least large portions of it came gradually into existence through a process, passed down from one generation to another acquiring their final form with assistance and contributions of many individuals and groups along the way' (1973: 633). Unsurprisingly, then, it has already been thoroughly and persuasively demonstrated that all extant versions of the book of Esther, too, are the result of a long process of textual development. Moreover, the story of Esther may also have existed in an oral, pre-textual version.[2] Hence, the story as it now stands is likely to be the result of an amalgamation of at least two distinct traditions, each with a lengthy prehistory, as has been argued by, among others, Henri Cazelles (1961), Hans Bardtke (1963), David Clines (1984) and Stephanie Dalley (2007) – to mention but a few. There is reason to believe that

---

1. Except in cases where I clearly state otherwise (such as when using my own translation), this chapter follows the NRSV. As if for emphasis, 2.20a repeats 2.10 almost verbatim.

2. For a concise treatment of how and when the extant versions of Esther may have come into being, see Clines 1984.

what the reader faces in the various ancient versions of Esther preserved in all of the Masoretic Text, Septuagint (Greek B text), the Greek A Text, Josephus and the Targumim, is more than just examples of distinct redactions. Instead, these different versions may represent numerous variations or manners in which the story of Esther was transmitted and received. The different versions, therefore, are not indicative so much of different textual stages over time but of multiple tellings in a multiplicity of settings for different audiences. In the book of Esther, I argue, we see a case where the line separating redaction from reception is nonexistent or, at best, very fine. What often passes as editorial or redaction interest is, in fact, a matter of a complete reworking of the narrative to have it make sense in a distinct setting. While the story of Esther may have had a central core narrative, the differences in the available extant versions of the story suggest a lot more than mere editorial work.

Empire as Gendered Space

The power of the colonizer, the authority assigned to the Temple in Jerusalem and the question of how to negotiate gender relations are three elements that recur in certain biblical texts with some frequency. The power dynamics at the core of all three may also have been instrumental in terms of shaping biblical traditions and I consider the hegemonic tensions wrapped up in these elements to be clearly manifest in the book of Esther. Feminist and womanist commentaries of this book abound and address both overt and latent gender issues. These readings frequently cast the character of Esther in negative terms, as an embodiment of 'full compliance with patriarchy' (Laffey 1988: 216). Exceptions to such readings can also be cited; hence, Jo Carruthers remarks, 'Esther would indeed be invoked as a model of female submission, but more often than not (and certainly outside theological contexts) she represented the sexually problematic woman, the heterodox woman and even the warrior woman' (2008: 3).

To be sure, the character Esther has to negotiate considerable obstacles and prejudices in her literary world. First, she is part of a Jewish community, living as colonized second-class citizens in the diaspora, in a space where Persians are politically and culturally dominant. Second, she is a woman in a patriarchal world in which men dominate and wield authority. Third, she is an orphan and, therefore, lacking the protection of immediate family members and likely to be economically (and otherwise) vulnerable. It has even been proposed that Esther is exposed to the threat of sexual abuse from a tender age: hence, one tradition has preserved that, being an orphaned damsel of exceptional beauty, her cousin Mordecai adopted and raised her for a wife: Επαιδευσεν αυτην εαυτω εις γυναικα (Greek B Text [LXX] Est. 2.7). While this expression can also be translated in a less sinister manner that does not suggest that Esther and Mordecai were a couple, the image of a powerful male over against a powerless orphaned female cannot be ignored. In any case, the fact that in the same verse, and repeated a few lines below, Esther is referred to clearly as της Θυγατρος Αμιναδαβ, meaning 'the daughter of Aminadab' (Greek B

Text Est. 2.7 and 15) shows that if it was a protective father–daughter relationship that was implied for Mordecai and Esther, the vocabulary with which to express such a relationship with clarity was available to the author.

The directionality of gendered oppression in the book of Esther is for the most part one perpetrated by powerful males on less powerful females. The comparative powerlessness of females is in evidence in a variety of ways. Hence, Esther and the other virgins do not actively enter a beauty pageant to compete for a place in the royal bed; rather, the girls צבקהב 'were gathered' and Esther תלקח 'was taken' into the harem (Est. 2.8): passive constructions apply. The storyline has men making the decisions and women acting as objects, being gathered and taken. The passive verbal construction here offers no justification for Lewis Bayles Paton's claim as to Esther's questionable sexual ethics, when he accuses her of actively joining the harem with the intention of winning wealth and power (1908: 96).

On the other hand, however, negating female passivity, it is also the case that several counts of action in the narrative, even brilliant ones, are associated with women: such as Vashti's bold stance in refusing the degrading demands of her intoxicated royal husband,[3] or Esther's heroic entrance into royal space without summons and her subtlety in exposing Haman's evil intentions. In the book of Esther then, for all the female gender stereotypes pertaining to the desirability of feminine beauty and submissiveness, women also shine with remarkable and sometimes subversive brilliance. Moreover, the men, while dominant, are also gently mocked – hence, their outrage and anxiety, transpiring in a nationwide decree, emerge as disproportionate and somewhat ludicrous. It is the women here who ultimately come to the fore as more formidable.[4]

Let me now turn from the context of colonized Jews and Judah to colonization in the modern era. In the last one and a half centuries, too, imperialist ideology found ample expression in colonial enterprise and once again its agenda operated within a carefully circumscribed gendered context. Consequently, those who set out to conquer and expand their territories were once again predominantly men, and those whom they encountered in the first instance, whom they fought and/ or brokered concessions with, were also mostly male. This is certainly how *history* depicts it. For example, according to the official version, the person who, almost single-handedly it seems (!), shaped the history of Southern Africa was Cecil John Rhodes (1853–1902) – to the extent that two nation states, today's Zimbabwe

---

3. As is attested in a collection of essays exploring the question of sex in antiquity (Masterson et al. 2015), it was commonplace as part of the excesses associated with banquets that secondary wives or harlots could be summoned to provide entertainment. This would happen at events from which officials' wives were excluded. In Esther 1, to ask the queen to provide such entertainment is (understandably) interpreted by Vashti as degrading because such a demand reduces her status.

4. Of note, too, is that alongside the rather gender-stereotypical male and female characters in Esther there is also repeated mention of gender-ambiguous eunuchs (e.g. 1.10-12).

and Zambia, were named after him: that is, Rhodesia and Northern Rhodesia, respectively. Yet Rhodes was not a 'lone ranger' in this enterprise but rather one man among many, riding on an expansionist ideology and promoting the British imperial interests of his time. It was during his long stint as a student at Oxford University that he became acquainted with the person and teachings of John Ruskin, a British philosopher, who envisaged a united Africa under British rule and who is remembered as challenging the young British men of his time with these stirring words:

> [This is] a destiny now possible to us, the highest ever set before a nation to be accepted or refused. Will you youths of England make your country for all the world a source of light, a centre of peace? This is what England must do or perish. She must found colonies as fast and as far as she is able, formed of the most energetic and valiant of men; seizing any piece of fruitful waste ground she can set her foot on. (cited in Tindall 1968: 137)

The language used here (and elsewhere) to describe the colonies-to-be suggests passivity – presumably, due to the lands' inherent inferiority. These lands lie fallow – unless rescued and redeemed: they are 'fruitful waste ground'. The language also appeals to patriotic bravado, British superiority ('a source of light, a centre of peace') and British entitlement (or 'destiny'). It also clearly assigns the business at hand to the (superior) British nation's young *men* ('the most energetic and valiant of men'). But on arrival in the territories, which the likes of Ruskin depicted as derelict and ready for seizure,[5] these valiant British men met stiff resistance, mounted by the men of the 'savage' communities who considered these same territories their home! Imbedded in its very nature, colonialism presented itself as a gendered endeavour where women waited at the fringes while the men of colonizer and colonized communities determined their fate.

Ruskin's position is likely to have made perfect sense in the tension-filled context of the Europe of the last half of the nineteenth century and the 'grab-and-take' policy of the colonial enterprise. Such was the seriousness of the tension that German Chancellor Otto von Bismarck convened a conference in Berlin in December 1884 aimed at regulating occupation of Africa by the powerful nations of Europe (Tindall 1968: 135). The audaciousness of this endeavour cannot be overemphasized: the fate of Africa was negotiated by a European political consortium, the larger percentage of whose members had never set foot on the continent. None the less, they took it upon themselves to decide on political border markings without much regard to realities (such as demographics) on the ground. In some instances, political borders were drawn cutting across tribal territories.

One example concerns the Ndau people of the southeast of Zimbabwe who found a portion of their land and their kinsmen on the Mozambican side of the

5. There are some resonances here with the ideology of the 'empty land' in the Hebrew Bible (see Carroll 1992).

border. The southwest portion of the land now called Zimbabwe, meanwhile, was home to the Ndebele people who would make forays into the lands of neighbouring tribes to plunder but never claimed hold of these lands. Working on the guidelines set at the Berlin Conference, Rhodes erroneously assumed that an arrangement made with the Ndebele would suffice for the entire region. He is said to have uttered, 'I have always been afraid of the Matebele king. He is the only block to central Africa, as, once we have his territory, the rest is easy' (cited in Rotberg 1988: 257–8). Yet the Ndebele people had settled in the southwest of modern-day Zimbabwe – a region known for its semi-aridness and susceptibility to droughts – fleeing from Chaka the Zulu. While agricultural enterprises such as livestock rearing could thrive (albeit on a small scale), crop farming would rarely yield much, due to the general nature of this region's soil type and climate.[6] Trade with neighbours, meanwhile, would be unsustainable for a number of reasons: (1) relations were generally poor, as tribes treated each other with suspicion and (2) using simple farming methods and equipment, the neighbouring tribes' agricultural outputs were barely at subsistence level and would hardly sustain their own needs. As a result the Ndebele would resort to raiding their neighbours and, when successful, would help themselves to grain, women, livestock and slaves. There was never an intention on the part of the Ndebele to take the lands of their neighbours. It is possible that Rhodes wrongly got the impression that the Ndebele were a warring people who controlled the entire region. The 1884 Berlin Conference referred to above, which provided one framework for occupation of Africa, was prone to significant errors and gross misrepresentations of reality; hence, this inaccurate interpretation of Ndebele actions and intentions is not surprising at all.

Rhodes sent three men as representatives of his de Beers Company to meet Lobengula, the Ndebele king and on 30 October 1888 Lobengula was 'assisted' in signing what is known as the Rudd Concession (Tindall 1968: 143). By means of this 'agreement' Lobengula granted exclusive mineral rights in all his territories and agreed not to enter into any negotiations with any other party without the permission of Rhodes. For their part, the colonizers pledged that Lobengula 'would receive a monthly payment of £100, a thousand rifles and a gunboat on the Zambezi or £500 instead' (Tindall 1968: 143).

One absurdity of the proposal to offer a gunboat on the Zambezi lies in the fact that Lobengula's royal homestead was in fact several hundred miles from the Zambezi River! Lobengula would never have use for the gunboat – but this is what those in power were offering. The imperial hegemony exemplified here in the exercise of colonial enterprise demonstrates that white settler males occupied the top positions and engaged with the most powerful of the indigenous populations – but not as equals but in ways that denigrated the colonized, even when the façade was one of respectfulness (as with Lobengula). Certainly in the frontline, there is

---

6. This is the region of modern-day Zimbabwe closest to the Kalahari Desert, a geographical fact that may explain its rather harsh climatic conditions.

no place for women – whether among colonizing settlers or the colonized. These historical realities, which have cast long shadows in Zimbabwe (shadows that persist), are in my mind as I read Esther.

Reading Esther in the Context of Colonization

The traditions emerging (in part) from the colonial enterprise only entrenched the marginalization and commodification of women and did not allow for much celebration of women's achievements. But in the account of Esther (named after a woman!) there are three points in relation to the two protagonists that leap out for me: (1) it is Mordecai who foolishly starts a conflict he cannot win; (2) it is Esther who steps in (albeit under some duress) employing her wit and charm to avert impending danger; and (3) it is Mordecai who reaps the greatest benefit by becoming elevated to prime minister of the Empire. Indeed, who the dominant character, or hero of the story is, is ambiguous. If piety is the measure of what it means to be a good Jew, the book is ambivalent: famously, the scroll of Esther contains no single reference to God. Mordecai will not bow down before Haman (3.2-5), possibly because he will bow down only to his god, while Esther, also, possibly, exhibiting piety, calls for a three-day community fast (4.16). But Esther exceeds, if not in piety, in both bravery (as demonstrated in her approaching the king without summons) and cleverness (as exhibited in her careful timing and contriving of banquets and of making her petition known to the king).

And yet contributions to Esther studies are sometimes characterized by 'the tendency … to exalt Mordecai as the true hero of the tale and to downplay or even vilify the role of Esther' (White-Crawford 1998: 133). Could this be due to the pattern also set by colonialism? The scroll is named after Esther but the jury is still out as to who is the main character of the story. Suggestions have been made to the effect that '[b]etween Mordecai and Esther the greater hero is Mordecai, who supplied the brains while Esther simply followed his directions' (Moore 1971: liii). I believe that the perception of Esther playing a secondary role to Mordecai is influenced in part less by what the text actually states than by the dominant understanding (including in colonial discourse) concerning the power balance between the sexes, which is tilted to favour males. It is for this reason that this chapter focuses on imperial dynamics and tradition-sanctioned hegemonic structures to explain the nature of the challenges associated with the reception of the book of Esther.

Very few books of the Hebrew Bible have courted the controversy that the book of Esther has. Despite the well-documented popularity of the festival of Purim – especially during but also well before and since the Middle Ages (Walfish 1993 *passim*) – it has also been noted that this Jewish festival, which emerged separately from Pentateuchal (or Torah) traditions to which it is nevertheless indebted (Berlin 2001: ix), has struggled to command acceptance and respectability among some Jewish communities as far back as antiquity. It is in this vein that Carey A. Moore has noted:

The festival of Purim was definitely not celebrated by the Jewish sect of Qumran as part of their sacred calendar; and so, not surprisingly the Book of Esther, which had as its *raison d'etre* the establishment of Purim, has not been found among the Dead Sea Scrolls. Moreover, according to the Talmud, some Jews continued to reject the book as late as the third or fourth century A.D. (*Megilla* 7a; *Sanhedrin* II). (1982: 370)

Therefore, to say the book of Esther is a strange book is axiomatic. The strangeness begins with the fact that it is (alongside the book of Ruth) one of only two eponymous books securing a place in the Hebrew Bible that bears the name of a female character. Another challenge is how to make sense of Mordecai as the image of a devout and model Jew, given that he willingly gives away in marriage to a foreigner (albeit a foreign king) a Jewish female relative under his care. This detail is further problematized when the story of Esther is read inter-textually alongside the restrictive marriage regulations in Ezra–Nehemiah (Ezra 9–10; Neh. 13.23-31), or certain stipulations in Pentateuch law (Exod. 34.11-16; Deut. 7.1-4).

In summarizing further anomalous features, Bernhard W. Anderson notes that 'in comparison to the frequent oases of inspired Scripture, [the book of Esther] is an uninviting wilderness' (1950: 32). This must be with particular reference to the Masoretic version of the book of Esther, where both Jewish and Christian traditions have noted the peculiarity of a canonical book that does not mention God or make reference to the land of Israel. As a result, it was widely viewed as uninspired and its canonization contested (Zeitlin 1972: 21–4). The additions in the Septuagint version of Esther can be read as an attempt to address this unusual situation by making pious interpolations into an otherwise not overtly religious story. The controversy associated with its inclusion in the Hebrew canon and its failure to command widespread acceptance as part of authoritative scripture has been discussed at length (e.g. Carruthers 2008). The observations that it is conspicuous by its absence among the Dead Sea Scrolls and that there is no reference to it in the New Testament have received ample attention. The list of reasons that can be given to assert the book of Esther's strangeness is long indeed. Next, by reading Est. 2.10 with a postcolonial lens, this chapter will move beyond the question of *how* the book is strange and attempt to address the question of *why* this is the case.

The preamble of the book marks out the expanse that was (allegedly) the Persian Empire, a sketch of the territory ruled by King Ahasuerus: 'This happened in the days of Ahasuerus, the same Ahasuerus who ruled over one hundred and twenty-seven provinces from India to Ethiopia' (Est. 1.1). The Persian province of Yehud is part of this vast territory. When the decision is made to replace Vashti, the search for the new queen is depicted as comprehensive and empire-wide: 'And let the king appoint commissioners in *all* the provinces of his kingdom to gather *all* the beautiful young virgins to the harem in the citadel of Susa' (Est. 2.3, italics added). While the likelihood of such a thing actually taking place is remote (cf. Allen 2005: 42), let me state that I am less concerned here with historical accuracy than with the ideological orientation of the book – especially with regard to expressions of imperialism, counter-imperialism and/or subversiveness. Hence, while the Persian Empire may not have *actually* been as immense and while Persian power may not *really* have extended to being able to gather *all* virgin women, the text chooses to impart matters in this way in an effort to assert absolute imperial authority and control and – as I will go on to develop – to contrast this with the underdog status of the Jews, more particularly Jewish women.

Attempts at reconstructing the history of the Persian Empire in recent years have shed light on marriage conventions and revealed that a Persian queen had to descend from the Great Seven Families of the oligarchy established by Darius (Allen 2005: 42). Again, this would throw into question the historicity of Ahasuerus's marriage to an unknown immigrant maiden. But the author of Esther chooses to present the situation here as including the daughters of the Persian province of Yehud. In other words, on the basis of the logic of the text, there is nothing to preclude eligible girls of Jewish descent from the contest. Perhaps, therefore, the story is not only a fiction but also a fantasy.

Also to be noted is that early on in the storyline, the clash between Mordecai and Haman is yet to happen: Mordecai is just a good Jew, dutifully serving in the kingdom. The explanation for his decision to enter his cousin in the royal beauty contest and, more importantly, the instruction to the young woman to keep her ethnicity a secret, have nothing to do with the crisis that is yet to happen – although these elements do ensure the exciting plot that is unfolding. The biblical narrative, moreover, contains several allusions to anti-Jewish sentiment, which may make sense of Mordecai's instruction to Esther. To say that the story has xenophobic overtones (and ethnic stereotyping of both Persians and Jews) is hardly far-fetched. And yet, even when the King becomes aware of the ethnic identity of Esther and Mordecai, there is no hint of disdain. In fact, at the end of it all, the King promotes Mordecai in the full knowledge that he is a Jew. Purely on the basis of the narrative of Esther, entering a Jewish girl into the pageant and then instructing her not to reveal her identity possibly constitute an element of irregularity. But is this purely for storytelling effect?

It seems to me that the strangeness of the book of Esther stems from nonconformity in terms of what was and still is perceived by both Jewish and Christian readers as orthodoxy. I propose a more nuanced consideration of what is going on here and suggest that full attention be paid to the important statement when Mordecai and Esther are introduced: 'Now *there was a Jew in the citadel of Susa* whose name was Mordecai son of Jair son of Shimei son of Kish, a Benjaminite. Kish had been carried away from Jerusalem among the captives carried away with King Jeconiah of Judah, whom King Nebuchadnezzar of Babylon had carried away' (Est. 2.5-6, italics mine). The emphasis here is that Mordecai is not resident in the province of Yehud but at the Persian citadel of Susa, where he has possibly lived all his life. His ancestor Kish, apparently (or so the NRSV implies), three generations before, was deported from Judah by Nebuchadnezzar. The Hebrew text leaves the identity of the actual deportee unclear although the NRSV translation is justified in that the likeliest antecedent is indeed Kish.

When all is said, the story of Esther makes best sense as a diaspora story; a story, moreover, focused more on telling a good yarn than on conveying historically accurate detail. Jon Levenson, therefore, affirms that the community behind the story is one that had managed to turn exile into diaspora (1997: 16). The distinction is profound, with 'exile' implying an unwelcome condition that is temporal *and* geographical and 'diaspora' referring to a condition of permanence and settlement – possibly, though not necessarily, with the implication of resignation to this state of affairs. This diaspora story, however, is not just one of survival but of triumph and vindication in the new homeland, of the success of Jews even when away from Judah. Susan Niditch also agrees with the idea of Esther constituting the work of a diaspora community: 'I am inclined to believe that the work was written in diaspora, for a cultural group surrounded by overlords in an alien setting, for a minority rather than for a conquered and culturally threatened majority in Palestine' (1995: 45). I see the community behind Esther as one not only needing to negotiate life within a powerful imperial hegemony but also as one living too close to the displays of that empire's power and glamour to resist its lure.

Postcolonial Reading: A Summary

In the book *Orientalism*, Edward Said offers a range of tenets defining this phenomenon, ranging from concrete geographical terms where the Orient (or East) is understood in relation to the Occident (or West, from the Latin *occidere* 'to fall/set [of the sun]'), to a complex political definition: 'a Western style for dominating, restructuring, and having authority over the Orient' (2003: 3).

Postcolonialism emerges from ideas similar to those of orientalism and also has geographical dimensions (given the concentrations of global wealth and ideological power in the geographic North and West in particular). According to postcolonialism, 'colonialism' incorporates more than the concrete plundering and exploitation of resources of the colonized and also more than the imbalanced and unjust world economic structures deriving from these. Colonialism also includes a targeted effort by one section of the global population (the colonizer) to dominate and impose demeaning thought-forms upon another (the colonized), transpiring in the internalized oppression and lack of self-worth of the colonized. Postcolonialism reveals, analyses and resists these insidious forms of colonialism.

Rasiah S. Sugirtharajah lists among the contributions of postcolonial biblical hermeneutics more particularly the fact that 'it has brought to attention the importance of biblical empires – Assyrian, Egyptian, Persian, Greek, and Roman – central to many biblical books and providing the social, cultural and political framework' (2012: 46). And this, in turn, raises ideological questions of power distribution, which are, again, central to postcolonial criticism. Hence, while much of mainstream biblical scholarship concerns itself with textual, theological and historical questions, postcolonial biblical hermeneutics has brought to the foreground of biblical scholarship the significance of power politics, focusing particularly on the perspectives of the formerly colonized and the effects on them of colonial domination that extend well beyond seizures of land and resources to internalized socio-psychological dimensions.

Traditionally, therefore, both in academic and liturgical contexts, historical-and theological-critical questions have dominated engagement with and reception of the book of Esther. The imperial dynamics defining the book's context and provenance, and the hegemonic structures within which the book was received have not, until recently, featured prominently in its interpretation. Postcolonial biblical hermeneutics, however, has begun to redress this. This method has also served to demonstrate how some more egalitarian biblical traditions came to be corrupted in order to perpetuate the male-dominated ecclesiastical hegemony developed alongside and hand-in-hand with colonial expansionism. Sugirtharajah cites the case of the New Testament figure of Mary Magdalene as one example: 'One such maligned figure is Mary Magdalene. Utilising the discarded Gospel of Mary, postcolonialism attempts to configure the story of Mary Magdalene, showing how a once exemplary leader has been turned into a repentant sinner by later ecclesiastical writers' (2012: 47). Interaction with the biblical texts must take into account that preservation and transmission of these traditions occurred in a context where, alongside colonial dynamics, gender relations placed males in a dominant power position over females.

The postcolonial hermeneutic retrieval process extends to include cases where imperial translational impositions contaminated 'some [of the] egalitarian values intrinsic to local cultures' (Sugirtharajah 2012: 50). In the culture of the Shona people of Zimbabwe, as an example, there is evidence of a strong religious consciousness prior to contact with Christian missionaries, with a conception of God that does not include any gender specification. This God of the Shona existed (and still does) in spirit form and is neither male nor female.[7] It is only when the Christian missionaries appropriated the Shona God and name to translate the name and concept of the biblical Judeo-Christian God that the male traits of the latter were imposed on the conception of the former. In a sense, Christianity robbed the Shona of their God (cf. Sugirtharajah 2012: 50). In so doing, the missionaries were able to influence the Shona into accepting a hegemonic structure that was characterized by imbalance of power; one where males were designated superior over females and the biblical God dominant over indigenous gods.

This was further extended to race relations, with one group (that of the colonizer) claiming a privileged relationship with the powerful He-God from whom ultimate power is said to derive. This group was, thereby, by inference, 'naturally' more entitled to power than the group being introduced to this deity (viz. the colonized peoples). Postcolonial biblical hermeneutics proceeds from an understanding that it is the empire's power politics that define the processes by which biblical traditions are preserved, transmitted and interpreted. In the case of Esther, the empire's over-exertion of power, as demonstrated in the Persian overlord's exercise

---

7. Editors' note: for a similar conceptualization pertaining to the Shona deity Mwari, see the contribution in this volume by Elizabeth Vengeyi.

of complete dominance, became imaginable and internalized – but alongside this the story also offers possibilities for subversion.[8]

Application of a Postcolonial Reading and Analogy

Approached this way, the applicability of a postcolonial reading of the book of Esther is entirely fitting. The biblical book of Esther in all its variations is testimony to the gripping influence of empire. The various versions, translations and readings, and the manner in which the characters of the story are cast, all testify to how politics shape both the plot of the story and the subsequent hermeneutic outcomes. I have already mentioned Esther's strangeness insofar that, at least in the Masoretic Text tradition, the story ends with certain Israelites comfortable at home away from home (but nonetheless colonized). In a framework that has the imperial structure at Susa as the dominant political power in sight and the idealized Jerusalem-centred hegemonic structures as putative religious authority, the powerlessness of the Jewish population, settled far away from home, separated from its religious hub, and constituting a minority with little political power, is palpable.

Moreover, there is no homage paid to diaspora realities in later hermeneutic processes. Hence, traditional interpretations of Esther have not included much in the way of express acknowledgment of economic, or political, or cultic problematics. Instead, the story and its interpretations have tended to point to ahistorical, even fantastical features, to a turning away from such realities and towards succeeding in adversity and the victory of an underdog, as is well exemplified by the triumph of a Jewish orphan woman. Diaspora realities are presented only indirectly.

I will now turn to an accessible analogy to demonstrate my reading. In the recent past, different colonial authorities are known to have used various methods to ensure continued control over their respective colonies' people and resources. Systems were designed that relied on a wide range of tactics, including brutal force and repressive policies, as exemplified in the draconian and institutionalized system of South African Apartheid, which deprived the majority population of even basic human rights and dignity. The Portuguese, meanwhile, employed a policy in their African colonies where natives were rewarded with the status of *assimilado* for being able to assimilate into their colonial masters' culture. The nature of this assimilation was expressed in a wide range of manners: including religious ideas (amounting to conversion), and acquisition of Portuguese language, dress, food and drink. Linda Heywood notes that this was a development codified in law and sanctioned by the Church:

8. The idea of the book of Esther as an example of subversive, or protest literature is proposed by, among others, LaCocque (1990).

The historic Missionary Accord of 1940 based on the Concordat between
the Vatican and the Portuguese, and the Missionary statute of 1941 were also
important. These laws spelled out the subordinate but vital role the colonies
and colonial peoples were to play in the Portuguese Empire, and the duty of
the government towards the 'native' populations. The laws stated the moral
obligation to promote, by all means, 'the moral improvement and material life of
the [native] population' and the Africans' duty of assuming their legal status in
Portuguese colonial society. (2000: 64)

A considerable number of local populations found the lure of their colonial
masters' way of life and the elevated status that came with it irresistible. Those from
the native population that left their kinsfolk to seek employment in urban and semi-
urban areas, establishing close contact with the colonialists as civil servants, domestic
workers, farm supervisors and similar occupations, were the most likely to attain
this special status. While there is likely to have been variegation between colonies,
it was common throughout the Portuguese colonial empire for those Africans who
had left their rural homes to establish close contact with their European masters to
become *assimilado* – and this may indeed have been their active pursuit.

The Portuguese colonial authorities, it must be added, operated on the
understanding prevalent at the time that Africans were an inferior people and as
such could never be truly assimilated, or truly become like Europeans. Alexander
Keese notes: 'Portuguese officials recognised that young "educated Africans" who
had even managed to study in Portugal merited – up to certain limits – good
treatment and consideration as elite' (2007: 103). This, however, was as good as it
got. There was no equality between Portuguese and *assimilados*. The *assimilados*,
at best, attained a status somewhere 'in-between' where they were perceived as
better than their kinsmen but below the colonizer Europeans.

For the colonial authorities, this arrangement made it easier to divide-and-rule,
as the favourable treatment of a section of the native population as 'more elite'
naturally bred resentment among those of their fellow people who were, by
contrast, branded as less civilized and, therefore, less advantaged.[9] For their
part, the 'uncivilized' kinsfolk perceived the *assimilados* negatively as sell-outs
to the extent where their families disowned them. In native population circles,
such calamities as lack of rains, disease outbreaks, and 'unnatural' deaths were
blamed on the *assimilados*. Again, dynamics between *assimilados* and those
kinsfolk resisting this status are likely to have been variable but some *assimilados*,

---

9. In Rwanda, too, the privilege conferred by colonizers on Tutsi over Hutu and the split
and hostility this engendered between the two, played out with devastating consequences
in the attempted Tutsi genocide of 1994. Also, in Apartheid South Africa there are plenty
of examples of those designated 'coloured' receiving rights and privileges denied to those
designated 'black' – again, indicating a divisive hierarchy imposed by the dominant 'white'
group most closely identified with the colonizer. There are many more examples of this
practice in colonialism.

considering themselves more enlightened, remained resolute in their endeavour to become like their masters, gladly cutting off ties with their relatives, picking up foreign names and new identities.

I must state here categorically that this is not a comparative study. The dynamics involved in Portuguese colonies and the traditions assumed in the biblical book of Esther are too disparate in terms of both time and space to make a meaningful comparison feasible. The one historical context might, however, provide a fillip for reflection on the other literary context, with regard to patterns or tendencies of colonizer–colonized dynamics.

From its classical formulation in the work of Aristotle, analogical reasoning has become common currency in epistemological discourses to this day (Bartha 2010). Aristotle recognized two major types of arguments: namely (1) the argument from example (*paradeigma*) and (2) the argument from likeness (*homoiotes*), both of which developed to become central to all later variations of the analogical argument (Bartha 2010). The consequent philosophical framework that emerged is best understood in terms of a special rhetorical syllogism (a three-part deductive argument) commonly employed in oratory presentations from antiquity and referred to by its technical name as enthymeme. Bertrand Russell credits to Aristotle the formulation of syllogism, which 'remained for some two thousand years the only type of argument recognised by logicians' (1959: 85).

One trait common to all enthymemes is that at least one premise of the argument is not expressed in explicit terms but rather bases its strength upon the employment of examples that arise from one or more similar cases, to arrive at a general proposition, and then to argue deductively towards a particular inference. In other words, the fact that something has happened so often in the past warrants an inference that it will happen again in the future. It is on the basis of such reasoning that Ernst Troeltsch, one of the most influential post-Enlightenment philosophers, in an essay first published in 1913, entitled 'Über historische und dogmatische Methode in der Theologie', gave expression to what has now become the principle of analogy (1991 [1913]: 13). It states that for anything that has happened in the past to pass as credible, it must find an analogy in the present. This takes away the need for comparative analysis, as analogical domains need not be exactly the same in all respects. However, I must emphasize that the more similar the analogical domains, the stronger the argument.

It is my considered opinion that there is sufficient *homoiotes* in terms of hegemonic structures, power dynamics and gendered prejudices in the communities behind first, the story of Esther and second, recent southern African contexts to warrant fruitful comparison. Considering the governance policies pertaining to Portuguese colonies alongside the narratives of my own people's collective memory of the realities of life under British colonial rule, I see sufficient analogical material for the kind of hermeneutic I am proposing to explain Esther's vow to identity secrecy. The power of the empire corrupts solidarity in the colonized communities by drawing one part of the colonized community (e.g. the *assimilados*) to its centre and pushing the rest further out to the margins. For the select few 'becoming like the colonizer' confers clear advantage. Marrying Ahasuerus, even though in all likelihood this was detestable to many in Esther's own Jewish community,[10] may still be regarded as elevating her status (much like that of the *assimilado*) – partly, no doubt, because Ahasuerus is king, but possibly also, because he is Persian, that is, of the ruling group. The loyalty with which Mordecai serves Ahasuerus is, likewise, rewarded by elevation within the structures of the empire, which would have the consequence of strengthening allegiance with the colonizer and, commensurately, weakening ties with his own people. All this and several other subthemes in the story of Esther constitute clandestine support systems for the notion that becoming more like the colonizer is advantageous and turns one into something better.

The temptations of the empire are certainly amply displayed in the book of Esther. The opening of the book dwells at length on the Persian king's wealth and power. Ahasuerus rules over a vast expanse of land (1.1, 20) and the court is much occupied with lavish displays of abundance – hence, the frequent reference to banqueting (e.g. 1.4, 9) and the reference to precious materials, such as fine linen, gold, silver, marble and mother-of-pearl (1.6). Moreover, the empire is depicted as having far-reaching power and a high degree of organization (1.22) – so, it is easy to see what is desirable and alluring about the colonizer.

Stephanie Dalley (2007) has put forward an intriguing case based on, among other things, the fact that the names 'Esther' and 'Mordecai' are not Hebrew names. In my reasoning, non-Jewish names for Jewish characters are indicative of succumbing to the pressure and seductions of the empire.[11] Again, it is not the

---

10. The secrecy surrounding Esther's Jewish identity (2.10, 20) can be variously explained. It might have been intended to protect Esther from discrimination on the part of Persians – although, as mentioned, Ahasuerus's discovery of Esther's Jewishness elicits no disapproval or rejection (ch. 8). It could also be explained as protecting her from disapproval of *other Jews* who may have objected to her marriage to a non-Jew. As in other colonial contexts alluded to here, assimilation is regarded in Esther with some ambiguity. It can advance one's prospects (as Esther's and Mordecai's are advanced: hence Mordecai even comes to wear Persian royal insignia, 8.15) but it can also dilute one's identity and one's community ties. The book of Esther is careful to emphasize that although Mordecai came to be second in rank within the empire, 'he was powerful among the Jews and popular with his many kindred, for he sought the good of his people and interceded for the welfare of all his descendants' (10.3). This closing statement may be intended to assuage concerns as to the threats posed to Jewish identity and customs on account of assimilation.

11. Names and renaming function in similar ways in a number of places in the Hebrew Bible. Hence, when the king of Egypt appoints Eliakim king over Judah and Jerusalem, he also renames him 'Jehoiakim' (2 Chron. 36.4). Both the king of Egypt's power to appoint and his act of renaming indicate his power over Judah's king. The change in name indicates Eliakim's subservience to the colonizer. In the book of Daniel, on the other hand, the renaming of Daniel and his friends by the palace master (Dan. 1.6-7) appears to be honorific and indicative of their acceptance in the Babylonian court. The preservation of Hebrew names in the biblical text, however, including that of 'Hadassah' for 'Esther' (2.7) might also indicate a degree of pride in Jewish names as well as of some resistance to such

historical accuracy of the book of Esther that is central to this chapter but, rather, the ideological values that the book conveys – and these values tend to promote a degree of assimilation. I must note that assimilation is not envisaged as total, as there remains evidence for the maintenance of Jewish traditions[12] – even in a text where God is not named or mentioned – and of the distinctiveness of the Jewish people.[13] Quite a number of details might indeed confirm conventional Jewish beliefs or customs: such as Mordecai's confidence that even if Esther decides not to act, deliverance will come from some other place (4.14); Esther's call for a three-day fast (4.16); the possibility of association between Purim and Pesach – and Pesach *is* explicitly associated with God's salvific intervention (Exodus 12–14) even if God is unmentioned in Masoretic Esther; and the plural Hebrew form of the name 'Purim'.

Mordecai and the community of Jews around the citadel of Susa represent the wider Jewish community, with the distinction that they are at the hub of the Persian Empire. The glitz of imperial power in their proximity must have exerted allure. If Esther, within the court itself, could remain in the harem for about a year *and* go on to win the approval of the king while keeping her Jewishness secret from imperial authorities, her level of assimilation must have been consummate. However, the vow to secrecy indicates that in the eyes of the ruling Persians, assimilation alone is still not good enough. Like in the case of the *assimilado* who was advantaged but still not equal to a European, admitting Jewish identity would have diminished Esther's chances. When understood this way, most of what has posed challenges in the long reception history of the book of Esther now makes sense. Here we have a story told from the perspective of the Jewish equivalent of the *assimilado* of the Portuguese empire, a story that would struggle to find acceptance in mainstream Jewish thought.

Conclusion

The vow to identity secrecy in Esther attests to internalization of hegemonic insistence on superiority of the empire. As the story now stands, it appears that

colonial power play. Notable in some colonial contexts is how using names of the colonizer can indicate prestige or assimilation. Conversely, in postcolonies, independence has often led to resurgence in popularity of indigenous names.

12. Mordecai's resistance to doing obeisance to Haman (3.5) is explained on account of his Jewishness (3.4). From this might be inferred his devotion to the Jewish God alone (cf. the story of Daniel 3 in which Shadrach, Meshach and Abednego refuse to bow down to Nebuchadnezzar's statue and are rescued from the furnace by their God).

13. While Mordecai's Jewishness must be explained to Haman (3.4) and while Esther can keep her Jewish identity a secret, indicating that physical markers are not an issue in terms of distinguishing 'the Jews' from other peoples of the empire, 'the Jews' are clearly understood as a discrete group and mentioned as such insistently (3.6; 4.3, 7; 8.1, 8–9, 13, 16–17; 9.1-3, 5–7, 10, 12–13, 15–16, 18–20, 22–25, 27–28, 30–31; 10.3).

suppressing markers of Esther's ethnic identity and traditions and assimilating to the empire enhanced her chances of winning the contest and subsequently, living prosperously in the very heart of the empire's power centre. Gaining status (as queen) and the trappings of wealth, however, come at the cost of self-denial and of internalizing the inferiority imposed on her by her colonizer. Only at this price can Esther survive. People in the sort of predicament that faces Mordecai, Esther and the community of Jews around Susa, can never get it right as they have to deal with forces pulling them in opposite directions. First, like in the case of the Mozambican *assimilado*, cultural solidarity and strong identity remain with those whose contact with empire is minimal. From the safety of their location – be it the native villages of Mozambique or Persia's province of Yehud – those at some remove from the centre (the colonial heartlands or Susa) can more easily reject and disdain what the empire represents. But not so those that find themselves at the hub of the empire's power. Mordecai and those around him, as Jon Levenson puts it, reflect 'a stratum of society with a very different understanding of Jewishness' (1997: 16). For them there is advantage in and temptation of adopting the colonizer's ways but no true prospect of full assimilation.

Given the trends of global population movements today, a considerable proportion of the world population lives in an in-between situation – for a multiplicity of reasons. More than ever before, large numbers of people are dislocated from their homeland – as refugees or economic migrants. The book of Esther's rising prominence is arguably because it resonates with such uprooted groups. Its strangeness, moreover, is now becoming its strength and in postcolonial and diaspora contexts the story makes good sense. In Jo Carruthers' words:

> ... it is precisely Esther's strangeness that other readers appropriate for its subversive potential. For those at the margins of orthodoxy, there is something alluring about this wilderness text that promises an alternative perspective from the mainstream, a heterodoxy to be tapped into for seditious means. (2008: 2)

It is my submission that when read in the context of the grip of a powerful empire, the vow to identity secrecy of Est. 2.10 represents the response of a powerless colony. Its inclusion and emphasis serve to illuminate the imperial power relations undergirding the plot of the story. That a story of compromised Jewishness, developed in a context of colonial subjugation would struggle to command widespread acceptance among the Jews is inevitable.

Works Cited

Allen, L. (2005), *The Persian Empire: A History*, London: The British Museum Press.
Anderson, B. W. (1950), 'The Place of the Book of Esther in the Christian Bible', *Journal of Religion* 30: 32–43.
Bardtke, H. (1963), *Das Buch Esther*, Gütersloh: Gütersloher Verlagshaus/Gerd Mohn.

Bartha, P. (2010), 'Analogy and Analogical Reasoning', in E. N. Zalta (ed.), *The Stanford Encyclopedia of Philosophy* (Winter 2016 edn). Available online: https://plato.stanford. edu/archives/win2016/entries/reasoning-analogy/ (accessed on 4 December 2016).

Berlin, A. (2001), *Esther*, Philadelphia: The Jewish Publication Society.

Carroll, R. P. (1992), 'The Myth of the Empty Land', *Semeia* 59: 79–93.

Carruthers, J. (2008), *Esther Through the Centuries*, Oxford: Blackwell.

Cazelles, H. (1961), 'Note sur la Composition du Rouleau d'Esther', in H. Gross and F. Mussner (eds), *Lex tua veritus: Festschrift für Hubert Junger*, 17–29, Trier: Paulinas.

Clines, D. J. A. (1984), *Esther Scroll: The Story of the Story*, Sheffield: JSOT Press.

Dalley, S. (2007), *Esther's Revenge at Susa: From Sennacherib to Ahasuerus*, Oxford: Oxford University Press.

Heywood, L. M. (2000), *Contested Power in Angola: 1940s to the Present*, Rochester, NY: University of Rochester Press.

Keese, A. (2007), *Living with Ambiguity: Integrating an African Elite in French and Portuguese Africa 1930–61*, Stuttgart: Franz Steiner.

Knight, D. A. (1973), 'Tradition History', in D. Freedman (ed.), *The Anchor Bible Dictionary* (vol. 6), 633–38, London: Doubleday.

LaCocque, A. (1990), *The Feminine Unconventional*, Minneapolis: Fortress Press.

Laffey, A. L. (1988), *An Introduction to the Old Testament: A Feminist Perspective*, Philadelphia: Fortress Press.

Levenson, J. D. (1997), *Esther: A Commentary*, London: SCM.

Masterson, M. N. Sorkin Rabinowitz and J. Robson (eds) (2015), *Sex in Antiquity: Exploring Gender and Sexuality in the Ancient World* (Rewriting Antiquity), New York: Routledge.

Moore, C. A. (1971), *Esther* (Anchor Bible), Garden City, NY: Doubleday.

Moore, C. A. (1982), *Studies in the Book of Esther*, New York, NY: KTAV.

Niditch, S. (1995), 'Esther: Folklore, Wisdom, Feminism and Authority', in A. Brenner (ed.), *A Feminist Companion to Esther, Judith and Susanna*, 26–46, Sheffield: Sheffield Academic Press.

Paton, L. B. (1908), *A Critical and Exegetical Commentary on the Book of Esther*, Edinburgh: T & T Clark.

Rotberg, R. (1988), *The Founder: Cecil Rhodes and the Pursuit of Power*, Oxford: Oxford University Press.

Russell, B. (1959), *Wisdom of the West*, London: Rathbone.

Said, E. (2003), *Orientalism*, London: Penguin.

Sugirtharajah, R. S. (2012), *Exploring Postcolonial Biblical Criticism: History, Method, Practice*, Chichester: Wiley-Blackwell.

Tindall, P. E. N. (1968), *History of Central Africa*, London: Longman.

Troeltsch, E. (1991 [1913]), *Religion in History* (trans. J. L. Adams and W. F. Bense), Minneapolis, MN: Fortress.

Walfish, B. D. (1993), *Esther in Medieval Garb: Jewish Interpretation of the Book of Esther in the Middle Ages*, Albany, NY: State of New York University Press.

White-Crawford, S. A. (1998), 'Esther', in C. A. Newsom and S. H. Ringe (eds), *Women's Bible Commentary*, 131–7, Lousville, KY: Westminster John Knox Press.

Zeitlin, S. (1972), 'Introduction – The Books of Esther and Judith: A Parallel', in M. S. Enslin (ed.), *The Book of Judith: Greek Text with an English Translation*, 1–37, Leiden: E. J. Brill.

Chapter 8

'MY WORDS DROPPED UPON THEM LIKE DEW': TOWARDS REIMAGING THE IDENTITY OF AFRICAN BIBLICAL INTERPRETERS

Mark S. Aidoo

Introduction

This chapter seeks to illustrate how communication between scholarly readers, on the one hand, and ordinary readers, on the other, is enhanced through recognition of affinity between speech art in the Hebrew Bible and in Akan[1] traditional contexts. My illustrations will focus particularly on an examination of Job 29.21-25 alongside that of the *okyeame*, or Akan traditional spokesperson for chiefs and other authorities. I seek to demonstrate how African scholars of the Bible may draw on their own traditions and imagery to facilitate and enliven dialogue with non-scholarly communities. One issue at stake is how West African biblical scholars might harness the power and beauty of both traditional and biblical speech art, in order to captivate and enthral ordinary readers, thus making them more willing and receptive to hear. Hence my question is, can the image of the *okyeame* inspire trust and effective dialogue between scholarly and ordinary readers of the Bible?

In his reflections on the articles published in *Semeia* 73: *'Reading With' – African Overtures* (1996), Eric Anum (2007) congratulates African interpreters because they have made significant efforts in reading the Bible with ordinary readers in a variety of contexts.[2] As he explains, the discrete local settings and cultural tools from which each contributor draws facilitate distinctive and mutually enriching dialogues between scholarly readers and ordinary readers and this, in turn, helps

---

1. The Akan peoples are comprised of ethnic groups with somewhat mutually intelligible cognate dialects. Among them are the Wassa, Fanti, Asen, Denkyira, Twifo, Akwapim, Akyem, Kwahu, Asante, Bono and Ahafo. Their dialects are spoken mainly in the western, central, eastern, Volta, Ashanti and Brong-Ahafo regions of Ghana. Other clusters of Akan people are found in mid-western Togo and south-eastern Ivory Coast.

2. Anum uses the congratulatory Akan expression *Ye ma wo mo*, which means 'well done!'

to close the gap between the worlds of the academy and grass-roots communities. Anum concludes with a further call to scholars to take another closer look at epistemological categories that could bring about yet more dialogues with ordinary readers (2007: 18). It is this call that motivates my choice of the *okyeame* as a model of a good speaker as enacted by Job.

Job, You have Done Well and Spoken Well

Job 29 is evocative of Job's role and identity in his community. It looks back to the time when he was prosperous, and describes his fall – a terrible turn of events that damaged his status profoundly. Conveying his contribution to society, Job, following three cycles of dialogue with his 'friends', enumerates his past glories. First, he attributes his rise to God (29.1-6); second, he points out that he used his advantages for the benefit of his society (29.12-20); and finally, he states that his former prestige validates his standing in public to act as a good speaker to whom people listen (29.21-25). That is to say, if Job's word refreshes people like dew, then this is because of his standing, which is able to empower the vulnerable, a quality that earns him respect across the classes, but especially with the poor and marginalized:

> When the ear heard, it commended me; and when the eye saw, it approved: *because I delivered the poor* who cried and the orphan who had no helper. The blessing of the wretched came upon me; my justice was like a robe and a turban. I was eyes to the blind, feet to the lame, I was a father to the needy, and I championed the cause of the stranger. I broke the fangs of the unrighteous and made them drop their prey from their teeth. (29.12-17)[3]

As a champion of justice, Job earns respect from all people including princes of the land (vv. 10-12). He specifically links his role as champion of justice for the vulnerable to the power and influence of his speech, and in this literary and social context Job's mellifluous words are heartening to his listeners. Job is fully aware that it is possible for the same people who were close to him in his 'good old days' to turn against him. So, with no wealth to give and only speech at his disposal, he dwells on his role as one-time celebrated speaker whose words might still sink deeply into the hearts of his hearers.

Let me demonstrate with an example the artfulness of Job's rhetoric in order to argue that his are skilfully crafted words spoken by a consummate speaker. I will then go on to suggest resonance with *okyeame* rhetoric. Job 29.21-25 may be divided into two movements: vv. 21-23, and vv. 24-25. Job's expressive description of himself in this pericope abounds with syntagmatic pairings, demonstrating facility with words: words//speech (v. 22); rain//latter rain (v. 23); smile//light on my face (v. 24); and chief//king (v. 25). Moreover, the progression from vv. 21-23 is

---

3. Translations are my own, unless otherwise indicated. Italics added for emphasis.

symmetrical. Structurally, while v. 21 and v. 23 refer to the listeners, v. 22 points to the speaker. There is also a correlation between the listeners keeping silent to hear from Job (v. 21b) and the listeners' mouths widening as they hear from Job (v. 23b), as though in awe when they register the impact of his word (v. 22b). Hence, the sequence of actions intensifies and climaxes in v. 23b. Those who are overwhelmed at the way he speaks are the ones whose mouths widen in awe. A chiastic pattern can be observed in vv. 21-23:

A   They listened to me and waited // (v. 21a)
B   Keeping silent // for my counsel (v. 21b)
C   After I spoke // they said no more (v. 22a)
C^1 My speech // overwhelmed them (v. 22b)
B^1 They waited for me // like the rain (v. 23a)
A^1 They spread their mouth wide // as for the latter rain (v. 23b)

This first movement (vv. 21-23) shows the reactions of the people to Job: 'waited' corresponds with 'keeping silent'; 'said no more' corresponds with 'overwhelmed them'; and 'waited' corresponds with 'spread their mouth wide'. A *Leitwort*, 'waited', opens the movement in Line A and also serves as a closure marker in Line B^1. In this unit, Job emphasizes how the people receive his words: they not only listen silently but also prepare their hearts in anticipation. Moreover, Job's words in v. 22 possibly recall Moses's song in Deut. 32.2: 'May my teaching drop like rain, my speech condense like the dew; like gentle rain on grass, like showers on new growth' (NRSV). The writer in Deuteronomy points to the falling dew or light rain that restores, renews and yields abundantly, likening this to the hoped for effect of Moses's instruction. Analogously, this is the desired impact of Job's speech; it, too, will provide sustenance and renewal.

The Hebrew text in Job 29.22 is very difficult to interpret:

אחרי דברי לא ישנו
ועלימו תטף מלתי :

This translates (rather literally) as: 'after my words, they did not repeat // and my speech drops over them.' Perhaps influenced once more by Deut. 32.2, some versions, like the French Nouvelle Edition de Geneve (1979), NRSV and NKJV, insert 'like dew' in Line B. Other versions reveal significant differences in translation. To cite some examples:

NJB
When I had finished, no one contradicted,
my words dropping on them, one by one.

NASB
After my words they did not speak again,
And my speech dropped on them.

NIV
After I had spoken, they spoke no more;
My words fell gently on their ears.

Such divergent translations give cause for further reflection. The word, תִּטֹּף 'drop/ secrete' (a *qal* imperfect of the root נטף) certainly is problematic and makes a literal reading clumsy. The NIV translates, 'My words fell' and qualifies it with 'gently' to express how speech flows from Job's lips gently, much like fluid secretes. The NJB inserts the phrase 'one by one', perhaps to indicate how the words come out one after another, like drops of rain. It seems these insertions are motivated by the concept of rain falling gently, or perhaps mellifluously (Hartley 1998: 394). Gerald Wilson sees it as a statement that draws on a symbol of luxury and abundance whereby the 'listeners heard Job's words as a gift of sweetness rather than harsh and unwelcome prodding and coercion' (2007: 320). Such a speech may be pleasing, soothing, or intoxicating to many people. H. H. Rowley's claim that Job is envisaged as speaking either slowly or unhurriedly is worth considering, too (1976: 189). One may, however, wonder why people would wait attentively for words that drop 'one by one': is there an expectation here that the message is about to become spectacular or revelatory – that is, are the drops rising to a climactic torrent? Or, is the 'drip-drip-drip' perhaps hypnotic or otherwise transfixing?

The expression 'my speech dropped over them' is in all likelihood not only metaphorical but also idiomatic. It could connote that the words have a deeply positive and quenching effect on the hearers. But the words could also, instead, be persistent and make the hearers feel uncomfortable. The Hebrew, תִּטֹּף, after all, can also denote 'speaking against'. In Ezek. 21.2-7 and Mic. 2.6, the same word is used to mean 'preach', 'prophesy', or 'make words flow' against the nations. Again, 'drop' can also point to some kind of negative connotations like careless words or something – either monotonous or accidental – ceasing, declining, or decreasing. Job's words were not necessarily prophetic or careless. Still, words that are spoken as drops – be it slow and deliberate, comforting and encouraging, or monotonous and careless speech – will not, in my view, captivate an expectant crowd.

In the African setting, too, any speech lacking a charismatic touch will not engage, let alone persuade an anxious or eager audience. Certainly, rain that drops as dew only refreshes the topsoil. If Job's words really have an impact on the hearts of his hearers (as the wider context indicates), then they probably do not merely *drip* from his mouth. It seems to me the watery movement used alongside 'over them' creates the impression of covering up completely and with some force, such as is captured, for instance, by the word 'surging' or 'foaming'. Consequently, I prefer a translation along the lines of: 'After I spoke they said no more // And my speech overwhelmed them.'

Isaiah uses the imagery of rain to emphasize the power of words. Hence, he likens speech to the watering of the field for plants to flourish, to yield seed and food (Isa. 55.10-11; cf. Song 4.11). Also in support of this, Marvin Pope, likewise, refers to a charismatic speaker who is compared to the rain that is vital and life-giving (1982: 211; cf. Prov. 16.15; Hos. 6.3). Noteworthy is that such speech is above all productive and energetic: it makes things happen. The metaphors combining 'word' with 'rain' or 'dew' thus confer a sense of something that is refreshing and also brings powerfully overwhelming action and satisfaction. It is not only the first rains that are welcome and anticipated but also the latter rains. Both rains come at a time of need for revitalization, and bring new life. Job's allusions to rain in his speech, then, are calculatedly dramatic. This is also echoed by Norman Habel who says that Job's speech shows him to be 'not merely a hero of justice but a beneficent source of life' (1985: 406, 412).

Job is not, apparently, the only one authorized to speak, but it appears the others present also love to listen to him – 'keeping silent for [Job's] counsel' (v. 21b). His compassionate care to transform oppressive situations of the poor and marginalized influences the reception of his speech. The implication is that those listening – perhaps including elders, nobles, chiefs and rulers – accord Job respect when he speaks (vv. 8-9). The context explains that Job is one who identifies with and helps the poor and orphan (v. 12), the widows (v. 13), the blind and lame (v. 15) and the needy and stranger (v. 16). Job seems to affirm that he is a man of the people. His relationship with the community operates on multiple levels and his actions bring positive impact to the lives of diverse members of his community: notably, advocacy for the vulnerable.

The second movement (vv. 24-25) is arranged in a staircase parallelism and depicts Job as a leader in the community. However, the pattern set in A to D deviates at D^1:

A   When I smiled on them, they scarcely believed it (v. 24a)
B   They did not let the light of my face fall (v. 24b)
C   I directed their course (v. 25a)
D   and sat as a chief (v. 25b)
D^1 I dwelt as a king among his troops (v. 25c)
E   I was like one who comforts mourners (v. 25d)

The similes in D and D^1 amplify C and make it clear that Job is not a chief or a king. His acting 'as a chief' and 'as a king' may point to the authority he possesses, but he nonetheless speaks as one of the people. He is comparable with a chief in that the expectant crowd looks to him for some direction. His role in relation to a figure of authority echoes that of Aaron when he is appointed to work with Moses to call the people of Israel out of Egypt:

> Is there not your brother Aaron the Levite? For I know *he can speak well*. Behold, he is already on his way to meet you, and when he sees you his heart will be glad. You shall speak to him and *put words in his mouth*. I will be with your mouth and his mouth, and I will teach you what to do. *He will speak to the people for you, and it will be as if he were your mouth and as if you were God to him*. (Exod. 4.14b-16. Italics are mine)

Aaron, in this text, is best understood as acting as a mouthpiece, interpreter and mediator on behalf of Moses. Aaron's ability to speak well is a virtue endowed by God. Indeed, God will be with his mouth, an expression that connotes divine enablement. Moses is to tell Aaron all that he desires for the people to hear and Aaron's duty is to speak well to the people on behalf of Moses. In this sense, Aaron could speak authoritatively because of divine enablement and on account of the authority conferred by Moses. Perhaps, Job is to be regarded in a similar vein: he is not a chief but he has qualities associated with a chief and the approval of divine and temporal authority. Stephen Hooks, thus, compares Job to Hermes of Greek mythology, the spokesperson and messenger of Zeus, highlighting how Job combines superior wisdom and rhetorical skill in his speech (2006: 340).

The meaning of the phrase in v. 24b – 'they did not let the light of my face fall' or 'the light of my countenance they did not extinguish' (NRSV) – is uncertain. A glowing countenance portrays a positive psychological effect. A falling face, however, signifies upset and/or shame, the body language of which includes blushing, lowering of the head and downcast eyes. This might recall Akan *animguase*, meaning 'shame/ disgrace': this word constitutes a compound of *anim* ('face') and *gu-ase* ('fall down'). If this is indeed the case, then Job affirms that the people did not put him to shame when he spoke. Their response, instead, motivates Job.[4] Carol Newsom, however, argues that the expression 'light of my face' is less about absence of shame than about God's presence (cf. Num. 6.25-26, the Priestly Blessing), and that 'Job uses these images because they characterize the ideals of leadership in his community, whether this is the leadership of either a patriarch, a king, or of God' (1996: 540).

Scholars also struggle with Line E – 'I was like one who comforts mourners' – because association with the words preceding is tricky (Gordis 1978: 322; Clines 1989: 943; Balentine 2006: 67): Do chiefs or kings typically comfort mourners? And yet, the metaphor of a comforter enlivens the imagination as to the relationship Job has with the people, not merely as a leader and speaker but also as someone who cares and empathizes. Switching to his care and compassion becomes another means to emphasize the influence of his speech.

Gerald Janzen (1985: 203) and Newsom (1996: 540), similarly, relate the royal imagery of Job to that in Psalm 72, a royal psalm in which the king is likened to rain falling on the fields causing the righteous to flourish and prosper (Ps. 72.6-7). Possibly, Job, too, is depicted as someone playing the ideal royal role, of one leading by example to facilitate piety. With such an image in mind, I will elaborate next on the spokesperson in the Akan cultural contexts and compare this with Job in relation to ch. 29.

The Cultural Identity of the Akan Spokesperson

Distinctive speech structures, especially those rooted in the institution of chieftaincy, are a distinguishing feature of traditional social forms in many parts of the continent

---

4. Although soon afterwards (30.1), Job reports that the situation has changed for the worse, 'now they make sport of me' (NRSV).

of Africa. Despite diminished emphasis given to traditional speech in modern democracies, effective speech continues to be admired and is integral for the preservation and continuing dynamism of indigenous African traditions. True, the institution of chieftaincy was offered up on the altar of colonialism – particularly during the period between the 1950s and 1970s, as many African countries struggled for independence, and when the desire for liberation and egalitarianism caused a backlash against not only colonial but also traditional rulers. Chieftaincy has come under heavy attack and it has been variously depicted as alien to certain societies or tribal groups or as a stumbling block to egalitarian living. It is equally true that democratic rule, with its diverse trappings from precolonial, colonial and postcolonial ideologies, has also contributed to damaging the efficacious and valuable traditions of African traditional speech art. While not suggesting that African traditions are only positive, I am asserting that many aspects of African traditions, more particularly those concerning influential and artful speech, can effect widespread social benefit and meaningful dialogue and that these traditions have been challenged and to some extent damaged by forces from within as well as without. My aim here, therefore, is to use a text from the Bible (again, a text *of* Africa and brought to Africa *by* colonialists, with positive *and* negative consequences) alongside indigenous Akan tradition for the mutual benefit of African biblical scholars and ordinary readers. I am doing so in a wider context that has seen renewed and intensive scholarly interests in African institutions, including chieftaincy (e.g. Nyamnjoh 2015: 4; Adu-Gyamfi 2012: 262–6; Rugarabura 2008: 111–12; Dankwa III 2004: 15).

As much as colonialism and neocolonialism tried to strip African peoples of their own cultural practices and traditions, some spaces for traditional systems persist within independent democratic systems of government (Nyamnjoh 2003: 96–110; Rugarabura 2008: 95–100). In fact, some African political leaders of the post-independence era, such as Kwame Nkrumah of Ghana, Julius Nyerere of Tanzania, Jomo Kenyatta of Kenya, Hastings Banda of Malawi, or Modibo Keita of Mali, succeeded in promoting African consensual political pluralism and thus allowed chieftaincy and its derivative values to thrive within democratic societies (van Binsbergen 1987: 156–66; Bediako 1995: 237–43; Searing 2002: 407–29; Boafo-Arthur 2006: 145–68). To give one example: Nkrumah, first president of independent Ghana, in a bid to promote Africanness and reclaim African cultural heritage as well as to appeal to his subjects and their cherished cultural memory, saw the symbolic trappings of chieftaincy as irresistible and embraced the tradition of the *okyeame*,[5] or traditional spokesperson, by appointing Okyeame Boafo Akuffo to speak and prepare the minds of the masses before he made presidential speeches. Okyeame Akuffo was given the title 'State Linguist', a position that, while not granted any official political authority, appears to have been prestigious and to have worked

---

5. This term is sometimes mistranslated 'traditional linguist' (Yankah 1995: 2; cf. Gyekye 1975: 111). Distinguishable from the academic philologist or linguist, there is no equivalent for the *okyeame* in Western contexts and no English word captures its full essence. Consequently, Akan *okyeame* is maintained.

greatly in the President's favour. Not only did Okyeame Akuffo earn admiration on account of his eloquence but he also attracted many listeners to the President.

Among the Akan, the *okyeame* exemplifies 'rhetoric competence *par excellence*' (Yankah 1995: 1), and his[6] role is comparable with that of speech functionaries of Burundi and the Limba of Sierra Leone (Finnegan 1970: 44–9, 80). In the Akan context, the role also has application beyond the sphere of chieftaincy, such as in ordinary family meetings and in marriage ceremonies. In other words, the model of *okyeame* pertains not only to the realm of traditional governance but also to other systems of social life where there is call for meaningful utterance. In traditional Akan culture, one cannot engage in significant ritual dialogue, especially with someone of elevated status and authority, without using an *okyeame*. Any person who has the gift of speaking poetically or skilfully can be appointed to the role, even on an ad hoc basis, if the situation demands such. Within the setting of traditional chieftaincy, however, the *okyeame* is a *de facto* official and member of the traditional councillors who steer the affairs of state. He sits at the right hand of the chief holding the royal staff on which the totem of the community is displayed, thus acting as the repository of the 'soul' of the tribe. Consequently, the *okyeame* wields some considerable amount of authority and status. Strictly speaking, an *okyeame* must not be chosen from within a royal family and Kwesi Yankah observes that, 'it is a taboo for an *okyeame* to become a chief' (1995: 85). In this sense, the *okyeame* (like Job in the text above) acts *like a chief*.

Whenever the chief speaks, the *okyeame* must convey the meaning of the speech to the audience in such a way that all will understand. Yankah further observes that:

> In the absence of the *okyeame*'s editorial art, the royal speech art is considered functionally and artistically incomplete. The public art of the *okyeame* thus turns on creativity. But his mode of accomplishing his duties also overlaps with the public enactment of power within the royal domain, for nobody speaks to the chief *in situ* except through the *okyeame*. (1995: 3)

The *okyeame* collaborates with and promotes the views of the chief by capturing the admiration of the audience, thereby upholding the authority of the chief. His task is to retell what the chief says so that all receive the intended meaning: hence, the maxim 'there is no bad chief but only a bad *okyeame*'; meaning, the *okyeame* takes the blame for every 'miscommunication' from the authorities. Oseadeeyo Addo Dankwa III adds that two important qualities of any *okyeame* are eloquence and wit: 'Even where the chief himself is not all that

---

6. I am using the masculine pronoun because the *okyeame* model, while in theory a gender-inclusive system, is in practice very much dominated by males. For instance, the Queen Mother of the Asante kingdom in Ghana uses between six and eight *akyeame* at a time, but rarely is more than one female (Stoeltje 2003: 3).

eloquent, still a good Linguist [*okyeame*] must make the best of an interpretation as wit and sapience could make of a speech. The Linguist [*okyeame*] must be suave, stylish, crunchy and crisp in repartee' (2004: 33). The potency of the *okyeame* lies in the ability to master language, use proverbs, interpret customs and traditions and direct proceedings. This means that the *okyeame* is expected to be conversant with history and traditions but also to keep abreast with what is going on in society at the present – not only in the royal echelons but also among the demos.

The *okyeame*, therefore, mediates between higher authorities and ordinary people. Hence, he captures and interprets the concerns of the community to persons in authority and vice versa. In this sense, the *okyeame* performs a dual and reciprocal role as a representative of those in authority and of the people, speaking 'for' both parties. The *okyeame* is not the originator of messages – but he facilitates dialogue between very different groups.

The *okyeame*, unlike chiefs, is free to operate in the lower as well as higher echelons of social life and can, therefore, explore knowledge within the public spaces where the ordinary people gather to work and play. Many look to the *okyeame* as a parent-figure, an advocate and a teacher. In other words, the *okyeame* occupies a dual space: firmly in the centre but leaning into the periphery. With his vested authority, the *okyeame* stands out as a translator, interpreter, mediator, legal expert and counsellor, ideally displaying charismatic leadership, sagacity, eloquence and knowledge.

African tradition places a high premium on wisdom and superior rhetorical skills, and the *okyeame* is expected to exhibit these to a particularly high standard. Good speech is essentially persuasive. The Akan have various terms to express what constitutes persuasive speech. The word *kasapa* ('good speech'), for instance, is a compound word with layered meanings. Hence, *ka* may mean 'bite, mix', *sa* means 'war' or 'drench' and *pa* means 'good'. As such *kasa* ('speech') may connote initiating war, but something less militant also. In analysing Akan speech forms, Kofi Agyekum observes that *kasapa* is 'persuasive language [that is] is sweet, pleasant, good, and positive; it strokes, flatters or deceives the addressees' (2004: 66). Other terms for good speech include *daadaa* ('to persuade/deceive'); *defedefe* ('palatable, fine and flattering speech') and *korokoro* ('fragrant, sweet smelling speech') (Agyekum 2004: 65). Perhaps, the notion is that, sweet and flattering speech may promote good and persuasive speech. As such, one may adopt various persuasive ways to reach the hearts of listeners. Instructive and strategic deployment of words, in turn, motivates admiration. But how may such an understanding of effective speech within the *okyeame* model play out well for *scholarly* readers? It is this to which I turn next.

The Scholarly Reader as the Okyeame

Focusing on Job as rhetorician alongside the *okyeame*, it can be observed that both act as leaders in the community. Neither, however, is a chief or king. Rather, each acts as a chief or a king, playing some quasi-royal role. They create spaces to represent both persons in authority and ordinary people. Both are advocates for the vulnerable and oppressed, but Job's role as a champion of justice is more emphasized than tends to be the case with the *okyeame*. Job's commitment and advocacy for the poor and needy makes an impact on the community so much so that when he speaks, the people listen and are overwhelmed. The people know him for his compassion and advocacy, hence find his speech refreshing. Job builds trust, and social transformation becomes more possible. Both Job and the *okyeame* endeavour to speak well: deploying words are intended to fall upon the people's heart like dew. The *okyeame's* stock in trade is mastery in using familiar cultural expressions, proverbs or stories, and to employ words that renew, restore and motivate. The same may be true of Job and, I argue, the scholar of the Hebrew Bible who is also versed in local tradition is well placed to adapt the qualities of Job, on the one hand, and of the *okyeame*, on the other, to create productive spaces within the community for championing the cause of justice as well as for transmitting the Word of God by means of conceptual categories that are relevant and persuasive for the ordinary reader. In this way, words of the Bible may become overwhelmingly enriching and refreshing, much as rain waters rejuvenate a parched land. A commitment to all of justice, the Bible and cultural propriety of language can in such a way promote effective and meaningful community well-being.

As Anum points out, African interpreters deserve praise for their efforts in reaching out to ordinary readers and exerting positive impact on non-scholarly communities. Indeed, the adventures of scholars who read with ordinary people using various techniques (as recorded in 'Reflections on *Semeia* 73, 1996' in Anum 2007) provide a useful inspiration and platform for identifying further areas for investigation. Jonathan Draper, for example, highlights the merits of using Gerald West's contextual Bible study approach with some members of the Anglican Church in Cape Town (Draper 1996). Musa Dube reports on reading with Batswana women in Botswana using the framework of *Semoya*, a postcolonial feminist approach (Dube 1996). And Megan Walker discloses the views of ordinary people at the margins of church and society by focusing on Marian devotion in Mpophomeni, Kwa-Zulu Natal (Walker 1996). These authors emphasize complementary dialogue between scholarly readers and ordinary readers, with scholarly partners taking up the role as listeners and mediators for the ordinary people. Other contributors present alternative readings of biblical texts from the perspectives of ordinary people. For instance, Justin Ukpong (1996) reads from the perspective of ordinary West African peasant farmers using inculturation biblical hermeneutics, while John S. Pobee (1996) reveals a form of contextual Bible study in the context of a forum where the leader reads selected Bible texts that speak to life situations, eliciting silent reflections from the congregation as they intuitively interpret and translate the words in the texts into their own life situation. Such readings highlight the role of the socially engaged biblical scholar as, I wish to argue, being much like that of the *okyeame* who speaks for those in authority *and* for ordinary people, and who also offers alternative interpretations to facilitate mutual understanding.

Let me also mention a notable publication comprising the writings of seventy African theologians, the *Africa Bible Commentary*, edited by Tokunboh Adeyemo, which constitutes the first one-volume Bible commentary produced by Africans and from African perspectives. In this volume, African proverbs, folklore and illustrations drawn from African contexts are used as tools to speak about distinctively African concerns and to address some questions that African life and culture bring to the Bible.

Despite all these significant achievements, there is, however, more to be done as what is there is not adequate. Tewoldemedhin Habtu's commentary on Job in the *Africa Bible Commentary*, for example, in making analogies between the Hebrew Bible and African wisdom refers to only six African proverbs: five in Tigrigna from Eritrea and one in Amharic from Ethiopia. It hardly quotes from African scholars, and all the illustrations (such as the tornado, snowman and Romanian pastor's experience) are unfamiliar to most African readers. Surely, the book of Job offers more scope to African readers than Habtu's commentary suggests! I would have expected to find some allusions to suffering in Africa, as well as references as to why the sick in Africa (those enduring the scourges of malaria, or Ebola, and, particularly, of HIV and AIDS) are sometimes misrepresented as deserving their affliction. The commentary also makes no reference to any African myth, or song, or drama. Considering how the book of Job has been received throughout generations (in terms of court-room drama, rhetoric investigation and the frame-story from mythology, to mention but a few topics for fruitful comparison with African traditions), this strikes me as seriously remiss. Significantly, Africans also have other creative arts, among them distinctive traditions of proverbs, music, dance and storytelling, which might also be fruitfully explored for further critical reflections on this biblical book. Musa Dube, for example, makes reference to 'communal interpretation, participatory interpretation through the use of songs, interpretation through dramatized narration, and interpretation through repetition' (1996: 120), which hold promise for an African-centred interpretation of Job. Much the same way, the model of the *okyeame* is another tool for navigating ways that facilitate dialogue and understanding between biblical scholars and ordinary readers in African contexts.

It is intriguing that the biblical 'writers' (or better, 'communicators') used what appears to be the colloquial language of their time and in it they communicated with their audiences rich and sophisticated insights that have continued to be appreciated by successive generations. Unfortunately, nowadays, communication of the biblical message has sometimes become restricted to elite circles. This is not only true of biblical academic scholarship more widely but also of contemporary biblical scholarship in Africa more particularly, where application to critical principles, analogies and symbols regularly does not reflect the practical faith concerns of ordinary Africans. Instead of using a language accessible to the majority of Bible-using people academic language is often used in its place – and such language is mostly inaccessible, except to those trained in the biblical languages and conversant with academic jargon.

While academic study has much to offer, I believe that Biblical Studies is functionally incomplete if it persistently overlooks the concerns of ordinary readers. It is equally incomplete if ordinary readers struggle to understand the contributions and criticism of scholarly readers. Biblical scholars continue to encounter profound challenges in their quest to relate to church and society, but they should not shy away from dialoguing with ordinary readers. West's admission of the difficulty is worth noting here:

> Our initial response as biblical scholars to dialogue was an overwhelming sense of the inadequacy and paucity of our resources in this context. And yet the community also helped us to recognize that we did have resources which might be useful, provided we were willing to read the Bible and do theology *with* them. (1996: 24, italics as in original)

It is in the light of such challenges and in an attempt to advise on how the scholarly reader may speak effectively and persuasively to ordinary readers that I propose the *okyeame* model as an apt West African model of facilitation of dialogue and as a springboard for a more critical engagement with the text, context and with the dialogue partners. Such reimaging, when appropriated critically, may make the necessary resources dear to the hearts of ordinary readers very clear so that the words, to appropriate the biblical writer, may fall on them as dew.

In recognizing the need for scholarly readers to engage in speech art that enhances dialogue, Sarojini Nadar argues that 'reading with' or 'speaking with' the ordinary community should only be a preliminary step. She rightly emphasizes that the scholarly reader, like Job, must be committed to social justice to effect social transformation (2006: 345). According to Nadar, to be a socially engaged biblical scholar 'requires that the scholar transfer from the "reading with" paradigm to a "reading to" paradigm' (2006: 345). What Nadar downplays is that even though the scholarly reader is a member of the community, s/he is not the originator of ideas, and does not have monopoly over interpretation. The scholar reader, like in the case of Job and the *okyeame*, is not a chief, but one who can provide counsel and interpretation, and who may be endowed to speak well so that a text is meaningfully understood. It may indeed be appropriate for the scholarly reader to be a person of the people, and to learn first from the people and gain access to indigenous data. Again, this is comparable with the *okyeame*'s consultation with the people and with Job, who is not just a person of status but also one who knows the plight of the disadvantaged. But the scholar is not a master of indigenous data any more than the holder of authoritative (or normative) interpretation, and may require the direction of the ordinary people who are more conversant with certain forms of knowledge. In my view, dialogue between the scholarly reader and ordinary reader is not a linear activity to require one step before moving to the next. The saying that 'wisdom is not found in one person's head' underlines that the ordinary reader has something to contribute to the ventures of the scholarly reader: the process is dynamic and collaborative.

I am inclined to believe that many African Instituted Churches (AICs) are thriving because of their adaptation to the *okyeame* model. J. Kwabena Asamoah-Gyadu seems to draw a similar conclusion when he argues that the tendency of the mainline churches in Africa to read sermons to the congregation along with promoting characteristically Western thought forms of speech epitomizes their failure to respond to Africans' deep-seated yearnings. Pentecostal and Charismatic ministries, on the other hand, are rising in popularity because they provide a significant countermeasure, adapting a strategy of speaking and reading *with* the people, and then addressing their needs directly with considerable application of African thought-forms (2005: 17–18). These ministries take a serious view of the ethos of the people and speak in ways that reflect African world views. They allow the Bible to speak directly to the life challenges of the people and explore ways of addressing these challenges rather than using Western Bible commentaries that tend to have less applicability and relevance (Clarke 2005: 61).

The scholarly reader, like the *okyeame*, can play the double function of imparting to and representing the text for the ordinary people. In this way, s/he, too, is a negotiator for mutual engagement. West African scholarly readers must not identify with the text alone, or engage just with the text and its interpretation. They must be champions of justice. Maintaining contact and engaging with the people at the grass-roots level to explore knowledge within public spaces is not only integral to African traditions but can result in new interpretations, and ensure greater visibility and dissemination of ideas. The most important step in this process is trust built not only by virtue of living within the community or building relationships with the people but also by earning it. The ordinary readers reserve the right to choose whom to dialogue with and whom to trust. As West avers, 'Trust of intellectuals is reserved, however, only for those with whom the people chose to speak' (1996: 28). One can stay within the heart of the community for a long time but remain a complete outsider if the person does not have a commitment to justice or is unable to speak well. Hence, it is not misplaced for ordinary readers to be suspicious. Trust might be established when scholarly readers, like Job and the *okyeame*, identify with and become absorbed within the community, which, in the Akan context, might entail walking in the strapless sandals of the people and with the loose cloth wrapped around the body, and doing so without mis-stepping.

The world of contemporary African scholarly readers may not be compatible in every way with that of the *okyeame* whose role is founded on traditional customs of the remote past. The role of each – biblical scholar and *okyeame* – has a distinct context, history and purpose. But I am arguing that African biblical scholars have much to gain from the contemporary *okyeame* who is *re*-imaged and *re*-branded, because in this way they may assert a fuller and more relevant identity and purpose for biblical scholarship in the midst of faith communities. In other words, scholarly readers do not only have to devise new epistemologies but also have to draw on an existing model of the *okyeame*. They can liberate themselves from the real and imaginary confines set in Western academia and other power circles and follow the call to be post-critical, plumbing their own African traditions for scholarly resources.[7] As West asserts, they should feel motivated in this endeavour to be distinct from the Western methods and models because the elements of interest and subjectivity that constitute corporate reading within the African space are also distinct (1996: 36). *Re*-casting in the form of the 'postmodern' *okyeame*, moreover, can draw strength and motivation from the figure of Job in ch. 29 of the eponymous book. Job himself shows some affinity with the Akan *okyeame* in a shared facility to navigate between the worlds of the privileged (the royal family, the elite strata of society, the academy) and the worlds of the ordinary peoples (the poor, the underprivileged, the laity). This can go a long way to allay the fear of ordinary readers about critical scholarship and strengthen the bond between scholarly and non-scholarly communities.

The use of culturally appropriate and familiar concepts may have a refreshing and renewing impact on the audience. But as Job 29 underlines, the credibility of such a speech to the listeners largely depends on the speaker's solidarity with the vulnerable and on their commitment to social justice. West African scholarly interpreters can use the palatable, fine and flattering speech of the *okyeame* to present their insights and words in a fashion that will overwhelm their hearers, not only to inform but also to transform them. In the words of Renita Weems, when interpreters expose their presence to ordinary readers, it brings hope, provides comfort and support. Such exposure 'forces us [the scholarly interpreters] to examine concrete ways in which our scholarship and our privileges as scholars rely upon the status quo' (1996: 260).

Conclusion

My discussion on Job 29.21-25 reveals how Job can help the reader to appreciate the model of the *okyeame* who like Job is an effective and enlivening speaker. Job's identity in the text seems to be that of an authoritative speaker. He is like a chief or a king who speaks to his listeners and gains their admiration. But he is also, alongside holding this status, in touch with the less fortunate of society – the orphan and the mourner – and able to communicate with and comfort them. Job captures the attention of his hearers and his words are eagerly anticipated. Such a charismatic speaker teaches, directs, comforts and empowers others by speaking well, speaking with authority and making speech efficacious. Similarly, the Akan spokesperson, the *okyeame*, exemplifies dexterity, eloquence and wisdom. In the light of Job's example, scholarly interpreters are called to see affinities with the

---

7. Some African biblical scholars, however, move beyond Biblical Studies to other fields that are significant for promoting African identities. Hence, Nancy R. Heisey (1998: 35–48) looks at trends among African-American and African scholars and claims that the intersection between Biblical Studies and African Studies is yielding fruitful results. Other scholars, however, are critical of this 'movement' of departure and towards interdisciplinarity. For a critique, see Maluleke (2000: 87–112).

okyeame who uses skilled verbal rhetoric to speak not only powerfully but to the hearts of ordinary people.

Biblical scholarship in Africa has made some advances in facilitating effective dialogue between scholarly interpreters and ordinary readers but there remains a need to focus on *how* to speak. For such dialogue to flourish, I call on the scholarly reader to present himself or herself as an *okyeame*: above all, because such verbal artistry has ancient and noble roots in African tradition. Moreover, such a traditional role is not only deeply rooted and instils pride but is also less affected by colonial and postcolonial trappings that are responsible for and implicated in the degradation of African cultural practices. The image of the *okyeame* continues to find a place in the West African sacramental world view and new religious practices. Such a commitment is both at the centre *and* the periphery, serving as a mediating presence, that is, to the academy *and* intuitive, non-scholarly interpreters. When scholarly readers reach out with familiar cognitive categories that affirm the ethos of their people, it may cause hearers to anticipate eagerly the discourses of scholarly interpreters.

Scholarly readers, like the *okyeame*, have a twofold responsibility: to make knowledge accessible and transmissible by means of their skilled speech, and to embark on dialogue with a willingness to listen and learn. And there may be a third one: to champion justice, as in the case of Job. This appeal to consider the significance of persuasive and compelling speech in our postmodern world cannot be overemphasized because calls are being made for dialogue between the privileged and underprivileged, North and South, East and West, the First and the Two-Thirds Worlds. Here then is one modest proposal, for the *okyeame* model may, like the rings of the pebble cast into waters, transpire in many more fruitful dialogues so that diverse peoples may better communicate and understand one another.

Works Cited

Adeyemo, T., gen. ed., *Africa Bible Commentary*, Nairobi, Kenya: WordAlive Publishers.

Adu-Gyamfi, Y. (2012), 'The Role of the Chief in Asante Society', in M. D. Palmer and S. M. Burgess (eds), *The Wiley-Blackwell Companion to Religion and Social Justice*, 256–67, Chichester, UK: Blackwell.

Agyekum, K. (2004), 'Aspects of Persuasion in Akan Communication', *RASK International Journal of Language and Communication* 21: 63–96.

Anum, E. (2007), '*Ye ma wo mo*! African Hermeneuts, You Have Spoken at Last: Reflections on *Semeia* 73 (1996)', in G. O. West (ed.), *Reading Other-Wise: Socially Engaged Biblical Scholars Reading with Their Local Communities* (*Semeia* Studies Society of Biblical Literature), 7–18, Atlanta: Society of Biblical Literature.

Asamoah-Gyadu, J. K. (2005), *Africa Charismatics: Currents within Independent Indigenous Pentecostalism in Ghana*, Leiden: Brill.

Balentine, S. E. (2006), *Job* (Smyth & Helwys Bible Commentary), Macon, GA: Smyth and Helwys.

Bediako, K. (1995), *Christianity in Africa: The Renewal of a Non-Western Religion*, Edinburgh: Edinburgh University Press.

van Binsbergen, W. (1987), 'Chiefs and the State in Independent Zambia', *Journal of Legal Pluralism* 25/26: 156–66.

Boafo-Arthur, K. (2006), 'Chieftaincy in Ghana: Challenges and Prospects in the 21st Century', in I. K. Odotei and A. K. Awedoba (eds), 145–68, *Chieftaincy in Ghana: Culture, Governance and Development*, Accra: Sub-Saharan Publishers.

Clarke, C. (2005), 'In Our Mother Tongue: Vernacular Hermeneutics within African-Initiated Christianity in Ghana', *Trinity Journal of Church and Theology* 15 (2): 59–72.

Clines, D. J. A. (1989), *Job 21–37* (Word Biblical Commentary 18a), Nashville: Thomas Nelson.

Dankwa III, O. A. (2004), *The Institution of Chieftaincy in Ghana – The Future*. Accra: Konrad Adenauer Foundation.

Draper, J. A. (1996), 'Confessional Western Text-Centered Biblical Interpretation and an Oral Residual Context', in West and Dube, *Semeia* 73, 57–77.

Dube, M. W. (1996), 'Readings of *Semoya*: Batswana Women's Interpretation of Matthew 15:21–28', in West and Dube, *Semeia* 73, 111–29.

Finnegan, R. (1970), *Oral Literature in Africa*, Oxford: Oxford University Press.

Gordis, R. (1978), *The Book of Job: Commentary, New Translation and Special Studies*, New York: The Jewish Theological Seminary of America.

Gyekye, K. (1975), *African Cultural Values*, Accra: Sankofa Publications.

Habel, N. C. (1985), *The Book of Job – A Commentary* (Old Testament Literature), London: SCM.

Habtu, T. (2006), 'Job', in T. Adeyemo (gen. ed.), *Africa Bible Commentary*, 571–604, Nairobi, Kenya: WordAlive Publishers.

Hartley, J. E. (1998), *The Book of Job*, Grand Rapids: Eerdmans.

Heisey, N. R. (1998), 'The Influence of African Scholars on Biblical Studies: An Evaluation', *Journal of Theology for Southern Africa* 101: 35–48.

Hooks, S. M. (2006), *Job*, College Press NIV Commentary, Joplin: College Press.

Janzen, J. G. (1985), *Job*, Atlanta: John Knox.

Maluleke, T. S. (2000), 'The Bible among African Christians: A Missiological Perspective', in T. Okure (ed.), *To Cast Fire upon the Earth: Bible and Mission Collaborating in Today's Multicultural Global Context*, 87–112, Pietermaritzburg: Cluster.

Nadar, S. (2006), '"Hermeneutics of Transformation?": A Critical Exploration of the Model of Social Engagement between Biblical Scholars and Faith Communities', *Scriptura* 93: 339–51.

Newsom, C. A. (1996), 'The Book of Job: Introduction, Commentary and Reflections', in L. E. Keck et al. (eds), *The New Interpreter's Bible* 4, 319–39, Nashville: Abingdon.

Nyamnjoh, F. (2003), 'Chieftaincy and Negotiation of Might and Right in Botswana's Democracy', in H. Melber (ed.), *Limits to Liberation in Southern Africa: The Unfinished Business of Democratic Consolidation*, 93–114, Cape Town: HSRC Press.

Nyamnjoh, F. (2 July 2015), 'Our Traditions are Modern, Our Modernities Traditional: Chieftaincy and Democracy in Contemporary Africa'. Available online: http://www.nyamnjoh.com/files/chieftaincy_and_democracy_in_contemporary_africa.pdf. (accessed 24 October 2015).

Pobee, J. S. (1996), 'Bible Study in Africa: A Passover of Language', in West and Dube, *Semeia* 73, 161–71.

Pope, M. H. (1982), *Job: A New Translation with Introduction and Commentary* (Anchor Bible 15), New York: Doubleday.

Rowley, H. H. (1976), *Job* (New Century Bible), London: Oliphants.

Rugarabura, P.-R. N. (2008), 'Traditional Chieftaincy and Decentralization in the Democratic Republic of Congo: Opportunities and Challenges', PhD Dissertation, Libera Università Internazionale Degli Studi Sociali, Rome.

Searing, J. F. (2002), ' "No Kings, No Lords, No Slaves": Ethnicity and Religion Among the Sereer-Safèen of Western Bawol, 1700–1914', *Journal of African History* 43 (3): 407–29.

Stoeltje, B. J. (2003), 'Asante Queen Mothers: Precolonial Authority in a Postcolonial Society', *Research Review New Series* 19 (2): 1–19.

Ukpong, J. S. (1996), 'The Parable of the Shrewd Manager (Luke 16:1–13): An Essay in the Inculturation Biblical Hermeneutic', in West and Dube, *Semeia* 73, 189–210.

Walker, M. (1996), 'Engaging Popular Religion: A Hermeneutical Investigation of Marian Devotion in the Township of Mphophomeni', in West and M. Dube, *Semeia* 73, 131–58.

Weems R. J. (1996), 'Response to "Reading With": An Exploration of the Interface Between Critical and Ordinary Readings of the Bible', in West and Dube, *Semeia* 73, 257–61.

West, G. O. (1996), 'Reading the Bible Differently: Giving Shape to the Discourses of the Dominated', in West and Dube, *Semeia* 73, 21–41.

West, G. O. and M. W. Dube (eds) (1996), *Semeia* 73: *"Reading With": An Exploration of the Interface between Critical and Ordinary Readings of the Bible – African Overtures*, 57–77, Atlanta: Scholars Press.

Wilson, G. H. (2007), *Job* (Understanding the Bible Commentary Series), Grand Rapids: Baker Books.

Yankah, K. (1995), *Speaking for the Chief: Okyeame and the Politics of Akan Royal Oratory*, Bloomington and Indianapolis: Indiana University Press.

Chapter 9

RESPONSE: LOCATING AFRICAN BIBLICAL SCHOLARSHIP AS ANOTHER GENERATION OF AFRICAN BIBLICAL SCHOLARS TAKES UP THE WORK

Gerald O. West

Introduction

In a recent publication I argue that African biblical scholarship has always been both postcolonial and tri-polar (West 2016a). In a yet more recent publication (2018) I develop both of these claims and add a third: that African biblical scholarship should be overt about the Bible as a site of struggle. These three 'claims' offer a useful way of locating African biblical scholarship within its global and local contexts. However, while the first two claims are *descriptive* of what African biblical scholarship is and has always been, the second claim is *prescriptive*, making an argument for what ought to be. Biblical interpretation has always been a site of struggle for African biblical scholarship, but African biblical scholars have not been as clear about the Bible itself as a site of struggle.

In this chapter I will engage with two case studies of a new generation of African biblical scholars, Mark Aidoo from Ghana (Aidoo 2017) and Tsaurayi Mapfeka from Zimbabwe (Mapfeka 2017). I will also add a third dialogue partner, Andrew Mbuvi, from Kenya, who has been teaching in the USA for some time, and has written the most recent 'mapping' (to use a European metaphor) or 'tracking' (to use an African metaphor) of African biblical scholarship (Mbuvi 2017).

Postcolonial

African biblical scholarship is intrinsically postcolonial, both because the Bible was brought to Africa as part of the missionary-colonial enterprise (1415–1787 and 1787–1919) (West 2016b:14–18) and because Biblical Studies as an academic discipline is itself an import into Africa from Euro-American contexts (from the 1930s) (Ukpong 2000: 12; Mbuvi 2017: 153) and therefore a postcolonial or, perhaps more accurately, a neocolonial reality. African biblical scholarship is historically postcolonial and ideologically postcolonial, adopting a default ideological postcolonial attitude towards the Bible and biblical scholarship.

Mbuvi is clear about this postcolonial orientation (Mbuvi 2017: 158–9). Mapfeka, in his essay 'Empire and Identity Secrecy: A Postcolonial Reflection on Esther 2.10', too, uses his emphasis on ancient (biblical) empires to reflect on Africa's and Zimbabwe's colonial realities. Both an engagement with Africa-wide experiences of colonialism and the particular colonial realities of a particular African context are a distinctive feature of African biblical scholarship, so that while Euro-American forms of postcolonialism tend to (anachronistically) project postcolonial theory (derived from recent colonial realities) back into the biblical past, African biblical scholarship engages with colonialism/neocolonialism as a recent or even contemporary African reality. Mapfeka is clear about this, reflecting as he does on the effects of British colonialism on the Ndebele people of Zimbabwe.

Aidoo similarly, in his essay "'My Words Dropped upon Them Like Dew': Towards Reimaging the Identity of African Biblical Interpreters', links notions of cultural identity with respect to 'chieftaincy' in contemporary Ghana to the colonialism of the 1950s to 1970s.

Tri-polar

There are three intersecting poles in this analysis: the African context, the biblical text and the ideo-theological forms of dialogue between African context and biblical text. While most characterizations of African biblical hermeneutics tend to portray a bi-polar approach, referring for example to 'the comparative method' (Anum 2000: 468; Ukpong 2000: 12; Holter 2002: 88–9), in which African context and biblical text interpret each other, it would be more accurate to describe African biblical hermeneutics as tri-polar.

Implicit in bi-polar-like formulations are aspects of a third pole mediating the engagement between the African context and the biblical text – the pole of appropriation. Justin Ukpong, a key commentator on the comparative method, refers overtly to the goal of comparative interpretation as 'the actualization of the theological meaning of the text in today's context so as to forge integration between faith and life, and engender commitment to personal and societal transformation' (2000: 24). What connects or entangles text and context, then, is a form of dialogical appropriation that has a theological and a praxiological dimension (Draper 2015). This ideo-theological third pole can take various forms, resulting in at least six intersecting yet different theoretical emphases in African biblical interpretation: inculturation (with an emphasis on culture and religion), liberation (with an emphasis on politics and economics), feminist (with an emphasis on gender and patriarchy), psychological (with an emphasis on individual and communal psyche), postcolonial (with an emphasis on missionary-colonialism) and queer (with an emphasis on gender and sexuality) biblical hermeneutics (West 2016a). Mbuvi offers a partially overlapping set of ideo-theological orientations, but includes an emphasis on reconstruction and democratization hermeneutics (2017: 163).

Both Aidoo and Mapfeka are properly tri-polar. Aidoo brings African context and biblical text into dialogue via an inculturation hermeneutic, and Mapfeka brings

African context and biblical context into dialogue via a postcolonial hermeneutic with some intersections with feminist hermeneutics. I say 'feminist' hermeneutics deliberately, not 'African feminist' hermeneutics, because surprisingly Mapfeka does not refer to any of the bountiful work of African feminist biblical scholarship. This may have to do with those looking over his shoulder as he completed his PhD in England, as Africans studying or working in Euro-American contexts are often coerced to bow the academic knee to neocolonial sources of biblical scholarship. Aidoo by contrast, doing his research within an African context, in Ghana, cites African sources extensively. Citing each other's work is a discipline among many African biblical scholars as we intentionally and deliberately construct our own sub-discipline within the hegemonic Euro-American guild. Talking among ourselves has become increasingly constitutive of what we do as African biblical scholars.

In each case Aidoo and Mapfeka construct a theory-laden conversation between African context and biblical text. Where one begins does not matter, for the hermeneutic cycle is a cycle, or, in Jonathan Draper's terms, borrowed from the liberation theology of Clodovis Boff, a 'back-and-forth' movement, each constituting the other through conversation (or even contestation) (Draper 1991: 243). Aidoo begins with the biblical text, the book of Job, as does Mapfeka with the book of Esther. As biblical scholars, responsible to their inherited disciplinary parameters, they use the methods common to and characteristic of biblical scholarship. Aidoo focuses on the literary rhetoric of Job, using inculturation theory to mediate an ideo-theological conversation with the rhetoric of 'the Akan spokesperson'. Mapfeka adopts the more usual, among African biblical scholars, socio-historical methods, locating Esther within its socio-historical context and then using postcolonial and gender theory to establish a conversation with different forms of African colonization, including (briefly) Apartheid and (more extensively) Portuguese colonization. In each case there is a 'back-and-forth' movement, with biblical text and African context conversing, each rereading the other.

Site of Struggle

Mapfeka's rereading of the biblical text demonstrates more clearly than Aidoo's that the Bible is itself a 'site of struggle'. In Africa's long and deeply ambiguous engagement with the missionary-colonial brought Bible (West 2016b), the predominant tendency among African biblical scholars has been to work with the Bible with a 'hermeneutic of trust', using inculturation theory to reappropriate the Bible over against missionary-colonial deprecations of African religion and/ as culture. Both Aidoo and Mapfeka recognize this damaging colonial legacy, with Aidoo explicitly arguing that 'colonialism and neocolonialism tried to strip African peoples of their own cultural practices and traditions', and demonstrating through his own rhetorical analysis the resonances between 'traditional' African rhetoric and the rhetoric of Job, using the biblical text to affirm and reclaim what the missionary-colonial enterprise tried to destroy. But Mapfeka, using his analysis of the Mozambican *assimilado* under Portuguese imperialism to illuminate the complicity of Esther with empire, recognizes the limits of a hermeneutics of trust with respect to this text. Because this text is complicit with empire, it must be read 'against the grain', to use Terry Eagleton's phrase which has been appropriated by South African Black theologian and biblical scholar Itumeleng Mosala (1989: 32).

Mosala is adamant that 'the texts of the Bible are sites of struggle' (1989: 185), and that any appropriation must foreground this reality of struggle. Unless the Bible is recognized and reread as itself, intrinsically, a site of struggle, there is always the risk that the oppressor's form of the text will have the final word (Mosala 1989: 28). Mapfeka follows Mosala (though not explicitly), recognizing and analysing Esther as a site of struggle, a struggle with empire that has left its mark on the biblical text. However, Mapfeka, as most of us African biblical scholars do, does not leave the biblical text unappropriated. Approaching it cautiously, recognizing its markings of empire, Mapfeka offers ways of appropriating its 'seditious' potential.

From Aidoo's chapter it is clear why the Bible must be appropriated, and a similar contextual logic may reside behind Mapfeka's reading. While Aidoo argues that 'academic study has much to offer', he 'believes' 'that biblical studies is functionally incomplete if it persistently overlooks the concerns of ordinary readers'. Biblical Studies must serve African communities for whom the Bible has become a sacred and significant artefact. Many of us adopt this stance (Mbuvi 2017: 154), a stance, which distinguishes our scholarship from the mainstream of Euro-American biblical scholarship. Echoing the words of the Latin American liberation theologian Gustavo Gutiérrez, we can say that while the primary interlocutor of Western biblical scholarship is the educated middle class, the primary interlocutor of biblical liberation hermeneutics is 'the poor, the exploited classes, the marginalized races, all the despised cultures' (Gutiérrez 1973: 241; West 2015).

And echoing the words of Black theologian Takatso Mofokeng, African biblical scholars must continue to work with an ambiguous Bible, alongside the African 'masses' until it becomes 'a formidable weapon in the hands of the oppressed instead of leaving it to confuse, frustrate or even destroy our people' (1988: 40). This is what, I think, Aidoo means when he says, more politely, that African biblical scholarship 'is equally incomplete if ordinary readers struggle to understand the contributions and criticism of scholarly readers'.

African biblical scholarship, much to the consternation often of our Euro-American mainstream compatriots, is accountable to 'ordinary' African readers/users/hearers of the Bible (Mbuvi 2017: 167), perhaps even more so than it is responsible to biblical scholarship in its familiar Euro-American forms.

Conclusion

Mark Aidoo and Tsaurayi Mapfeka locate themselves more or less (respectively) overtly within the parameters of African biblical scholarship as it has emerged over the past ninety years. As more and more African biblical scholars do their work within the neocolonial Euro-American zone of our globalized world the challenge that will face them is how accountable they are to African realities and African dialogue partners. For those who do their biblical scholarship at home (West 2008), context is undeniable, intruding into the African academy and demanding that we account for what we are doing with our scholarship.

Works Cited

Anum, E. (2000), 'Comparative Readings of the Bible in Africa: Some Concerns', in G. O. West and M. W. Dube (eds), *The Bible in Africa: Transactions, Trajectories and Trends*, 457–73, Leiden: E. J. Brill.

Draper, J. A. (1991), '"For the Kingdom Is Inside of You and It Is Outside of You": Contextual Exegesis in South Africa (Lk. 13.6–9)', in P. J. Hartin and J. H. Petzer (eds), *Text and Interpretation: New Approaches in the Criticism of the New Testament*, 235–57, Leiden: E. J. Brill.

Draper, J. A. (2015), 'African Contextual Hermeneutics: Readers, Reading Communities, and Their Options Between Text and Context', *Religion & Theology* 22: 3–22.

Gutiérrez, G. (1973), *A Theology of Liberation: History, Politics and Salvation*, Maryknoll, NY: Orbis.

Holter, K. (2002), *Old Testament Research for Africa: A Critical Analysis and Annotated Bibliography of African Old Testament Dissertations, 1967–2000*, New York: Peter Lang.

Mbuvi, A. M. (2017), 'African Biblical Studies: An Introduction to an Emerging Discipline', *Currents in Biblical Research* 15 (2): 149–78.

Mofokeng, T. (1988), 'Black Christians, the Bible and Liberation', *Journal of Black Theology* 2: 34–42.

Mosala, I. J. (1989), *Biblical Hermeneutics and Black Theology in South Africa*, Grand Rapids: Eerdmans.

Ukpong, J. S. (2000), 'Developments in Biblical Interpretation in Africa: Historical and Hermeneutical Directions', in G. O. West and M. W. Dube (eds), *The Bible in Africa: Transactions, Trajectories and Trends*, 11–28, Leiden: E. J. Brill.

West, G. O. (2008), 'Doing Postcolonial Biblical Interpretation @home: Ten Years of (South) African Ambivalence', *Neotestamentica* 42 (1): 147–64.

West, G. O. (2015), 'Africa's Liberation Theologies: An Historical-Hermeneutical Analysis', in S. D. Brunn (ed.), *The Changing World Religion Map: Sacred Places, Identities, Practices and Politics*, 1971–85, Dordrecht, Heidelberg, New York, London: Springer.

West, G. O. (2016a), 'Accountable African Biblical Scholarship: Post-colonial and Tri-polar', *Canon&Culture* 20: 35–67.

West, G. O. (2016b), *The Stolen Bible: From Tool of Imperialism to African Icon*, Leiden and Pietermaritzburg: Brill and Cluster Publications.

West, G. O. (2018), 'African Biblical Scholarship as Post-colonial, Tri-polar, and a Site-of-Struggle', in Tat-siong Benny Liew (eds), *Biblical Interpretation* (Present and Future of Biblical Studies: Celebrating 25 Years of Brill's *Biblical Interpretation*), 240–73. Leiden/Boston: Brill.

Part III

Chapter 10

THE DARK HEART OF BIBLICAL SCHOLARSHIP: WESTERN READERS AND AFRICAN READINGS

Hugh S. Pyper

Introduction

For a number of years, I taught students in Sheffield a module on 'The Postcolonial Bible'. Most of the students were British or European. My aim for the module was to encourage the students to become aware that they as much as anyone were part of the global nexus of economic and intellectual interchange that was shaped by the history of European colonialism. I hoped they would realize that the access to the Bible, to education, to the resources of the university, which often they took for granted, were privileges denied to the majority of people and that there were historical, political and economic reasons why they, in this place, had the luxury of academic study of the Bible. Sheffield, like any British city, is in its own way postcolonial; its buildings, its industry and its population are irrevocably marked by the experience of empire and its decline.

At the same time, I wanted the students to reflect on the fact that at least some of the ideological justification for the systems that set up and preserved this inequality was grounded in readings of the Bible. Furthermore, we could use the techniques developed by postcolonial critics to look at the biblical texts themselves and read them as the product of a history of conquest and resistance in the Ancient Near East. By looking at the experience of readers in other contexts, Africa among them, I hoped that they would have a deeper understanding of their own privilege and perhaps of the responsibilities that that might entail. Reading the Bible as interpreted through African eyes was a key part of that learning.

Yet the following words of the Kenyan novelist Ngũgĩ wa Thiong'o have haunted me ever since I came across them: 'In the eighteenth and nineteenth centuries, Europe stole art treasures from Africa to decorate their houses and museums; in the twentieth century, Europe is stealing the treasures of the mind to enrich their languages and cultures' (1986: xii). Could we add, 'and in the twenty-first, Europe is stealing Africa's critical tools'? Postcolonial theory is itself a commodity in an academic economy that is still marked by colonial tension. Western universities fund the salaries of their biblical scholars by inducing students from their former colonies to come to the West to study postcolonial readings of the Bible, thereby recapitulating an older economy of exploitation.

In what follows, I want to explore some of the inescapable ironies that are entailed when Western readers seek to appropriate African readings, although both those terms 'Western' and 'African' already beg many questions. I shall do this by looking at two examples where Western readers meet non-Western readings. The first is a parable by Walter Dietrich which recasts the encounter between Western scholarship and non-Western readers on the analogy of the journey of the Magi; the second is the critical debate over Chinua Achebe's reading Joseph Conrad's novel *Heart of Darkness*. In different ways, these point to the dark colonialist legacy of the Enlightenment which is at the heart of Biblical Studies, as suggested by juxtaposing Walter Mignolo's postcolonial account of the Renaissance and Enlightenment with Stephen Moore and Yvonne Sherwood's analysis of the Enlightenment roots of Biblical Studies as a discipline. Having acknowledged this darkness, Edouard Glissant's understanding of 'opacity' may then help both Western and African readers to find a positive way forward by resisting the Enlightenment valorization of clarity and transparency.

Learning from the Magi

One attempt to address this issue is to be found in a parable Walter Dietrich offers 'instead of a conclusion' to the collection of essays he edited with Ulrich Luz under the title of *The Bible in a World Context* (2002). The parable is called 'Theological Astronomy' and recounts the visit of two wise men and one wise woman from afar to a great European astronomical observatory that has all the latest equipment and the latest scientific knowledge. The scientists there, however, are still at a loss to discover what a star is and how it comes about.

The three visitors politely point out that working inside a brightly-lit observatory is not the only way to find out about stars. What about going out into the streets of their impoverished hometowns where the lack of electricity means that everyone can actually see the stars? What about taking whatever inexpensive telescopes you can afford, sharing them with ordinary people, and then listening to what those ordinary people say they can see? (What about studying with ordinary readers, sharing with them at least the rudiments of Western biblical scholarship and helping them to articulate their insights into the text?)

The Western astronomers acknowledge the force of this criticism but wonder whether there are not more important things than stargazing that their visitors should be doing in order to fight for economic and technical development. Yes, the visitors reply, but the stars themselves encourage you to seek and show you the direction of the search.

In Matthew's version of the nativity, Dietrich muses, the magi, or 'Astronomers from the East', play much the same role: 'They too, came from far away, from parts of the world that were less in the center of interest; most probably, they had the wrong astronomical background knowledge, wrong basic convictions, and questionable equipment. But in the end, they were at the right place' (2002: 80).

This parable seriously annoyed the doyen of postcolonial Biblical Studies, R. S. Sugirtharajah. He levels his guns at it in his contribution to a collection of essays he edited entitled, rather glumly, *Still at the Margins*. This appeared as a reflection on what had changed in Biblical Studies in the fifteen years since the first publication of his groundbreaking collection *Voices from the Margin* (1991), one of the first publications that brought together a range of readers from outside the Western academy.

He takes Dietrich's parable as proof of 'business as usual' in Biblical Studies. First, he points to the assumption of the superiority of Western equipment and resources. Second, he views the reference to the *magi* as 'unleashing a Pandora's box of every kind of Orientalism' (2008: 8). The implication he draws from the use of this word is that these tricksy easterners are going to subvert the order and logic of Western thought. He accuses Dietrich of implying that Western biblical scholarship has the status of the infant Jesus, an immaculate innocent that risks being corrupted by alien sorcery. Third, he contends, the economic standards of the North are set up as the benchmark to which everyone else should aspire; he might have added that the responsibility of rectifying this injustice seems to be laid on the visitors, not their wealthy hosts. Fourth, Dietrich ends his parable by saying that the wise visitors had come to the 'right place', in this case to Berne, a centre of European enlightenment, which Sugirtharajah reads as a value judgement and claim to quasi-imperial superiority.

This is quite a list of indictments of what may seem to most readers as at worst a slightly sentimental and occasionally tactless story, but one that is essentially harmless. Sugirtharajah himself admits, 'I may have over-read Dr Dietrich's parable' (2008: 9). Whether he is fair in his criticism or not, the lesson Sugirtharajah draws from this story is of the unintentional damage Western scholars and readers can do to the very people they wish to help. His overreaction just goes to show how difficult the issue is. Dietrich, for his part, does provide a number of hostages to fortune.

On the other hand, does Sugirtharajah suggest that the visitors should not have come? Should they be excluded from learning techniques and using equipment provided by resources that are superior in some ways to their own? Dietrich's parable may not provide an ideal model of such an encounter, but what should he have been willing to hear from his guests and how could he best address the message they bring? At the very least, Dietrich and his colleagues did invite their colleagues, rather than depending on their taking the initiative, and expressed the wish to listen.

Can Biblical Scholarship Be African?

However, this raises the question of what is it that they want to listen to? What is distinctive about the interpretation of the Bible that can come from beyond the West? In the particular case of Africa, what makes for an African reading? Gerald

West raises this issue in his article 'Mapping African Biblical Interpretation: A Tentative Sketch' (2000). He acknowledges that 'African' is a colonial designation, which has been claimed as a mark of pride and solidarity by those who have had it imposed upon them, but he also warns that it hides the diversity of readings in a continent with peoples of many ethnic groups, languages and political histories. The idea of 'an African reading' also elides the very different ways in which people in Africa receive the Bible and go about interpreting it. The world of academic discourse about the Bible represents a tiny fraction of those in Africa who engage with biblical texts, orally as well as through reading, in a multitude of languages, social locations and religious traditions.

Even within literate circles, what makes an interpretation 'African' is open to question. As an example, Mark McEntire (2000) records that his Ethiopian students were unable to accept the validity of the political readings of the Cain and Abel story that Allan Boesak and Itumeleng Mosala offered in the context of the struggle against Apartheid in South Africa and were puzzled that the two had come up with radically different readings. His students' way of reading the Bible was shaped by the American Protestant missionaries who had introduced the Bible to them. Is their literalist reading of the text, which sought to uncover its one true meaning and refused to countenance a political interpretation, not an African reading? For that matter, how African is Mosala's reading, with its dependence on Marxist analysis and source criticism?

The dilemma for African scholarship is put succinctly by Robert Bernasconi. He is referring particularly to philosophy, but the point still holds for biblical scholars: 'Western philosophy traps African philosophy in a double bind. Either African philosophy is so similar to Western philosophy that it makes no distinctive contribution and effectively disappears; or it is so different that its credentials to be genuine philosophy will always be in doubt' (1997: 188).

The problems run even deeper than that, however. The term 'African biblical scholar' leads us to ask what exactly defines a biblical scholar and who gets to determine the definition? In their *The Invention of the Biblical Scholar* (2011), Stephen Moore and Yvonne Sherwood draw on the work of Jonathan Sheehan (2005) to support their argument that contemporary biblical scholarship is beholden to the Enlightenment project in specific and fundamental ways. As they put it,

> almost all biblical scholarship has been enacted within the massive edifice of the Enlightenment Bible, it seems to us, by which we mean that almost all biblical scholars have thoroughly internalized Enlightenment modes of relating to the Bible – modes anxiously marked as distinct from the devotional and the confessional, the pietistic and the homiletical, through a fetishistic display of methodological expertise as the primary badge of professional identity. (2011: xii)

The 'Enlightenment Bible' is the product of scholars who were seeking to justify their continuing interest in the Bible in the wake of the questioning of the institutional authority that had formerly insulated from criticism. They recast it as the foundational document of European culture. In the process, Moore and Sherwood argue, the Bible became 'a key site where foundational, but unsustainable, "modern" separations were made' (2011: 128).

The implications of this in a postcolonial context are brought out in a series of works by Walter Mignolo in which he has argued that Enlightenment and what he calls 'coloniality' are inextricably linked in a way that goes back to the Italian Renaissance.[1] With all their insistence on recapturing the clear light of Greek reason, the Renaissance thinkers ignored the dark shadow of slavery and colonialism. The rethinking of what it meant to be human that was provoked by the discovery of the Americas and the problem of how to account for their different cultures ushered in a new hierarchy based on race. This legacy is further developed in the Enlightenment. Biblical scholarship as practised in universities, freed from the dogmatic authority of the church, thus inevitably bears with it a hidden coloniality along with its search to uncover the rational and moral core of true religion buried within the aggregate rubble of the present biblical text. Moore and Sherwood's Enlightenment Bible is by definition a colonial Bible, by this argument.

If this is so, then African biblical scholarship cannot escape the taint of colonialism simply by adopting the adjective 'African'. All biblical scholarship carries, from its Enlightenment roots, a dark side. The Enlightenment ideals of universal reason and universal human rights prove to be, in Moore and Sherwood's phrase, 'European-universal' (2011: 71), masking expansionism and exploitation under a discourse of bringing education and culture to the dark places of the earth. The metaphors of light that underlie the Enlightenment with its valorization of clarity, transparency and lucidity give permission for those who bear the light to intrude into anything that is secret or hidden. At the same time, the light can be used to dazzle the denizens of the dark and conceal the appropriation of goods, human and material.

The Dark Heart of Biblical Studies

In the African context, the adjective 'dark' carries difficult political freight. Mignolo recalls the debate he had with himself before choosing to include the adjective 'darker' in the title of his book *The Darker Side of the Renaissance* (see 2011: xix). A student pointed out to him the negative implications of calling Africa the 'Dark Continent' and how this was epitomized in Joseph Conrad's *Heart of Darkness*.

In this regard, the Nigerian novelist, Chinua Achebe, intensifies the discomfort that a Western reader may, and indeed should, feel in engaging with African readings. For once, an African reading of a canonical text in Western literature caused something of an earthquake in literary studies when Achebe denounced Conrad's *Heart of Darkness*

---

1. His three works form what Mignolo himself describes as an accidental trilogy (1995; 2000; 2011).

as a racist text.[2] This complex, multilayered story of the discovery of Kurtz, a talented and charismatic European who has become the centre of a perverse cult in the Congo, and whose dying words 'The horror! The horror!' are among the most well-known of any literary character, had been read until then as a technical tour-de-force of narration and a savage satire on the enterprise of colonialism. In 1975, Achebe gave a public lecture in the United States entitled 'An Image of Africa: Racism in Conrad's *Heart of Darkness*' where he accused Conrad of using Africa as the antithesis of Europe to contrast its triumphant bestiality with the civilization of Europe.[3] This intervention provoked strong reactions and a long-lasting debate in literary studies.[4] Even those who do not agree with Achebe acknowledge that the question needed to be raised.

In a later conversation with his fellow novelist Caryl Phillips, Achebe made it clear that he was incensed by the reduction of the whole of Africa to a backdrop for the investigation of the self-destruction of a single European mind (Phillips 2003). Insofar as Conrad raised doubts over colonialism, this is done at the expense of the humanity of the Africans in his stories who are troubling precisely because they show signs of humanity. 'You cannot compromise my humanity in order that you explore your own ambiguity', retorts Achebe to Phillips, who records his own realization that, as a black man raised in Europe, he has no right to overlook the offensiveness of this strategy to an African reader. For Achebe, Conrad is a particular disappointment because he was a consummate artist who, Achebe feels, had therefore a special responsibility to transcend the mores of his time.

Whether we agree with Achebe's verdict on Conrad or not, the fraughtness of Western reception of African readings of any text, let alone the Bible, cannot be gainsaid. If that is where we end, then the implication is that biblical scholarship, as the West understands it, is itself intrinsically colonial. The unease which Ngũgĩ wa Thiong'o's accusation of culture and intellectual colonialism provoked would thus be justified.

Yet perhaps there are other ways to deal with Conrad's *Heart of Darkness*. In another provocative reading of that text, Phillipe Lacoue-Labarthe offers in passing the following characterization of the West: it is 'that which will always have recoiled from the dread of knowing [*savoir*] ... by taking refuge in knowing how [*savoir-faire*]' (2007).[5] In other words, the West is afraid of what it might learn and thus makes a virtue of elaborating and refining the techniques of knowledge. We might say it uses the labour spent on refining and polishing its lenses as an excuse never to look through them. This is another way of expressing Moore and Sherwood's charge of what they term 'methodolatry' in Biblical Studies: Western

2. *Heart of Darkness* was first published in three parts in *Blackwood's Magazine* in 1899. Its first appearance in book form was in 1902.

3. The lecture was first published in 1977 and revised and reprinted under a modified title in 1988.

4. For an example of a counter to Achebe's argument, see Watts (1983).

5. An English translation, 'The Horror of the West' (2012: 111–22), together with a number of critical responses to the article, is to be found in Lawtoo (2012). The quotation above is my translation from a phrase in the article's online version.

biblical scholarship is obsessed with developing and refining its methodologies, not so much to read the Bible better but as a way to keep narrowing the range of those who are accounted reliable readers and to prescribe what counts as a reliable reading.

Furthermore, for Lacoue-Labarthe, the West is itself defined as a giant colony since Greek and Roman times. This is an insight that he finds in Conrad as well. Near the beginning of his narration in *Heart of Darkness*, Marlow, the main storyteller, addressing his fellow sailors on the deck of a ship moored in London, reminds them that this too was once one of the dark places and imagines the dread of a Roman ship's captain steering his boat up the same river into a sinister and untracked land. Marlow's use of the past tense is grist to the mill for those who see Conrad contrasting the now civilized London of his time with the still barbaric interior of Africa. However, the darkness of London is not simply a matter of the past. The narrator, as he sets the scene for Marlow's narration, describes the scene thus: 'And farther west on the upper reaches the place of the monstrous town was still marked ominously on the sky, a brooding gloom in sunshine, a lurid glare under the stars.'

Although Lacoue-Labarthe does not mention this detail, it reinforces his point that 'beneath this colony, there is the horror'. London remains monstrous, gloomy and, in other places in the tale, 'sepulchral'. He goes on,

> This horror is less the *de facto* horror of savagery than the power of fascination that savagery exerts over the 'civilized' who suddenly recognize the void upon which their will to ward off the horror rests – or fails to rest. It is its own horror that the West seeks to dispel ... The West exports its intimate evil. (2012: 119)

In one way, Lacoue-Labarthe breaks down the binary opposition between London and Africa, metropolis and primeval jungle. Both poles of the opposition carry the horror that comes with being the colonized. Yet perhaps this conclusion is still too wedded to the dualisms of the Enlightenment. The opposition between colonizer and colonized is itself such a binary. Perhaps what is needed is another way of understanding the core metaphors that the 'Enlightenment' has embedded in the discourse. Rather than always giving priority to the light, clarity and revelation, what is needed is a way of valuing darkness, obscurity and the hidden.

In Praise of Opacity

I want to suggest that one resource that we could turn to is the work of the Martiniquan novelist and critic Edouard Glissant and in particular his use of the concept of *opacité*. Glissant's work stems from his argument that the Creole of his native Martinique, which metropolitan French culture regarded as a debased form of French, was not a product of a failure of the African slaves to learn French properly but was a strategy of resistance. Forcibly removed from their homes in different parts of Africa, once thrown together on the plantations of the West Indies, the slaves had no common language or culture. What Creole represented was their ingenuity in using the language of their masters, together with precious remnants of their native tongues, to create ways of communicating among themselves that crucially remained incomprehensible to their masters.

For Glissant, the other's opacity is a key point in his or her freedom to escape my appropriation. It is a defence against my attempt at 'understanding', which Glissant reads as often an aggressive appropriation: it is the right *not* to be understood. The Enlightenment assumption that human community thrives on openness and transparency and the lack of secrecy is also the logic of the panopticon where the whole world becomes a prison under constant scrutiny. Curiosity slips over into intrusion and ultimately control. For Glissant, community depends on my ability to accept that I *cannot* understand you as the other side of retaining the dark heart of my own identity.

Reading in this way, I found, brings out aspects of the familiar story of the tower of Babel in Genesis 11 that had eluded me. Glissant himself refers to this story in his *Poetics of Relation* (1997), where he simply attempts to reverse it, calling for the rebuilding of the tower out of a diversity of languages. I think, however, that we need not read against the text so blatantly to make the point. Daniel Delas in an essay on Glissant's reading points to the many ambiguities in these verses, which are full, in his words, 'of a misleading clarity' (1999: 296, my translation). In a Glissantian context, that is a telling oxymoron.

Given that, it is rather surprising that neither he nor Glissant seize on the way that the builders of Babel explain their own project to themselves. The people, after all, specifically state that their object in building the tower is to prevent themselves being scattered over the world. In most readings, God's actions are then interpreted as punishment. Human hubris of attempting to build a tower is thwarted by a God who seems threatened by this evidence of human solidarity and cooperation. The confusion of languages and the scattering of the people is thus the result of divine retribution and the disruption of an original Edenic unity.

Could we not read this, however, as a positive story of God saving human beings from their own capacity for self-limitation? After all, the efforts of the people in building of the tower to prevent themselves being scattered fly in the face of the divine command in Gen. 2.8, whereby human beings are directed to 'fill the earth' as part of God's good creation. The desire for unity and safety is also a refusal of the invitation to explore, to travel and to risk change through exposure to new and diverse environments. Just as the expulsion from Eden is necessary for the invitation to humans to people the earth to be fulfilled, so is the scattering from Babel. A key concept in Glissant's work is *errance*, often translated 'errantry', by which he means something not dissimilar from this paradoxical notion that identity is not found by clinging to one place or one time, but grows out of wandering and encounters. This too he traces, but here positively, to the Bible and other founding texts.

Furthermore, the root *bll*, most often translated 'confuse' or 'confound' in this context, is elsewhere used in the mixing of ingredients for baking. In the economy of the Hebrew Bible, the idea of mixing carries a strongly negative connotation in the context of the maintenance of purity laws, but that is not its only connotation. To get bread, we need to make a mixture. Is there a counter-reading of the Babel story that could see God's mixing of language as a positive way to provide each group with its own capacity to retain a core of opacity?

This in turn leads to the diversity which is the prerequisite for true relation, as opposed to the sterile unity of a human race shut up in its tower, speaking one language in a condition which renders each person transparent to all the others, melding them all into one homogeneous entity. I suggest we can revise the standard translation of the final clause of Gen. 11.6, as found for instance in the NRSV: 'nothing they propose to do will now be impossible to them'. This implies that human ambition has become a threat to divine power. The same words, however, could more literally be translated as, 'let not all that they could do be cut off from them'. In this case, the text does not need to be rewritten in order for it to give the message that it is precisely the desire for uniformity and shared identity that will lock humanity into a deathly stasis of uniformity. God acts to ensure diversity and therefore the possibility of relation. His confusion of language increases rather than diminishes human possibility.

Conclusion

There is a fascinating footnote in Søren Kierkegaard's *Concluding Unscientific Postscript to Philosophical Fragments* where he considers the problem of communicating with someone who already knows too much (1992: 275fn). He uses here the metaphor of a man whose mouth is so full of food that he cannot swallow and who is thus in danger of dying of hunger. Paradoxically, in such a situation the way to feed the man is not to give him more, but to remove food from his mouth so that he can chew and swallow what he already has.

Kierkegaard applies this metaphor to his own mission of bringing Christianity to the Christians in Denmark, who already know, or think they know, all about it, but whose lives are actually lived in terminal despair. What he is required to do is not to clarify things for them so that they become all the more confident over their grasp of Christianity, but to make things more difficult, to point out their ignorance, so that they realize what they have to learn. Rather than clarifying their readings of the Bible, his goal is to make the Bible more obscure, or rather to recover and celebrate the obscurity that it always has.

This may be the most important gift that biblical readers who challenge the all-knowingness of Western scholarship offer to Western readers. Western scholarship is all-knowing not in the trivial sense in having answers to all possible questions, but that it thinks it has sorted out what questions it can or cannot answer. It knows too much about the Bible to be able to read it, but is still wedded to the idea that the way to read it better will be to know more.

This is one place where Glissant may help us. The following passage from Glissant's *Traité du Tout-Monde* encapsulates much of what I believe he has to contribute to the discussion of how European scholars might approach African readings of the Bible:

> It is not necessary to 'comprehend' whomsoever it may be, individual, community or people, to 'apprehend them for myself', thus to lose them in an all-engulfing totality which I manage, in order to accept living with them, building with them and risking with them.
>
> May opacity, ours when it is discovered by another, and that of the other for us when we meet it, not close down into obscurantism or apartheid; let it be a celebration for us, not a terror. (1997: 29, my translation)

What Glissant shows is that such opacity can be a tool for resistance and freedom. Glissant's vision is of a decoupling of language and identity in a true community of those who accept the incomprehensible in each other and can make a strength of lack. The Bible, with its strange lack of fit between its genres, its languages and its ideologies is actually a powerful counter to the myth of a pure and realized identity.

Challenging this is the positive contribution of encountering the *opacité* of the other. The people of Babel know too much. Traditionally, we read the story of God's intervention as showing that God feels jealous and threatened by their knowledge. Maybe we should read this as a story showing divine compassion. The only way to help those who know too much is to remove some of what they know. By scattering them and confusing their language, they are given the chance to encounter each other as something unknown and unfathomable and as a result to realize the incompleteness of their knowledge and that that is not a lack, but a gift. Of course, they may choose to react by trying to eradicate or assimilate what they encounter in order to deny what is perceived as a lack. Much of the West's encounter with Africa bears witness to the consequences of reacting in the second way. But another way is possible.

In this way, Glissant's work seems to me a fruitful way forward in the spirit of Moore and Sherwood's work. They see a positive role for a new approach to the Bible, which sees it as a resource for questioning and troubling the assumptions that underlie the Enlightenment project. Precisely because it was a key site for the setting up of foundational but untenable separations, they argue that interrogating the history of biblical scholarship with this in mind means that the Bible becomes 'a resource for unsettling settled identities and shaking up the way we think about established concepts' (2011: 129).

This is an enterprise in which African readers and especially non-specialist readers can contribute significantly. It may also be a way in which we can mediate the tension between global and local by finding our common ground in the dark rather than the light by making a virtue rather than an obstacle of opacity. African and Western biblical scholars alike need to find ways of knowing less. Reading with biblical readers who are not wedded to the methodolatry of the discipline of Biblical Studies may be one way to do this.

It is undeniable that there is irony in teaching postcolonialism in a British university to British students. That irony does not mean that the enterprise is without meaning or value: far from it. If encountering African readers of the Bible can do no more than teach European readers a sense of humility not only about what they can know but what they should know by helping to show them the value of the darkness and opacity of the biblical texts, there is hope that we can all learn to read the Bible better.

Works Cited

Achebe, C. (1977), 'An Image of Africa', *Massachusetts Review* 18: 782–94.

Achebe, C. (1988), 'An Image of Africa: Racism in Conrad's *Heart of Darkness*', in C. Achebe, *Hopes and Impediments: Selected Essays*, 1–20, London: Heinemann.

Bernasconi, R. (1997), 'African Philosophy's Challenge to Continental Philosophy', in E. Eze (ed.), *Postcolonial African Philosophy: A Critical Reader*, 183–96, Oxford: Blackwell.

Conrad, J. (1902), *Youth: A Narrative and Two Other Stories*, Edinburgh: William Blackwood.

Delas, D. (1999), 'Reconstruire Babel ou la notion de créolisation chez Glissant', in J. Chevrier (ed.), *Poétiques d'Edouard Glissant*, 285–97, Paris: Presses de l'Université de Paris-Sorbonne.

Dietrich, W. (2002), 'Instead of a Conclusion: Theological Astronomy – A Parable', in W. Dietrich and U. Luz (eds), *The Bible in a World Context: An Experiment in Contextual Hermeneutics*, 77–80, Grand Rapids, MI: Eerdmans.

Glissant, E. (1997), *Poetics of Relation* (trans. Betsy Wing), Ann Arbor, MI: University of Michigan Press.

Glissant, E. (1997), *Traité du Tout-Monde: Poétique IV*, Paris: Gallimard.

Kierkegaard, S. (1992), *Concluding Unscientific Postscript to Philosophical Fragments* (trans. H. V. Hong and E. Hong), Princeton: Princeton University Press.

Lacoue-Labarthe, P. (2007), 'L'horreur occidentale', *Lignes* 22: 224–34. Available online: http://www.parole-sans-frontiere.org/spip.php?article243 (accessed 16 January 2017).

Lacoue-Labarthe, P. (2012), 'The Horror of the West', in Lawtoo, *Conrad's* Heart of Darkness *and Contemporary Thought*, 111–22, London: Bloomsbury.

Lawtoo, N. (ed.) (2012), *Conrad's* Heart of Darkness *and Contemporary Thought: Revisiting the Horror with Lacoue-Labarthe*, London: Bloomsbury.

McEntire, M. (2000), 'Cain and Abel in Africa: An Ethiopian Case Study in Competing Hermeneutics', in G. O. West and M. W. Dube (eds), *The Bible in Africa: Transactions, Trajectories and Trends*, 248–59, Leiden: Brill.

Mignolo, W. (1995), *The Darker Side of the Renaissance: Literacy, Territoriality and Colonization*, Ann Arbor, MI: University of Michigan Press.

Mignolo, W. (2000), *Local Histories/Global Designs: Coloniality, Subaltern Knowledges and Border Thinking*, Princeton: Princeton University Press.

Mignolo, W. (2011), *The Darker Side of Western Modernity: Global Futures, Decolonial Options*, Durham: Duke University Press.

Moore, S. and Y. Sherwood (2011), *The Invention of the Biblical Scholar: A Critical Manifesto*, Minneapolis: Fortress Press.

Ngũgĩ wa Thiong'o (1986), *Decolonising the Mind: The Politics of Language in African Literature*, London: Heinemann.

Phillips, C. (2003), 'Out of Africa', *The Guardian* (22 February 2003). Available online: https://www.theguardian.com/books/2003/feb/22/classics.chinuaachebe (accessed 4 February 2017).

Sheehan, J. (2005), *The Enlightenment Bible: Translation, Scholarship, Culture*, Princeton: Princeton University Press.

Sugirtharajah, R. S., ed. (1991), *Voices From the Margin: Interpreting the Bible in the Third World*, Maryknoll, New York: Orbis.Sugirtharajah, R. S. (2008), 'Muddling Along at the Margins', in R. S. Sugirtharajah (ed.), *Still at the Margins: Biblical Scholarship Fifteen Years after* Voices From the Margin, 8–21, London: T&T Clark.

Watts, C. (1983), '"A Bloody Racist": About Achebe's View of Conrad', *The Yearbook of English Studies* 13: 196–209.

West, G. O. (2000), 'Mapping African Biblical Interpretation: A Tentative Sketch', in G. O. West and W. Dube (eds), *The Bible in Africa: Transactions, Trajectories and Trends*, 29–53, Leiden: Brill.

Chapter 11

MWARI AND THE SHONA BIBLE: COLONIAL AND PATRIARCHAL IDEOLOGY IN TRANSLATION

Elizabeth Vengeyi

Introduction

Missionaries' introduction of Christianity to Zimbabwe in the late 1800s brought with it a number of significant changes in the lives of ordinary Zimbabweans. One such change, which had a profound impact on the Shona people, was the imposition of a new deity whom they were to worship and revere to the exclusion of all others. This Christian God was masculine and was to be served by the Shona according to a Westernized form of Christian tradition. The task of this chapter is to give a short history of how missionaries colonized the traditional spiritual values of the Shona. The colonization of the Shona Supreme Being was achieved in part through the translation of the Bible. The chapter makes reference to Mt. 5.48 as one indicative example demonstrating the colonial and patriarchal nature of missionaries' translation.

The Colonization of Zimbabwe

Before I discuss the colonization of Zimbabwe by explorers, missionaries and those who followed them, it is important to explain that Zimbabwe divides into two predominant and distinct regions: Matabeleland and Mashonaland. The main languages of these regions are Ndebele and Shona respectively. Both Ndebele and Shona peoples of Zimbabwe acknowledged and respected Mwari as the Supreme Being but this chapter shall focus on the Shona.[1]

In the sixteenth century Zimbabwe witnessed the arrival of white hunters, gold seekers, traders and explorers. Christian missionaries also started their enterprise at this time but, in spite of some efforts, did not make many inroads, or

---

1. In Matabeleland, Ndebele worship of Mwari was centred in the Matopo Hills. Rituals were entwined with agricultural practice and performed by many peoples in a variety of dialects (Mbuwayesango 2001: 63).

establish successful missions, for about two centuries (Needham, Mashingaidze and Bhebe 1998: 96). As Zimbabwe came to be colonized and invaded more concertedly by various missionaries, the London Missionary Society (LMS) came to the fore and opened their first mission station at Inyati in Matabeleland in 1859 (Togarasei 2013: 21–2). In the late 1880s Lobengula, the king of the Ndebele, signed the Rudd Concession which gave Charles Rudd and his associates 'complete and exclusive charge' over all metals and minerals (Zvobgo 1996: 2). At around 1890, the Mashonaland province also saw a number of missionary societies, such as the Pioneer Column, the British South Africa Company and the Dutch Reformed Church of South Africa, with each establishing mission stations (Zvobgo 1996: 3).

In the course of their activities, the Christian missionaries began to translate the Bible and other related literature, such as prayer books and hymns, into local languages. It was the Dutch Reformed Church missionaries who pioneered the translation of the Bible into Ndebele and Karanga (Zvobgo 1996: 125). As will be discussed shortly, this translation was not a neutral endeavour (is translation ever?), or of just substituting words from one language into another. It was also a process of imposition, which saw the Shona people's understanding of their Supreme Being colonized.

When the missionaries arrived in Zimbabwe, they came with many misconceptions about Zimbabweans. They perceived them as 'heathens, evil and wicked people' whose souls were in dire need of salvation (Kamudzandu 2010: 159). James Baur argues similarly that 'in the eyes of the European colonizers, the Africans were "savages" to be civilized, "cursed sons of Ham" to be saved, "big children" to be educated. For them, there existed no African culture, only tribal customs, no religion, only foolish superstitions and devilish cults' (1994: 421).

The missionaries' professed motives were to bring civilization, religion and education to 'the Africans' and they fully expected Zimbabweans to convert to their – by implication, superior – religion of Christianity. In their ministry European missionaries looked forward to seeing Africans reject their traditions. To them, salvation was only achievable if Africans renounced their past, their beliefs and their practices and demonstrated willingness to live in accordance with Christian principles. The transformation envisaged was wholesale because African ways of life and blackness were to the European missionaries indicative of evil (Amanze 1998: 52). The missionaries had a pressing motive for colonizing African peoples: it was, essentially, conceived of and cast by them as a battle of good versus evil.

As P. J. Paris among others points out, however, religion was not something being imported to Zimbabwe but something very much already there: 'The missionaries who introduced the gospel to Africa in the past 200 years did not bring God to our continent. Instead God brought them. They proclaimed the name of Jesus Christ, but they used the names of God who was and is already known by African peoples' (1995: 29). Next follows a discussion of how the Shona perceived and understood their Supreme Being, Mwari, who was worshipped long before the advent of missionary activity in Zimbabwe.

The Shona Understanding of Mwari

Prior to the colonization of Zimbabwe and for some time after, the Shona referred to their Supreme Being by the name 'Mwari' (see Hannan *ad loc)*. The Shona were once spiritually united by their belief in Mwari and yet, the missionaries' *first* observation when they arrived was that Zimbabweans were ignorant of God (Kamudzandu 2010: 159)! Mwari was believed to be above any other spirit and to be very powerful. The Supreme Being was responsible for everything on earth: be it fertility of humanity, or of land and forests. The Supreme Being sometimes could cooperate with territorial spirits, which might be male or female. For example, during the First Chimurenga,[2] Mwari spoke to Mbuya Nehanda, a female spirit. Nehanda was stronger than Kaguvi, a male spirit medium who converted to Christianity before he was removed by colonizers (Vengeyi 2013: 221). The territorial spirits could cooperate with the Supreme Being: for example, when a natural disaster happened. D. N. Beach also argues that mediums possessed by spirits of ancestors interceded with Mwari on behalf of the people in rituals that were visually more impressive than anything offered by Christianity. Moreover, these rituals were also more directly linked to the specific needs of Shona, for example, the need for procuring rain in times of drought. Christian ritual imported from Europe was less adapted to such needs and worship of Mwari and rituals associated with spirits and ancestors are likely to have been compelling (Beach 1973: 27).

Rituals involving ancestors and Mwari and indications of cooperation between them were misinterpreted by the missionaries as elevating the spirits (who are with Mwari) to being deities (alongside Mwari) – in other words, as polytheism (Bourdillon 1976: 278). Yet from a Shona perspective, Mwari ought not to be approached directly: to do so indicates deficient respect. Territorial spirits, mediums and messengers, therefore, are understood as being intermediaries between the Supreme Being and people (Kamudzandu 2010: 163). The Shona, moreover, claim that no one has ever seen the Supreme Being but that the ancestors are the bridge to Mwari. Thus, people call upon Mwari through messengers or mediators who (unlike humans) could make contact with Mwari (Aschwanden 1989: 200).

The Shona concept of the Supreme Being Mwari, indeed, was never polytheistic. The various names for Mwari reveal a number of functions associated with fertility, rain and matters of national interest rather than indicating the existence of multiple deities. Mwari is considered as the preeminent but also as a remote authority above and behind the ancestors who are beings more directly linked to the day-to-day lives of ordinary people (Daneel 1971: 80; Verstraelen 1993a: 221). Below are some of the praise names for Mwari, which add insight into the deity's qualities and attributes.

---

2. The First Chimurenga (Shona for 'revolutionary struggle') occurred between 1896 and 1897. It constituted an uprising of indigenous Shona and Ndebele communities for political dignity and against British colonization.

Shona Praise Names of Mwari

J. S. Mbiti notes that in several African societies the meaning of a person's name discloses aspects of their personality, or being. In other words, names can have significance beyond mere identification: they can yield clues about character and personal ontology (Mbiti 1990: 35). In the case of Mwari, while the deity's essential nature could not be apprehended, due to Mwari's remoteness, Mwari's epithets do say something about the deity's activities, traits or emanations. According to M. F. C. Bourdillon, Mwari was known by various titles, which include: *Nyadenga* or *Dedza* ('Lord of the Sky'), *Musikavanhu* ('Maker of People'), *Chikara* ('One Inspiring Awe'), *Dzivaguru* ('The Great Pool'), *Chirazamauya* ('The One Who Provides for Good and Bad') and *Mutangakugara* ('One Who Existed at the Beginning') and Mbedzi ('Giver of Life' or 'One Who Gives Birth') (1976: 277). Some of Mwari's titles are (unlike *Dedza*) suggestive of feminine traits, in particular *Tateguru* (meaning 'Great-Great-Great Grandmother'), *Ambuya* ('Source of Life', 'Grandmother') but also the praise name *Zendere* (meaning 'Young Woman') (Shoko 2007: 39).[3] Given that the Supreme Deity of the Shona was not gendered, this versatility or fluidity should not surprise. Taken together Mwari's names and titles suggest an eternal, all-powerful creator-deity.

Strikingly, a number of commentators glibly ascribe divine powers to a male god and depict Mwari, too, using masculine pronouns. William van der Merwe provides a typical example referring to 'His [Mwari's] powers of creation and fertility' (1957: 44), which suppresses both the possibility of coexisting feminine aspects of Mwari, or (alternatively) of the genderlessness of the deity. Since the possessive pronoun 'His' is used also for the Supreme Being Ambuya,[4] female or gender-ambivalent nuances are again suppressed or downplayed (Taringa 2004). The various names and titles for Mwari honour the deity with traits respected among males *and* females in the human realm. Additionally, they praise Mwari for non-human attributes, too, such as power over the elements and eternity. The names reflect what is close to the hearts of the Shona as well as the awe that Mwari inspires (Aschwanden 1989: 211). The Christian missionaries, however, utterly misunderstood the Shona concept of the Supreme Being, instead interpreting Mwari, like their own god, in masculine terms and mistaking Mwari as one deity of many in a polythestic scheme.

---

3. Taringa (2004) and Kamudzandu (2010: 162) note that Ambuya is regularly used in place of Mwari by one of the oldest Shona tribes, the VaHera.

4. The common noun 'ambuya', refers to a grandmother, someone who is understood to be generous and giving and welcoming to all. When Mwari is called Ambuya, however, this need not mean that the deity *is* feminine. Instead, it may point to qualities associated with female elders (Aschwanden 1989: 203).

Early Missionaries and the Name of Mwari

Before the missionaries settled on the name 'Mwari' to translate 'God' into Shona, they used quite a number of names such as *Mudzimu* ('Ancestor'), which was used by the Lutheran and Dutch Reformed Churches who were operating among the Karanga around 1899–1912. Another name was *Wedenga*, used by both the Dutch Reformed Church and the Church of Sweden in 1909 and 1927 respectively (Mbuwayesango 2001: 65). Dora Mbuwayesango argues that one Roman Catholic priest, Father Richartz, was opposed to adopting the name Mwari for the dominant Shona deity, 'because it did not connote the notion of judge – an essential ingredient of the Christian belief – nor the notion of creation in the strict sense'. He also demeaned the views of those who went to the Mwari shrines as concerned only about material matters (2001: 66). As time passed, however, from around the 1960s, some missionaries, such as Jesuits, joined other Christian missionaries in using the name Mwari, particularly due to the influence of the Roman priest Father Michael Hannan who was instrumental in standardizing the Shona language and who used the name Mwari (Mbuwayesango 2001: 66).

Missionaries' Translation of the Bible and Colonial Ideology

On arriving in Zimbabwe, the missionaries discovered that they need not explain to the Shona about the concept of God. This is because the Shona already believed in the Supreme Being named Mwari. The challenge for the missionaries thus became to make their own Christian deity of the Bible relevant and acceptable to Shona (Mbuwayesango 2001: 65). One step towards this endeavour was translation of the Bible into Shona.

Translation theory claims that 'translation is a communication process that moves the message or meaning from the source language to the receptor language' (Kumbirai 1979: 62). This implies that the Bible is the 'source text' that does not change while Shona and other African languages are 'receptor languages' that should be adapted to the Bible. For this reason, Gomang Seratwa Ntloedibe-Kuswani points out that translation theory in itself belongs to a colonizing ideology (2001: 80). Given that language is imbedded in culture and human societies, this has the possible implication, too, that the colonial forces that bring the Bible signify the standard, ideal, norm, or source towards which the colonized cultures and human societies should strive and to which they must adapt as best as possible. And this, in turn, implies deficiency and inferiority of the colonized – and completeness and superiority of the colonizer.

Translation can be horizontal: from one contemporary language into another, for example from English into Shona. It can also be vertical, from a language of the past into a language of today: for example, from ancient Hebrew into French. Translating the Bible into Shona seems to be a blending of both horizontal and vertical translations (Kumbirai 1979: 62). J. C. Kumbirai notes that if a translation is to be of any useful application, it must be addressed to the people and times for which it is produced (1979: 64). But if this is so, we do not seem to have a good translation in the Shona Bible produced by missionaries because it contains notions at odds with Shona beliefs. Hence, as discussed, while the Shona knew and understood their Supreme Deity as genderless, the Shona Bible gave them a male God.[5]

The Bible was translated into the vernacular languages of Zimbabwe in the nineteenth and twentieth centuries. These translations were carried out primarily by missionaries and heavily informed by colonial ideology. In this vein, Lovemore Togarasei argues that the translation of the Bible was never an objective process (2009: 19). In his article on the politics of Shona Bible translation, Togarasei highlights, for example, how the missionaries interpreted debauched banquetings in 1 Pet. 4.3 as *mabira* ('rituals') instead of the far more apt *kuraradza* ('to get drunk') (2009: 37). There is a considerable difference between rituals and getting drunk. In the Shona context, rituals are performed at different levels; for example, at family level, people can gather to brew beer for someone who is about to go to look for a job in the urban areas. Hence, the missionaries had the wrong – and derogatory – idea of the meaning of *mabira*. Musa Dube mentions that, similarly, in the Setswana Bible, the missionaries translated 'demon' with *badimo* ('ancestor'), thereby (literally) demonizing a revered spiritual entity of Tswana religion (1999). The missionaries perceived their Christian God as the only Saviour and their translations reflect dismissal and negative portrayal of African spirituality.

Togarasei traces the history of translation of the Bible by missionaries from around the 1890s until the time when the first Shona Bible became available to the Shona in the 1940s. First, the missionaries began translation within a few months of arriving in Zimbabwe. This immediately raises the strong possibility that they knew rather little about the Shona language, let alone Shona world view and culture. Also of note is that the Bible was translated into Shona not from the original languages (i.e. Hebrew, Aramaic and Greek), but from other translations of the major languages of the colonial powers – in the case of Zimbabwe, English. Consequently, the Shona Bible was a (deficient) translation of translations (Mojola 2002: 206; Togarasei 2009: 26).

Togarasei also argues that the missionaries came up with their own orthography since the Shona were non-literate. But this in turn, resulted in numerous errors, suggesting a lack of either a careful understanding of Shona, or of close collaboration with Shona speakers (2009: 23). Hence, the Bible in Union Shona, which was

---

5. Hebrew (the original language of the greater part of the Hebrew Bible or Old Testament) is a gendered language, which uses masculine verbs and pronouns for the God of Israel. Many of the prominent metaphors for this deity are also reminiscent of males in the human realm (e.g. metaphors pertaining to God as the father, husband, king, shepherd or warrior). There are, however, also occasional feminine metaphors used for God. Over time (for all the anthropomorphic divine depictions in the Hebrew Bible) both Judaism and Christianity have come to understand God in incorporeal terms and as not having male or female sex. Some modern Bible translations reflect inclusive or gender-neutral language for God.

translated by missionaries around 1949, has wrong transliteration or consonants missing in quite a number of words – including very common ones. One example is Mt. 5.47-48, where *vaŋwe* ('others') should read and be spelled as *vamwe*. Moreover, the incorrect word means 'to drink'. To give another example from Mt. 5.48, the Shona word, *naizozo* ('therefore') should read and be spelled as *naizvozvo*.

The reader of the Shona Bible, consequently, needs to be circumspect regarding such a translation because the indication is that missionaries with faulty understanding of Shona were in charge of the translation process. Given this situation, the elementary errors in the translation are no surprise[6] – nor should the accompaniment of missionary (i.e. colonial) ideology be any surprise. So, while the missionaries' Shona translation uses traditional and indigenous names to translate the Christian God, such as 'Mwari', no fuller understanding of this deity is reflected or taken into account – including Mwari's genderless or gender-ambivalent qualities. In all sorts of ways, moreover, African Traditional Religion emerges in the translation as evil and inferior compared to Christianity, which is portrayed as the true and superior religion (Togarasei 2013: 208). Christianity, a religion that emerged from Judaism in what womanist Wil Gafney aptly calls Afro-Asia was thereby imported to Zimbabwe in a westernized form and used to denigrate and erase African Traditional Religion. Explaining the reorientation that is so urgently needed, Gafney expands and advises as follows:

> In order to unmask whiteness in scholarly and ecclesial biblical interpretation, I must first help my students identify and name it. My introductory courses begin with maps of Africa and Asia. Naming the context, literature, peoples, and languages of the Hebrew Scriptures 'Afro-Asiatic' immediately calls into question the white imagery applied to the biblical world. This depiction manifests in the construction and consumption of white images and icons produced for religious and popular audiences, which are often imposed on peoples of color by their conquerors and colonizers. We talk about the sanctification of whiteness by aligning with the biblical text and the inevitable subsequent demonization of blackness in an interpretive world given easily to binary thinking. (2017: 206)

With the Shona Bible, too, the power dynamics were clearly set and missionaries had the final say in the interpretation and translation of the Bible (Mbuwayesango 2001: 73). They chose what to say and how to say it (Verstraelen 1993b: 157).

---

6. I am informed by the Bible Society of Zimbabwe (whose chief goal is to translate the Bible into vernacular languages) that many people continue to prefer to buy the first edition of the Union Shona Bible (published by missionaries in 1949) instead of revised and more recent and accurate translations. Wendland argues that 'such people do not want anyone to "tamper" with the Word of God, even if they cannot understand it' (2004). This indicates that the strategies of missionaries have been highly effective and to the detriment of those receiving the text.

Kumbirai cites a revealing passage about the work of the Rev. Michael Hannan, a Bible translator and author of the first Shona Dictionary. In the citation the Shona team leader has this to say about Hannan:

> Fr Hannan knew his Shona grammar and we did not know it; so he helped us out when we got stuck in matters of grammar. His knowledge of Shona was unparalleled. He was knowledgeable and knew what he was doing. I appreciated his critical ability, which enabled us to improve very much the present New Union Shona Bible. His dictionary was also very useful for our translation work. His knowledge of the various dialects helped us tremendously, as our goal was to produce a multi-dialect Bible. In short, I can say that he added certainty to uncertainty. After he had read, made suggestions, and approved of what we had done, we felt confident. (1979: 61)

According to this assessment, the Shona translators felt they were not doing an adequate job until a white Roman Catholic priest, namely Father Hannan, evaluated their work and suggested important improvements. But how likely is it really that Hannan, who was not a native speaker of Shona and had not been inculturated in Shona ways, was a superior linguist and translator who could advise authoritatively in matters of Shona diction, semantics and grammar? Instead, this seems to be a case of what Gafney has called 'sanctification of whiteness'. Perhaps the Shona team leader had internalized such sanctification, or the words may not have been his own. Whatever the case, it is implausible that if he said these words he was speaking the truth.

The Christian missionaries who came to Zimbabwe (super)imposed their own ideologies on the Supreme Being of the Shona people. The Shona people's only way to Mwari was no longer to be through their ancestors but through Jesus Christ alone. Jesus was not to be understood as an ancestor, or as fulfilling a role analogous to the ancestors. The ancestors of the Shona people were discredited by the missionaries. They were rejected and considered non-existent, or the stuff of superstition, or evil (Mbuwayesango 2001: 66). The missionaries condemned and suppressed traditional beliefs and values of the Zimbabweans and replaced them with their own westernized Christian beliefs. Their language became the official one which was to be used in church, schools and in job market (Kamudzandu 2010: 159). As I have mentioned before, the first Shona Bible translation of 1949 still sells better than the revised version of 2002. The 1949 version, which was translated by missionaries continues to be widely used by churches in Zimbabwe.

The Bible, which in a way is a colonial text, was accompanied by a colonial concept of God, and therefore was used in schools to teach about a Supreme Deity rather different from the traditional conception of Mwari. The Bible was also presented as more authoritative and reliable than the oral traditions about Mwari. Shona values, customs and beliefs had been transferred from generation to generation through folk tales, but this practice gradually receded and was mostly replaced and certainly overshadowed by the written word. Shona folk tales were not accorded the same validity as the Bible because they were called 'myths' or unrealistic stories (Mbuwayesango 2001: 74).

In line with the tendency that saw the accentuation of masculine and suppression of feminine divine traits of Mwari, the missionaries also forbade a long list of African ceremonies in which women were prominently involved: for example, ceremonies in honour of the ancestors were banned, as were ceremonies for rain making. For instance, at Chishawasha Mission,[7] around November 1985, people who brewed beer to honour their ancestors were charged with devil worship and forced to leave their land, which supposedly belonged to the mission. These ceremonies had been dominated by women who fulfilled the important roles of brewing and presenting the ritual beer as well as leading in singing and dancing (Schmidt 1992: 87). Instead of appreciating and accepting the gospel that was brought to ordinary Africans by the missionaries, the Africans often perceived the so-called good news as a thorn in the flesh as it stripped them of the various significant roles they had fulfilled before the coming of colonialism.

Mt. 5.48: A Colonial and Gendered Text

The colonization and patriarchalization of Zimbabwe was assisted by missionaries in considerable ways through the process of translation of the Bible into indigenous languages. Mt. 5.48 says (in English, RSV), 'You, therefore, must be perfect, as your heavenly Father is perfect.' This reflects the Greek original and the dominant divine metaphors of the Bible more widely, which favour masculine over feminine imagery. It also reflects the patriarchal ideology of the colonizers. When the Shona Bible translation of this verse depicts Mwari as Baba ('Father') it goes against the genderless or gender-ambivalent understanding of the Shona Deity. Moreover, the masculine divine image here renders the deity as 'perfect', with the implication that to be perfect one has to be masculine. Conversely, to be feminine or of indeterminate gender is imperfect. Although Shona (like many indigenous African languages) has no gendered pronouns (e.g. 'her', 'him') and although Mwari was traditionally depicted in gender-fluid ways, the Bible taught the Shona to worship God the Father and Jesus Christ the Son, transmitting therewith a clear gender hierarchy (Ntloedibe-Kuswani 2001: 92; Dube 2001: 6). Mbuwayesango says, 'With no written records to concretize th[e oral] traditions, the missionaries replaced the unwritten records of the Shona with the Bible. As a result, the Bible now talks about Mwari, but whose Mwari?' (2001: 70). To call the Supreme Being 'Father' represents the projection of colonial ideology that was dictated to the Shona people.

The language used by the Bible and by the missionaries, therefore, depicts Mwari as masculine and translation has not taken into account Shona world

---

7. Chishawasha Mission is located just outside Harare. During the colonial period the Chishawasha mission was headed by Jesuit missionaries.

view – even though a case could be made for the Bible (in spite of predominance of masculine divine imagery) depicting a God who, like Mwari, is neither masculine nor feminine. The translation reflects in the first instance the patriarchal ideology of the colonial missionaries. It also reflects their practice of imposing their values rather than seeking to understand Shona culture. Colonial, missionary and translation ideology are all entwined.

Conclusion

This chapter analysed the colonization of Zimbabwe from the 1800s focusing particularly on the role played by missionaries, including their part in the hijacking and westernization of traditional and spiritual beliefs of the Shona people. The missionaries managed to colonize and subvert the Supreme Being of the Shona people through their translation of the Bible with the Christian God replacing Mwari. The Shona had revered a Supreme Being who was genderless, only to be taught by the missionaries that the rightful God, as revealed in the Bible, was male. In this way Shona translations, too, came to reflect the colonial and patriarchal God, as in the case of Mt. 5.48, where God is Baba, the Father in heaven who is perfect (certainly by implication) on account of his maleness. The feminine or – more accurately – genderless or genderfluid manifestations of Mwari came to be suppressed, which has, in turn, seen negative outworkings for Zimbabwe's men and women.

Works Cited

Amanze, J. N. (1998), *African Christianity in Botswana*, Gweru: Mambo Press.

Aschwanden, H. (1989), *Karanga Mythology*, Gweru: Mambo Press.

Baur, J. (1994), *2000 Years of Christianity in Africa*, Nairobi: Paulines Publications.

Beach, D. N. (1973), 'The Initial Impact of Christianity on the Shona: The Protestants and the Southern Shona', in J. A. Dachs (ed.), *Christianity South of the Zambezi*, vol. 1, 25–40, Gweru: Mambo Press.

Bourdillon, M. F. C. (1976), *The Shona Peoples: An Ethnography of the Contemporary Shona, with Special Reference to Their Religion* (Shona Heritage Series), Gweru: Mambo Press.

Daneel, M. L. (1971), *Old and New in Southern Shona Independent Churches*, vol. 1, The Hague: Mouton.

Dube, M. W. (1999), 'Consuming a Colonial Cultural Bomb: Translating Badimo into "Demons" in the Setswana Bible (Matthew 8.28–34; 15.22; 10.8)', *JSNT* 73: 33–59.

Dube, M. W. (2001), 'Introduction', in M. W. Dube (ed.), *Other Ways of Reading: African Women and the Bible*, 1–19, Atlanta: Society of Biblical Literature.

Gafney, W. (2017), 'A Reflection on the Black Lives Matter Movement and Its Impact on My Scholarship', *JBL* 136 (1): 204–7.

Hannan, M. (1987), *Standard Shona Dictionary*, Harare: College Press.

Kamudzandu, I. (2010), *Abraham as the Spiritual Ancestor: A Postcolonial Zimbabwean Reading of* Romans 4. Leiden: Brill.

Kumbirai, J. C. (1979), 'Shona Bible Translation: The Work of the Reverend Michael Hannan', *Zambezia* 7 (1): 61–74.

Mbiti, J. S. (1990), *African Religions and Philosophy*, Oxford: Heinemann Education Publishers.

Mbuwayesango, D. R. (2001), 'How Local Divine Powers Were Suppressed: A Case of Mwari of the Shona', in *Other Ways of Reading: African Women and the Bible*, 63–77.

Mojola, A. O. (2002), 'Bible Translation in Africa', *Acta Theologica Supplementum* 2: 202–13.

Needham, D. E., E. K. Mashingaidze and N. Bhebe (1998), *From Iron Age to Independence*, Nairobi: Paulines Publications.

Ntloedibe-Kuswani, G. S. (2001), 'Translating the Divine: The Case of Modimo in the Setswana Bible', in *Other Ways of Reading: African Women and the Bible*, 78–97.

Paris, P. J. (1995), *The Spirituality of African Peoples*, Minneapolis: Fortress Press.

Schmidt, E. (1992), *Peasants, Traders and Wives: Shona Women in the History of Zimbabwe, 1870–1939*, Portsmouth: Heinemann.

Shoko, T. (2007), *Karanga Indigenous Religion in Zimbabwe*, Farnham: Ashgate Publishing.

Taringa, N. T. (2004), 'African Metaphors for God: Male or Female', *Scriptura* 86: 174–9.

Togarasei, L. (2009), *The Bible in Context: Essay Collection*, Bamberg: University of Bamberg Press.

Togarasei, L. (2013), 'African Traditional Religion in the Study of the New Testament in Africa', in A. Adogame, B. Bateye and E. Chitando (eds), *African Traditions in the Study of Religion in Africa: Emerging Trends, Indigenous Spirituality and the Interface with other World Religions*, 205–18, Farnham: Ashgate Publishing.

Van der Merwe W. J. (1957), *The Shona Idea of God*, Morgenster: Morgenster Mission Press.

Vengeyi, O. (2013), *Aluta Continua Biblical Hermeneutics for Liberation: Interpreting Biblical Texts on Slavery for Liberation of Zimbabwean Underclasses*, Bamberg: University of Bamberg Press.

Verstraelen, F. J. (1993a), 'The Christian Bible and African Cultural and Religious Realities', in I. Mukonyora, J. L. Cox and F. J. Verstraelen (eds) *'Rewriting' the Bible: The Real Issues*, 219–48, Gweru: Mambo Press.

Verstraelen, F. J. (1993b), 'Mission and Bible in Historical and Missiological Perspective', in *'Rewriting' the Bible: The Real Issues*, 141–67.

Wendland, E. R. (2004), 'The Challenge of Bible Translation in Africa Today' [*WLS* 80 (4)]. Available online: http://wlsessays.net/handle/123456789/779 (accessed 24 April 2017).

Zvobgo, C. J. M. (1996), *A History of Christian Missions in Zimbabwe 1890–1939*, Gweru: Mambo Press.

Chapter 12

RESPONSE: THE POLITICS OF APPROPRIATION

Adriaan van Klinken

Recently I wrote a blog post for the Religion and the Public Sphere blog run by the London School of Economics and Political Science. The post is about my current research on the ways in which LGBT activists and communities in Kenya relate to, and engage with, religion, specifically Christianity (van Klinken 2017). On Twitter, the social media officer of the blog had tweeted the following message to draw people's attention to my post: 'The Bible and the Christian faith have been appropriated by African LGBT activists in support of their cause.' In response to this tweet, somebody replied: 'Why "appropriated"? Who has decided this is not a legitimate interpretation?' The suggestion made here is that the word 'appropriated' is not adequate in this context because, apparently, it raises the question of il/legitimacy. This social media user had clearly read the message, and possibly also my post, as making a negative judgement of the use of the Bible by Kenyan LGBT activists, as if this usage is illegal.

Maybe it is because I am not a native speaker of the English language, but I was not aware of this strictly legal denotation of the word 'appropriate'. Checking the Oxford Dictionary, I was surprised to see that the first meaning of the word was indeed cited as '[t]ake (something) for one's own use, typically without the owner's permission'. In other words, 'to appropriate' comes rather close to 'to steal'. However, on second thoughts I realized that the use of the word 'appropriate' in the above-mentioned context is not ill-informed and has nothing to do with me being a non-native speaker. Instead, it reflects a strong tradition of postcolonial theory in which the term 'appropriation' functions exactly to problematize the question of ownership, permission and il/legitimacy. As a key concept in postcolonial studies, appropriation is

A term used to describe the ways in which post-colonial societies take over those aspects of the imperial culture – language, forms of writing, film, theatre, even modes of thought and argument such as rationalism, logic, and analysis – that may be of use to them in articulating their own social and cultural identities. (Ashcroft, Griffiths and Tiffin 2000: 15)

Thus, appropriation is a political category referring to processes through which colonized, subjugated or otherwise marginalized groups resist hegemonic uses of certain cultural expressions, and reclaim these to articulate and affirm their own identities. Indeed, it is about 'the ways in which the dominated or colonized culture can use the tools of the dominant discourse to resist its political or cultural control' (Ashcroft, Griffiths and Tiffin 2000: 16). This is exactly the point I was trying to make by using the verb 'to appropriate' in my blog post in which I discuss various ways in which Kenyan LGBT activists have made use of biblical texts and Christian-inspired notions to advocate for a recognition of their human dignity and rights. Hence I conclude:

> This clearly demonstrates that the Bible and the Christian faith are not only sites of struggle where the debate on homosexuality is being fought by homophobic African religious and political leaders, but that the same sites are appropriated by African LGBT activists in support of their cause. (van Klinken 2017)

For LGBT people in Kenya and elsewhere in Africa, both the Bible and the Christian faith are, to use Audre Lorde's words, 'the master's tools' with which they try to dismantle 'the master's house' (1983) – in this case, the house of homo- and transphobia and heteronormativity. Of course this stands in a long history of the Bible in Africa.[1] In the same way as black Africans have appropriated the Bible from white European missionaries, and African women have appropriated the Bible from a male-dominated church, now LGBT Africans appropriate the Bible from a heteronormative society, resisting the ways in which the same text has been used to silence and marginalize them, and reclaiming this text to affirm their identities and carve out a space of existence.[2]

In different ways, the two chapters in this book to which I have been invited to respond somehow raise the question of appropriation and its underlying politics. Elizabeth Vengeyi, in her chapter 'Mwari and the Shona Bible: Colonial and Patriarchal Ideology in Translation', is not concerned with appropriation as such. Instead, she is concerned with imposition, in this case the colonial imposition of the Bible by European missionaries on to the Shona people in what is now called Zimbabwe. She argues that the translation of the Bible into Shona language has had particular colonizing and gendered effects, such as the replacement of the gender-neutral or gender-ambiguous supreme being of Shona indigenous religion, called Mwari, by the masculine imagined biblical God of the missionaries. Also in other respects the Shona translation of the Bible is deeply problematic according to Vengeyi, not only because the missionary-translators in fact knew very little of Shona language and culture but also because of the ideology of European and Christian superiority that guided their translation efforts. As a result of the latter, Shona deities and rituals were demonized. One might expect that the Shona

---

1. For a rich mine of evidence, see West and Dube (eds), 2000.
2. For a wealth of examples, see Chitando and van Klinken (eds), 2016.

people, after the independence of Zimbabwe, as part of a process of decolonization would get rid of this colonial Bible.[3] However, the opposite appears to be the case.

As Vengeyi comments in a footnote that expresses her surprise, 'many people continue to prefer to buy the first edition of the Union Shona Bible (published by missionaries in 1949) instead of revised and more recent and accurate translations'. She explains this with reference to Ernst Wendland who has argued that 'such people do not want anyone to "tamper" with the Word of God, even if they cannot understand it', and then she concludes that apparently 'the strategies of missionaries have been highly effective and to the detriment of those receiving the text'. Reflected in this footnote are some striking assumptions: First, that the Shona people do not understand the Bible they have received from the missionaries, and second, that their use of this Bible is to their own detriment. Vengeyi overlooks, and apparently rules out the possibility of appropriation in the sense outlined above. However, I am left wondering: Could it be that the colonial Bible is one of the aspects of imperial culture that Shona Christians have used to shape their own social and cultural identities? I have not done any study into the use of the Bible by Shona Christians, so I do not know how this may shape their identities, and whether this could possibly be read in terms of resistance and reclaiming. However, I do believe that a reading through the lens of 'appropriation' could potentially be more interesting and productive than a reading through the lens of 'imposition', in which the Shona people are powerless victims lacking agency and creativity who simply stick to a Bible they cannot understand. What might be important to acknowledge here is that 'appropriation' is, of course, a complex and ambiguous process. It is not necessarily a tool of resistance of political or cultural control; instead of radically dismantling the master's house it can be used to make strategic room within the master's house, in this case the house of a Christianity that was originally introduced by European missionaries but that provides contemporary Zimbabweans a space to negotiate identity in a modern, globalized and postcolonial world. For these Zimbabweans, Shona religion and its gender-neutral Mwari may be remnants of the past, while Christianity is appropriated as an entrance to modernity and the first translation of the Bible has become, to paraphrase Gerald West (2016), a Shona icon.

Hugh Pyper, in his chapter 'The Dark Heart of Biblical Scholarship: Western Readers and African Readings', struggles much more explicitly with the question of appropriation. Interestingly, his concern is with what he describes as 'the inescapable ironies that are entailed when Western readers seek to appropriate African readings'. The context of his article is his experience of teaching postcolonial Biblical Studies, specifically African biblical hermeneutics, at an English university to mostly British or European students. One obvious irony of this context is that appropriation does not refer here to a process where formerly colonized groups appropriate aspects of the imperial culture to what they perceive as their own

---

3. Interesting in this regard is that one of Zimbabwe's independent churches, the Friday Masowe Apostles, is known for *not* reading the Bible (see Engelke 2007).

advantage and benefit, but to a process the other way around, in which formerly colonizing societies appropriate the readings developed by colonized groups to . . ., yes, to what purpose? What are the politics of appropriation when the power dynamics change? Is this an example, to paraphrase the words of Lorde, of the European master stealing Africa's critical tools, perhaps to dismantle the project of decolonization? Of course these questions are relevant, not only for teaching postcolonial Biblical Studies but also for any form of teaching where we (and I use 'we' here to refer to European academics teaching in the European academy) make use of, or appropriate, knowledge from the global South. In my own teaching, which is mostly in the field of religion, gender and sexuality in Africa, I encounter similar questions when introducing students to African postcolonial theology, African feminism and African queer studies. At stake here is, again, the question of ownership, permission and il/legitimacy, but perhaps the question is more pertinent now because of the power dynamics in place.

Pyper suggests that engaging with African readings is a way for students to be confronted with the 'dark colonialist legacy of the Enlightenment which is at the heart of biblical studies', meaning that there is a critical pedagogical value in using postcolonial knowledge. I have embraced the same value to guide my own teaching practices where I use knowledge produced in Africa to challenge the deeply rooted and widely spread tendency of 'othering' Africa. As Achille Mbembe puts it, 'Africa still constitutes one of the metaphors through which the West represents the origin of its own norms, develops a self-image, and integrates this image into the set of signifiers asserting what it supposes to be its identity' (2001: 2). Especially in Western (both academic and popular) discourses about gender and sexuality in Africa, this tendency can easily be recognized. It takes a while for students (and some of them never seem to get it) to understand that Africa is not a patriarchal and homophobic country that can be contrasted to a liberal, progressive and tolerant West. Using African feminist and queer texts helps to debunk such myths, to interrogate the underlying assumptions and normativities and to develop not just a critical but a humble hermeneutics. As Pyper puts it with reference to his Biblical Studies classes: 'If encountering African readers of the Bible can do no more than teach European readers a sense of humility not only about what they can know but what they should know by helping to show them the value of the darkness and opacity of the biblical texts, there is hope that we can all learn to read the Bible better.' I greatly sympathize with this line of thought and the postcolonial pedagogy it reflects. However, there may be a risk. Again in the words of Mbembe, 'narrative about Africa is always a pretext for a comment about something else, some other place, some other people. More precisely, Africa is the mediation that enables the West to accede to its own subconsciousness and give a public account of its subjectivity' (2001: 3). This is not the place to point out ways how to solve this conundrum of complex questions about the politics of appropriation of postcolonial knowledge (if only I could!). This conversation has only just begun and should continue.

One of the Kenyan LGBT texts I work with in my current research project is the music video *Same Love*, released in 2016 by Kenyan musicians and activists as a contribution to African debates on same-sex love and gay and lesbian human rights (Art Attack 2016). Interestingly, the video ends with a quotation from the Bible, the Pauline text about love in 1 Corinthians 13, concluded by the statement, 'love is God and God is love'. It is an excellent illustration of postcolonial and queer appropriation in the sense of resisting and reclaiming, and of affirming identity. In response to the tweet asking, 'Why "appropriated"? Who has decided this is not a legitimate interpretation?', I would say: Indeed, appropriated, exactly because there is no authority to decide about legitimate interpretation, and any interpretation claiming such authority should be resisted using the master's tools.

Works Cited

Art Attack (15 February 2016), Same Love (remix), *YouTube*. Available online: https://www.youtube.com/watch?v=8EataOQvPII (accessed 21 June 2017).

Ashcroft, B., G. Griffiths and H. Tiffin (2000), *Post-Colonial Studies: The Key Concepts*, London and New York: Routledge.

Chitando, E. and A. van Klinken, eds (2016), *Christianity and Controversies over Homosexuality in Contemporary Africa*, London and New York: Routledge.

Engelke, M. (2007), *A Problem of Presence: Beyond Scripture in an African Church*, Berkeley: University of California Press.

van Klinken, A. (1 June 2017), 'Beyond African Religious Homophobia: How Christianity Is a Source of African LGBT Activism', *Religion and the Public Sphere*, London School of Economics and Political Science. Available online: http://blogs.lse.ac.uk/religionpublicsphere/2017/06/beyond-african-religious-homophobia-how-christianity-is-a-source-of-african-lgbt-activism/ (accessed 21 June 2017).

Lorde, A. (1983), 'The Master's Tools Will Never Dismantle the Master's House', in C. Moraga and G. Anzaldúa (eds), *This Bridge Called My Back: Writings by Radical Women of Color*, 94–101, New York: Kitchen Table Press.

Mbembe, A. (2001), *On the Postcolony*, Berkeley: University of California Press.*Oxford Dictionary* (online). https://en.oxforddictionaries.com/definition/appropriate.

West, G. O. (2016), *The Stolen Bible: From Tool of Imperialism to African Icon*, Leiden: Brill.

West, G. O. and M. W. Dube, eds (2000), *The Bible in Africa: Transactions, Trajectories, and Trends*, Leiden and Boston: Brill.

AUTHOR INDEX

INDEX OF BIBLICAL REFERENCES (NRSV ORDERING)